A Kind of Order,
A Kind of Folly

Also *by* Stanley Kunitz

A Kind of Order,
A Kind of Folly

Essays and Conversations

by Stanley Kunitz

An Atlantic Monthly Press Book

Little, Brown and Company · Boston · Toronto

A

LIBRARY OF CONGRESS CATALOGING IN PUBLICATION DATA

Kunitz, Stanley Jasspon, 1905–
    A kind of order, a kind of folly.

    "An Atlantic Monthly Press book."
    Includes index.
    1. Poetry — Addresses, essays, lectures. I. Title.
PS3521.U7K5   808.1   75-2024
ISBN 0-316-50698-2

ATLANTIC–LITTLE, BROWN BOOKS
ARE PUBLISHED BY
LITTLE, BROWN AND COMPANY
IN ASSOCIATION WITH
THE ATLANTIC MONTHLY PRESS

Designed by D. Christine Benders

Published simultaneously in Canada by Little, Brown & Company (Canada) Limited

PRINTED IN THE UNITED STATES OF AMERICA

To Emily Morison Beck
*for the years of trust as my friend
and editor*

The Timber

Sure thou didst flourish once! and many springs,
Many bright mornings, much dew, many showers
Passed o'er thy head; many light hearts and wings,
Which now are dead, lodged in thy living bowers.

And still a new succession sings and flies;
Fresh groves grow up, and their green branches shoot
Toward the old and still enduring skies,
While the low violet thrives at their root.

—*Henry Vaughan*

Contents

5 Tête-à-Tête

6 Works and Lives

7 On the Threshold: Five Young Poets

8 Recapitulations

Foreword

A collection of critical and reflective prose, produced over a span of years and mostly for specific occasions, must inevitably bear the random aspect of a miscellany; but in assembling the contents of this book I have learned more than I anticipated about the durability of the psyche through the changes and vicissitudes of a lifetime. I will not say that since the heady outpourings of my youth I have been consistent in my concerns and views, but I have certainly been stubborn. One of my unshakable convictions has been that poetry is more than a craft, important as the craft may be: it is a vocation, a passionate enterprise, rooted in human sympathies and aspirations. The dream of perfection that all artists share is touched with noble pathos, and the poet who pursues excellence too relentlessly and too long runs the risk of narrowing his mind and chilling his heart. If the causes that have agitated me in this unquiet century do not figure overtly here, it is because I felt no need to spell them out — their traces are to be found in anything I have ever written.

Rather than defer unconditionally to chronology I have arranged the contents, under several broad headings, in a sequence designed for consecutive reading. I have not done any rewriting for the sake of improving or squaring my opinions, but I have tried to eliminate matter that seemed peripheral to the main thrust of this volume, or patently ephemeral, or boring, or redundant. A writer's obsessions and quotations are the indispensable baggage he carries with him from year to year and from page to page. Certain repetitions I have left for emphasis or simply because they could not be expunged without leaving too big a hole in the text.

Since most of these pieces were written on request, I have had only limited control over the table of contents. One of my chief regrets is that I have lacked the occasion to write about some of my contemporaries and ancestors who mean most to me. On the other hand, I have not been compelled or, as a rule, felt inclined to animadvert on those who leave me cold. My basic approach to society, as a complex of institutional forces, is adversary; to the arts, affectionate.

Painters and sculptors, it can be seen, are prominent citizens in my community of friendships and admirations. What I have learned from them, corresponding to what Rilke learned from Rodin, has helped to clarify my thinking about the delicate relationship between technique and imagination and between life and art.

In the medium of prose a poet walks more naked than in his verse. Deprived of the cover of his *persona* and of parabolic speech, he is likely to feel more exposed than is congenial to his nature. But the differences may be more illusory than he supposes — certainly all the arts and the modalities of art in our time are converging. Whatever he is up to, the same spirit and the same imagination are operating behind the scenes of his performance, and he may as well own up to them.

S.K.

I

The Style of an Age

Why do you complain? Poetry is respected only in this country — people are killed for it. There's no place where more people are killed for it.

— Osip Mandelstam

Today the fight for life, the fight for Eros, is the *political* fight.

— Herbert Marcuse

A Kind of Order

Our period demands a type of man who can restore
the lost equilibrium between inner and outer reality.
... who can control his own existence by the process
of balancing forces often regarded as irreconcilable:
man in equipoise.

— Siegfried Giedion

The vision of reality that marks the man of our time, a vision
that is ever changing and yet is always thought to be reality
itself, owes an incalculable debt to a familiar quartet of intellectual giants, the prime agents in the revolution of modern
thought: Darwin, who destroyed the innocence of nature;
Marx, who destroyed the innocence of the state; Freud, who
destroyed the innocence of the mind; Einstein, who destroyed
the innocence of time and space. These are the scientists of
our new world, those who employed reason to overthrow the
reasonable world into which they were born.

And how much does our vision owe, as we compose the
scene of an era, to the fabrications of Cézanne and Picasso,
Rimbaud and Eliot, Whitman and Lawrence, Dostoievsky and
Joyce? They were explorers at the frontiers of the creative
intuition. Their images brought us news. I think too of our
debt to Kierkegaard and Nietzsche, artists in the realm of phi-

losophy and theology, the broad dominion of the speculative mind.

We are the children of Kierkegaard, who meditated on dread, on the sickness-unto-death, on fear and trembling; who fought against Hegelian rationalism; who defined the significance of the act of choice as an expression of Being; who rejected the claims of objectivity, insisting on truth as inwardness, relational truth, realizable only by an individual in action; who stressed the necessity of commitment, the greatest commitment being the irrational act of faith, the faith that is priceless because it is absurd.

And we are the children of Nietzsche, who wrote, "All truths are bloody truths for me"; who questioned the whole structure of good and evil; who attacked the Christian ideal of asceticism as a flight from life, the expression of a diseased will; who deplored the nausea, the sickness, of self-contempt; who heard in himself man's desperate voice crying, "I have got lost; I am everything that has got lost." And who replied implacably, "What does your conscience say? You shall become who you are."

These two men are curiously prophetic. Who but Kierkergaard could have invented Kafka? And who but Kafka could have invented Adolph Eichmann? When Kierkegaard declared, "The more consciousness the more self," he cleared the ground for Freud's pronouncement: "Where id was, there ego shall be."

It was Nietzsche who said, before it really happened: "We live in a period of atoms, of atomic chaos"; who foresaw the Nation State; who predicted, "The hunt for happiness will never be greater than when it must be caught between today and tomorrow; because the day after tomorrow all hunting time may have come to an end altogether."

Truth is not the exclusive property of scientific intelligences. New intuitions, new modes of perception, new ranges of metaphor are aspects of the same reality as theirs and potentially even more comprehensive in view, since they incorporate, into a world of thought, a world of feeling. Artists and scientists comprise a fraternity of the imagination, subject to the same pressures of history, and interdependent in their development.

The central observations of modern science are to be found crystallized in Planck's Quantum Theory, Einstein's Theory of Relativity, and Heisenberg's Principle of Uncertainty. They imply a universe bereft of time and space, which have been pushed back into the human consciousness as forms of intuition; a universe without cause and effect, the cornerstones of the old science, which have been replaced by fields of statistics and probabilities; a universe, then, of indeterminacy and caprice, not stabilized by things but storming with energy and motion; a universe whose objective reality, if it has any, we can never hope to know.

The most recent explorations of inner and outer space lead us further along the road to nowhere. The atom, which used to be immutable and eternal, turns out to be neither. It has been broken down into more than two hundred elementary particles — or what are called particles — and the quest is far from ended. Beyond matter we hear strange stories about the properties of anti-matter, the most rabid inhabitant of the zoo of modern physics, since it destroys both itself and ordinary matter at once when the two approach each other. And now astronomers point to the existence of "black holes" in the sky as signals of the ultimate collapse of the entire universe into a superdensity of nothingness: a forever without matter, Shakespeare, or physical law.

Three centuries ago Pascal could write in words that still ring majestically: "Man is only a reed, the feeblest reed in nature, but he is a thinking reed. There is no need for the entire universe to arm itself in order to annihilate him: a vapor, a drop of water, suffices to kill him. But were the universe to crush him, man would yet be more noble than that which slays him, because he knows he dies, and the advantage that the universe has over him; of this the universe knows nothing."

The pride of Pascal, who gloried in the blessed gift of reason, rests on the conviction that man is man, nature is nature — the one subject, the other object. Though the king can be killed by a knave, the knave can never deprive him of his royalty. But a man of our time no longer stands separate from and superior to the natural universe. He has become part of his very field of perception; he is scattered into the drifting cosmic dust; and the dust blows through him.

Heisenberg, who demonstrated that the very act of observation changes the phenomena to be observed, quietly asserted, without feeling the need for an exclamation point: "Modern physics, in the final analysis, has already discredited the concept of the truly real." Probing the universe, man finds everywhere himself. "We are both spectators and actors in the great drama of existence," wrote another Nobel Prize physicist, Niels Bohr.

These are speculations that offer us at least an entrance to a new vision of heaven and hell, a vision that may have its portents of terror but is not without grandeur. Its equivalent in art would be works of spiritual assertion, of heroic confrontation, of tragic dimension.

We live in one of the most violent epochs of history, in which none of us can claim ignorance of the many faces of disorder. A man of this century has witnessed great seismic shifts of power; the rise and fall of dictators; the convulsions of nations; the slaughter of innocents; unprecedented scandals in high places, brutalities, terrors. "Things fall apart; the centre cannot hold."

Since the Industrial Revolution the mainstays of order have been religion, science, and bourgeois morality. We need not discuss the last, since it scarcely exists, save as hypocrisy or parody. As for religion, the rationalists who preoccupied themselves with setting up proofs of divinity have perished and we are left with the followers of Nietzsche, proclaiming, "God is dead," and of Kierkegaard, preaching, "Believe — but know that your belief is absurd." The third member of this trinity of order, science, is the craziest of the lot — that is, if common sense is your criterion. No scientist worth his salt would pretend for a moment that ordinary reason is equipped to cope with the structure of the universe. Science, in fact, has fathered a crucial paradox: on the one hand, by way of technology, it has served to effect the triumph of mechanization and mediocrity; on the other, by way of theory, it has opened the gates of the universe to mystery. "Pure logicality," wrote Einstein, "cannot yield us any knowledge of the empirical world."

He also remarked that common sense is nothing more than a deposit of prejudices laid down in the mind prior to the age of eighteen.

People are always complaining that modern art is unintelligible. Is there anything else on earth of any importance that they can truly profess to understand?

The first symptoms of the disintegration of our ordered universe appeared in the arts before it became generally obvious. The landscape begins to tremble in the paintings of Cézanne. A century ago Carlyle stated that the fine arts had got into "an insane condition and walk abroad without keepers, nobody suspecting their bad state, and do phantastick tricks."

Irrationality may well be the safest of all disguises for the modern artist — the Mask, or Persona, that permits him the greatest freedom of expression with a certain degree of immunity, though there is a danger, to be sure, that the Mask may eventually usurp the Face. As Yeats noted, "Seeming that goes on for a lifetime is no different from reality."

At a time when man does not have a steady gaze on a fixed

reality, when reality as such is atomized, and when the psyche, separated from society, split between thought and feeling, no longer appears to be a coherent entity, poetry inevitably tends to become increasingly aware of itself, to turn inward. The medium becomes the subject, the flow of the poem is equated with the flow of the mind, the associational flow. The poetry is in the *process*.

> *Poetry is the subject of the poem.*
> *From this the poem issues and*
>
> *To this returns. Between the two,*
> *Between issue and return, there is*
>
> *An absence in reality,*
> *Things as they are. Or so we say.*
>
> *But are these separate? Is it*
> *An absence for the poem, which acquires*
>
> *Its true appearances there, sun's green,*
> *Cloud's red, earth feeling, sky that thinks.*
>
> *From these it takes. Perhaps it gives*
> *In the universal intercourse.*
>   *—Wallace Stevens,*
> *"The Man with the Blue Guitar," XXII*

The difficulty with so impersonal a theory of poetics is that it takes no note of the indispensable encounter between the artist and his medium. Art doesn't simply happen: the artist must *do* something. After Franz Kline had abandoned representational painting and turned to the conversion of feeling and gesture into bold ideograms, he made a typically wry comment: "The subject has become the problem. You can say 'painting is the subject,' but you just can't stand by with a shelf full of paint cans." Once he said to me, "Art has nothing to do with knowing, it has to do with giving." Stevens would have resisted that dictum as romantic overstatement, but in the passage quoted he stresses the same verb: "Perhaps it *gives*/ In the universal intercourse."

One of the characteristic postures of the modern poet is the contemplation not of his own navel, but of his own mind at work. "An idea cannot be fixed," wrote Valéry. "The only thing that can be fixed (if anything can be) is something that is not an idea. An idea is an alteration — or rather a mode of alteration — indeed, the most discontinuous mode of alteration." His M. Teste remarks: "I am existing and seeing myself; seeing myself see myself, and so on." The work modifies the author, we are told, as a woman modifies herself in front of a mirror. I think of those women in the paintings of de Kooning who sit in front of a window that is also a mirror and also a picture on a wall. How can you tell the inside from the outside, the reality from its reflection? Yeats had asked the question before, "How can we know the dancer from the dance?" In a letter to Mallarmé, Valéry abandoned the distinction between form and content: "What they call the content is only impure (that is to say, *muddled*) form."

To perpetuate any kind of truth about human experience is ultimately to be on the side of order, but the concept of order is among the things that change. Consider, for example, how lunatic the flow of traffic in our streets would seem to our pre-automotive ancestors. We ourselves would be inclined to throw a fit every time we crossed the street if we did not believe, however mistakenly, that the mobility we have gained through the invention of the automobile is worth the risk we take with our pedestrian lives. The disorder becomes bearable because it fits into the structure of our twentieth century values. The human organism is equipped to tolerate only a limited amount of confusion. One of the prime tasks of the imagination is to create an illusion of order.

Cubism followed hard on the heels of Relativity in the first decade of the century, but it would be foolish to argue that Picasso or Braque was illustrating Einstein. Scientist and painter made the same metaphysical leap, discovering for themselves, each according to his genius, the equivocations of space, time, and location, where neither the scene nor the implied observer of the scene is at rest.

Since the art of our time is the only art we can get, I must defend it against the enemies of art, however much I quarrel with certain of its aspects. One can no more make a case against modern art than one can make a case against history. The argument from within is the only one worth listening to. The first obligation is the effort towards compassionate understanding, tied to the realization that it is the artist's historic consciousness that prevents him from being optimistic, as it is his aesthetic conscience that prevents him from becoming popular.

Every work of art of any interest must be considered an event. The word "event" has a peculiar vibration in the vocabulary of contemporary physics, for it is tantamount to a definition of reality. It is not the particle of matter or the point in space or the instant in time at which something happens that has physical reality, but only the event itself, the event embedded in its four-dimensional continuum. Einstein was born into a world of substances; he died in a world of events.

In the fifties a painting began to look like a scarred battleground in which there was as much evidence of destruction as of creation. The corrections, the rejections, the mistakes had become incorporated into the final work. It is as though the artist were intent on showing us the painting as a process rather than a thing. Behind this aesthetic lurks the ghost of the Dada movement, which — against the background of the Russian Revolution in a time of the breaking of nations — had borrowed from the revolutionary Bakunin the slogan: destruction is also creation.

Though the Dadaists loved nothing more than to create a scandal, their purpose was serious. The art that they rejected was an art they despised for serving as a safety-valve for the preservation of bourgeois society. They were against all systems that stultified human spontaneity. If they did nothing else, they demonstrated the creative power of unreason and violence — how they could be used for the sake of man instead of against him. Their cult of spontaneity is still very much with us. And all the arts, since the moustache was painted on the Mona Lisa, have moved in the direction of anti-art.

When belief in miracle was an article of faith, the irrational could enter art ceremoniously by way of the front door, with hat and calling card in hand, and be confident of a gracious welcome. Today, when the house is burning, we hear the irrational trampling up the cellar stairs, but we cannot be really sure, hearing the blows of its axe, whether it comes to kill us or to save. It seems to me no accident that so many wizards, astrologists, magicians and clairvoyants, readers of Tarot cards, not to speak of primitivistic fetishes less than half-believed in, populate our poems. They are the mocking agents of the degraded miracle. To misquote Emerson: "When the Gods go, half-gods arrive." No doubt it would be preferable to have full-time, hard-working gods to light up our verses, but they do not seem to be in supply at the moment.

With young writers I make a nuisance of myself talking about order, for the good reason that order is teachable; but in my bones I know that only the troubled spirits among them, those who recognize the disorder without and within, have a chance to become poets, for only they are capable of producing a language galvanic with the contradictions of the actual.

It was Lionel Johnson, of the child's body and the hieratic brain, who said to Yeats on one occasion, "Yeats, you need ten years in the library, but I have need of ten years in a wilderness." The library and the wilderness, order and disorder, reason and madness, technique and imagination — the poet to be complete must polarize the contradictions.

I would not even try to put my finger on the exact spot where craft ends and art begins. The match spurts fire, and flame begets flame. Clichés of speech, clichés of observation and thought, clichés of feeling — when these are driven from the temple, the Self stirs and the Imagination begins to taste its freedom. That is one reason why all poetry, no matter how tragic its theme, seems strangely rooted in joy. Of course, nobody goes to school to learn about wildernesses. Each artist can be trusted to discover his own.

Yeats taught us that out of our quarrel with others we make rhetoric; out of our quarrel with ourselves, poetry. Different quarrels make different kinds of poems, and our quarrels today are quite different from those, let us say, of the eighteenth century. Our quarrel with Sex, for example, is enormously complicated by our quarrel with Mechanization. The kind of poetry we get is not so much what the age demands — our age demands nothing from the artist but his submission — as what it deserves, and sometimes better than it deserves.

The arts do not characteristically attack the ills of an age with drastic remedies, for the artist is more than merely the physician: he is, in good measure, the patient as well. Order is treated with homeopathic doses of order; disorder with disorder. One might say, stretching the point, that the Age of Reason died of a surfeit of heroic couplets. Fine couplets, too, so many of them were!

> *Nature and Nature's laws lay hid in night:*
> *God said "Let Newton be!" and all was light.*

Who among us today could match the brilliance and sublime confidence of Alexander Pope's lines? A twentieth century parodist could only reply:

> *It did not last: the Devil howling "Ho,*
> *Let Einstein be," restored the status quo.*

The more man achieves, the more aware he becomes of his

limitations, including the limitations of his senses. The human eye, for example, is sensitive only to the narrow band of radiation that falls between the red and the violet. Most of the "lights of the world" are suppressed. For those missing lights we must substitute the light of the imagination. The prison-house, said Plato long ago, is the world of sight. One of the characteristic escape routes, for the modern artist, is to dive into the flux of his own sensibility, the space-time river, and to ride with the current. In the opposite camp are those who seek the purity of a system, the crystal palace of geometry. A few dare to submit themselves to the ordeal of walking through the fire of selfhood into a world of archetypal forms.

To make any kind of affirmation, in the midst of this random and absurd universe, one must begin by affirming the value of one's own existence; but the affirmation must not be too glib or too cheaply won; it must rise out of the wrestling with all that denies it, to the very point of negation.

That order is greatest which holds in suspension the most disorder; holds it in such precarious balance that each instant threatens its overthrow. In life and in art, consistent with the precept of Paul Tillich, "the self-affirmation of a being is the stronger the more non-being it can take into itself."

Where else but in the free country of art is it possible to tell the whole unspeakable truth about the human condition?

The Search for a Style

Misery kept me from believing that all was well
under the sun, and the sun taught me that history
wasn't everything.

— Albert Camus

It was not only to do a study that I came to be with
you — it was to ask you: how must one live? and you
replied: by working.

— Rilke to Rodin

I never met a poet who was not convinced of his uniqueness,
but some of us must be wrong, for clearly there are many more
poets than there are voices. Every artist, Malraux has said, is
born the prisoner of a style, by which I take him to mean that
the stamp of the age on our work is inescapable. *Anon.* still
flourishes, through a multiplicity of signatures. More than we
like to admit, the art of any given period is an unconscious
agitation of the collective sensibility, precipitating at calcu-
lable intervals a non-toxic sediment of reputations. This art
cannot be turned from its course by logic or willed into greatness. Even the most powerful of critics is incapable of creating
the style that will dominate a generation: he can at best clarify
it so that its outlines become unmistakable. In so doing he
makes it easier, it is true, for mediocrities to incorporate into
their work the fashionable floating materials that will make
them seem for a while newer and better than they are. Does

Based on a talk given at the National Poetry Festival, Library of Congress,
October 22, 1962.

that matter so much? In time a handful who have listened to the prevailing tune will play it back, but different — modified by the accents of the great dead, set to their own living voice, beating in their own true measure.

The persistence of vitality in the literary tradition is dependent on its stomach for change. Since no stomach, however, is equipped to digest everything, the process is not indiscriminate. Historically, one notes, the decay of a style is always preceded by an odor of sanctity. What can follow decorum but a hard rage? Art, we have been told, by Goethe among others, exists in limits. True enough. But the imperative of the artist is to keep testing those limits.

Each literary generation requires the existence of an *avant garde,* not because the latter are more original than the writers of reputation, or superior to them, but because the prevailing style of a period needs always to be resisted if it is not to grow lax, needs always to be modified to keep it supple. Even the mimeographed production of a small and desperate band of semi-illiterates serves a purpose, if only to remind us that a writer is either experimental or dead.

Since the fifties a good part of the commotion in the world of poetry has had to do with the rejection of what is called academic verse and with the effort to convert poetry into a popular art. The difficulty with this enterprise is that in an open society, such as ours, where the poet is free to pursue his deepest and most arcane thoughts and feelings to their source, his art tends to embrace the personal and to prefer an intimate tone. Who speaks more concretely or remains more secret? Through all the weathers of his spirit, which constitute his theme, the poet exults that nobody pins him down. This form of immunity is such a blessing that poets are shrewd enough to cultivate the myth of their difficulty. Under that cover they can apply themselves, with the compulsiveness that would seem to be their birthright, to the quest that gives their lives shape and meaning, the search for a style.

When a poet in a democracy strives for popularity through a public style — deliberately aiming at the mass ear — he soon loses himself in endless and shapeless vulgarity. Whitman did not entirely escape this pitfall, but what saved him was the polarity of his concerns, alternating between ego and cosmos. The common man preferred to listen to Longfellow, who demanded less of him and made him feel more comfortable. It was largely other poets and intellectuals who greeted Whitman and responded to the paradox of his art:

> *One's self I sing, a simple separate person,*
> *Yet utter the word Democratic, the word En-Masse.*

In a closed society a private and secret art is held impermissible, because who knows what dark subversive thoughts a subtle lyric or an abstract painting might conceal. "The age," wrote Pound, "demanded an image of its accelerated grimace." What the Soviet State demands and what, by force of its dictatorship of taste, it mostly gets is an open art that celebrates the Soviet way of life. The poems it favors are like speeches in a public square. In the dogma of socialist realism, everything must be hung out on the line. Even when Yevtushenko, as a young man, created a furor with his poem exposing the evil face of anti-Semitism, he did so in the most blatant and obvious rhetoric. The offense of Pasternak was that he dared to remain a closed, an esoteric poet in a closed society. The State could not tolerate this withholding of himself: it was an injury not to be borne.

Although I think that the effort to convert American poetry into a "pop" art is doomed to fail, I find that the works of my contemporaries that interest me most at this stage are poems that, stemming out of the great closed art of this century, are nevertheless relaxed in the line, fluid in their development, organic in their form, and immediate in feeling. I begin to see the possibility of a poetry that will recapture from the novel much of the territory that has been forfeited to it. I ask myself whether poetry, following the lead of other industries, has not become over-specialized, too different from prose, so that its connection with the whole body of modern literature seems strained or broken. Why should not all men of imagination feel that poetry is their medium, as long as they have a language of the imagination to offer — not necessarily a language designed for polite versification, but one, to borrow the words of

Ortega y Gasset, born of "the terror of facing single-handed, in their own persons, the ferocious assaults of existence"?

I do not think it is admirable to live by words, for words, in words. In the best poetry of our time — but only the best — one is aware of a moral pressure being exerted on the medium in the very act of creation. By "moral" I mean a testing of existence at its highest pitch — what does it feel like to be totally one's self?; an awareness of others beyond the self; a concern with values and meanings rather than with effects; an effort to tap the spontaneity that hides in the depths rather than what foams on the surface; a conviction about the possibility of making right and wrong choices, even symbolic choices. Lacking this pressure, we are left with nothing but a vacuum occupied by a technique.

A Visit to Russia

> We are witnesses of the greatest moment of summing-up in history, in the name of a new and unknown culture, which will be created by us, and which will also sweep us away. That is why, with fear or misgiving, I raise my glass to the ruined walls of the beautiful palaces, as well as to the new commandments of a new aesthetic. The only wish that I, an incorrigible sensualist, can express, is that the forthcoming struggle should not damage the amenities of life, and that the death should be as beautiful and as illuminating as the resurrection.
>
> — Serge Diaghilev (1905)

I came back from the Soviet Union in the spring of 1967 full of affection for the writers I had met, sharing the frustrations and anxieties of their predicament, and, to a degree, strangely envious of them. A writer is dignified by the attention of the State, even when it is the wrong kind of attention. As Mandelstam remarked, there is no denying the importance of poetry when people are killed for it.

I returned just before the convening of the fourth national congress of the Union of Soviet Writers, which everybody assured me would be a dreary event. It was no surprise that the congress ended with a reaffirmation of the orthodox pieties: "We regard our literature as part and parcel of the Communist party cause. . . . We do not have nor can we have other interests besides the interests of the people expressed by our party. . . . Soviet literature is essentially optimistic. It is permeated with the theme of building Communism. . . . Sound literature

Originally published in *The New York Times Magazine*, August 20, 1967.

is called upon to accord with the need of society. Its purposes are not meaningless experiments in the sphere of form." Only the party hacks take such sentiments seriously. The rest are perfectly capable of recognizing stupidities, but have to live with them anyhow.

To preserve an illusion of harmony, all was supposed to remain quiet on the literary front during the fiftieth year of the revolution, a period of celebration throughout the U.S.S.R. But Alexander Solzhenitsyn made a shambles of the Writers' Congress by circulating his heroic petition for the abolition of literary censorship. In the course of his plea he exposed to view the redundant chronicle of repression, exile, vilification, persecution, suicide, and extermination that stains the history of Soviet literature. During the period of the greatest terror, he charged, the Writers' Union had "obediently handed over to their fate in prisons and camps" more than 600 writers. He himself had spent eight years of his life under Stalin in forced labor camps; and his recent writings, since the furor created by *One Day in the Life of Ivan Denisovich,* had been deliberately "smothered" and "gagged." The tone of his conclusion was ominous: "I am, of course, confident that I will fulfill my duty as a writer under all circumstances, from the grave even more successfully and unobstructedly than in my lifetime. No one can bar the road to the truth, and to advance its cause I am prepared to accept even death."* In his support 82 Soviet writers, out of 6,500 in the Writers' Union, dared petition the Central Committee of the Soviet Communist Party. Though Solzhenitsyn's manifesto was suppressed in the Soviet Union, it was leaked abroad.

Among those who came to Solzhenitsyn's defense was the poet Andrei Voznesensky, not usually embattled, who proposed the issue of an omnibus volume of all the older writer's published work, including stories that had appeared only in magazines; and who called for the appointment of a committee of writers to examine the unpublished and rejected manuscripts of Solzhenitsyn. Following this proposal, the Writers' Union abruptly canceled Voznesensky's long-

* Solzhenitsyn was expelled from the Soviet Union in 1974; he is now living in Zurich.

planned visit to New York for a reading of his poems at Lincoln Center. The contradictory explanations offered to foreign journalists was that Voznesensky was ill, that he had neglected to book his plane tickets, and that he was free to go any time he wanted. Meanwhile Moscow buzzed with rumors of his "pro-Americanism."

"Nothing could be more idiotic," wrote Voznesensky indignantly about the treatment accorded to him, in a letter to *Pravda,* with a duplicate sent to the Writers' Union. "Such a practice of telling lies, of playing off writers against each other, is common in the Writers' Union. This has been done to many of my friends. Sometimes we don't get our mail. Sometimes our letters are replied to by others without our knowledge."

One of the friends to whom Voznesensky apparently referred was Vasili Aksyonov, a favorite novelist of Soviet youth, whose trip to Britain was also canceled at the last moment on the spurious grounds that he was ill.

Pravda, of course, never published Voznesensky's letter.

The next step, in the war of cultural exchanges, was the sudden cancellation in July of the scheduled American tour of the Russian Festival of Music and Dance, an action calculated to express Soviet displeasure at Israel's military triumph in the Six-Day War and at our Middle East policy. It would be a pity if such behavior, reminiscent of a child who refuses to play anymore because his feelings have been hurt, should result in the abandonment or suspension of the Soviet-American cultural exchange agreement. My own trip was a reactivation by our State Department of the lamentably fitful program of swapping writers.

Before I flew to Moscow, by way of London, late in March, my friends among the Sovietologists, on whose linguistic finesse and rarefied special knowledge I had often leaned in the course of my translations of Russian poetry, told me precisely what to expect. As an official guest of the Soviet Union, under the provisions of the agreement, I would be subject to constant surveillance; I would be permitted to see only those writers who were in the pocket of the bureaucracy; I would have no opportunity for private conversations or meetings; my audiences, whether for lectures or for poetry readings, would be hand-picked and scanty — they might be non-existent; I would be heckled and harassed about Vietnam.

My informants turned out to be wrong, dead wrong, on every count. I knew that they were wrong the moment that I saw Voznesensky, whom I knew well from his American visits, separate himself from the official greeting party at the airport in Moscow and rush forward to embrace me. Later I noted down my first reflection on Russian soil: "Even when Andrei grins, he has the pathetic face of a child." In the following five weeks, everywhere that I went, from Moscow to the Caucasus, I learned to rely on the good will and hospitality of strangers, who became instant guides and friends, overleaping the language barrier. No doubt the vodka helped. It is a great solvent. And so is poetry.

The Russian appetite for poetry is simply enormous. Voznesensky commented that his latest collection, *An Achilles Heart,* had been published in an edition of "only" 100,000. The book had half a million orders in advance of publication and went out of print practically overnight. For a poet of national reputation a printing of 100,000 copies is not uncommon. When the word gets round that an important new book is in stock, people make a run for it, since there is no expectation that it will be reprinted, regardless of public demand. Poets are paid, I was told, in direct ratio to their popularity, from as little as forty kopecks a line for beginning and local poets, who are usually printed in editions of 3,000 to 10,000 copies, to as much as ten rubles a line for the best sellers. Successful writers, including poets, are conspicuously among the most prosperous citizens of the Soviet Union, often with a housekeeper or cook and with a comfortable *dacha* in the woods. When I was asked how many copies of my poems were sold in the States, I felt embarrassed to tell the truth. Towards the end of my stay I found that I could double or triple the figure without batting an eye. After all, it was a small lie to tell for my country.

Books are the best value for the money in the Soviet Union. Poetry is on sale, for a few kopecks, in the subways, at sidewalk stalls, and in specialized poetry bookshops, which are always crowded. Verse in translation is gobbled up as fast as the domestic variety. In one of the most capacious of the poetry shops, in Kiev, I watched my interpreter, a studious young woman from Moscow, snatch a volume from the shelf with a triumphant air. "What is it, Valentina?" I asked. She showed me her find: Apollinaire in Russian. When the collection had been issued in Moscow a few weeks before, she had tried assiduously to acquire a copy there, but like all such tidbits it had sold out immediately. The size of the edition, indicated according to custom on the last page, astonished me — 115,000 copies!

Appropriately enough, books were the subject of the wildest boast I heard during my trip. I was visiting the Lenin Library in Moscow — unquestionably one of the world's biggest and busiest depositories, though its plant is sadly in need of renovation and its classification system is shockingly archaic. Soviet technological progress is so uneven, on the basis of socially determined priorities, that this kind of contradiction in the quality of the pattern is everywhere visible. The students who jammed the reading rooms and even cluttered the corridors, at badly lit makeshift worktables, were impressive in the intensity of their concentration. One felt that they were much less relaxed in the pursuit of learning than their American counterparts; nor had they yet arrived at the stage where they might question the validity of the educational system itself. My guide, who had been mercilessly reciting statistics, revived me by inquiring, "Do you know that there are more books in the public library system of Moscow alone than in all the libraries of the United States, England, France, and Italy combined?" "You don't say!" I replied. "Where did you get that fantastic calculation?" "It's true!" she insisted. "I read it in an official handbook." Later, during our inspection of the labyrinthine stacks, which are guarded at each level by armed soldiers at the hallway doors, she remarked sententiously, "What could be more worth defending than books?" Most of the time, fortunately, my escorts were writers or scholars, who proved to be charming companions as well.

The simplest way for the bureaucracy to cope with a visitor such as myself is to fill in his time with sightseeing and with perfunctory meetings at the official level. I made it clear from the beginning that my primary concern was to meet with writers, particularly with poets, and most particularly with young poets. I also expressed a desire to talk with students at the universities. Once the word got round that my motives were above suspicion, my hosts went out of their way to keep me occupied and happy. Unfortunately, exchange visitors from Russia to the United States do not return with an equally favorable report on American hospitality. No doubt the contacts of the Writers' Union with the literary community of the U.S.S.R. are superior to those of the State Department in this country.

Most of the poets I met — in Moscow, in Leningrad, in Kiev, in Tbilisi (old Tiflis), capital of Georgia — were in their twenties and thirties. I was enchanted by their beautiful seriousness, by the way they carried themselves as heirs of a great and proud and tragic tradition. For them Russian poetry begins in the blood of Pushkin and Lermontov, both of whom died young and senselessly in duels, as though they had gone out deliberately to find their assassins. The destiny of the poet is a recurrent theme in Russian literature, as in these lines by Voznesensky:

> *The sense of my life*
> *is to pay for Lermontov, Lorca,*
> *an everlasting debt.*
>
> *Payable in blood*
> *the terrible charges mount. . . .*
>
> *But who will pay for me,*
> *who will close the account?*

In Moscow I spent a fair share of my time in the wood-paneled, balconied dining room of the Writers' Club, an auxiliary of the union. At the club, which still retains traces of its previous existence as a Masonic lodge, some of the best food, drink, and conversation in the city can be enjoyed. It is a place for gossip, banter, flirtation, shoptalk, confidences, and compulsive table-hopping. In other Russian communities the Writers' Union is much more cut off from the daily life of the writer and does not attempt to offer equivalent social facilities. Typically the situation of the writer in Moscow, at the political center, differs from that of his colleagues outside the capital. The young poets of Leningrad, for example, tend to cling together privately as if in self-defense. I met a number of them at one apartment and felt that I had been admitted to a circle of devoted friends, the sort of circle that gathered round Keats.

Americans who respond to the passionate declamation of Yevtushenko and Voznesensky, the only poets whom the bureaucracy regularly chooses to export, mistakenly consider their platform style to be the epitome of modern Russian verse. Actually Yevtushenko's contemporaries and juniors deplore the theatrical abuse of his talent and are rather cynical about his foreign reputation. Voznesensky, who is a much less flamboyant personality, with little natural taste for politics, has managed to become a national figure without sacrificing his intellectual mobility or his instinct for privacy. Although the young poets generally speak of him with affection and praise, they reject for themselves the grand style, the concept of the poem as a form of public address, the rhetoric of causes. "All that belongs to Mayakovsky . . . and to Moscow," I was told. The influence of Mayakovsky, whose verse embodied the revolutionary spirit and became the archetype of Soviet (as opposed to Russian) poetry, is diminishing. Voznesensky descends from Mayakovsky, but claims Pasternak as his spiritual father.

I find it difficult, from hundreds of possibilities, to choose a single poem that may serve as representative of the other voice; but here is a quiet lyric that I remember listening to in a hotel room in Tbilisi, while my escort, himself a Georgian, offered a line-by-line interpretation. The fine-spun poet in his early thirties who read his lines to me was Otar Chiladze, of whose merits the Russians are only beginning to become aware, since for them too his poems must be translated from the original Georgian, a totally unrelated language of doubtful origin.

Expectation

I have become blind to branches, chimneys, wires ...
I can see nothing at all,
and like a black cube of ice
the telephone locks itself silent.

But expectation gradually loses
its terrible meaning,
and I hear a wall talking to a wall,
one thing talking to another;

though I no longer have the right
to cherish any feelings for you,
and my free and doomed passion
settles down like dust upon my surface.

And yet I must divert myself somehow
and bear the brand and the fatigue
because the role I play now

is becoming my whole performance.

More than a century ago a Muscovite described Moscow as the heart of Russia; St. Petersburg was its head. In Moscow they have long dreamed of holy Russia; in Petersburg they studied the masters of the French Enlightenment and aspired to open a window to Europe and to the west. Now Petersburg goes by the name of Leningrad, but the historic dialectic persists, incorporated into the grain of Russian life, as ineradicable as the ancient contradiction between the Dionysian and the Apollonian spirit. The poets of Moscow and of Leningrad reflect the difference of their cities.

Moscow is raw, bustling, aggressive, conscious of its power, crazy for progress, impatient to get on with the job of destruction and creation, showing its scars and its muscle as it bulldozes outward, in ever-widening circles, to the smoking suburbs. What holds Moscow together, gives it form and meaning, is the Kremlin at its core, secret and sacred heart, fortress and dynamo.

Leningrad is one of the great water-cities, like Venice and Amsterdam, and like them it makes a water-music, but colder, stricter, more measured. Peter's city rose out of the miasma of the Neva delta, domesticated its swamps, and called them canals. The very stability of its foundations represents a triumph of the will. It is not so much something born as something planned, elegantly plotted, sprung full-blown out of the heads of imported French and Italian architects. The design is horizontal in plane, fanciful but controlled in its ornament, correct in its proportions. The productions of Leningrad have the formal splendor of the baroque tuned to the oblique northern light.

In Leningrad, as elsewhere in the Soviet Union, the best of the young poets are unobtrusively returning to the formal modes, to the subjectivity and intimacy of the lyric tradition. Without assuming heroic postures they openly acknowledge their debt to the poets of an older generation who suffered suppression and persecution under Stalin or Khrushchev and who are still barely tolerated by the party hacks. They tend to think of themselves as the heirs of Anna Akhmatova, imperishably identified with Leningrad, whose first husband, the poet Gumilev, was executed by a Soviet firing squad, whose only son was deported to a concentration camp for more than fifteen years, and who was herself expelled from the Writers' Union in 1946 and condemned to silence; of Osip Mandelstam, Jewish in origin, whose bitter lines on Stalin led to his death, late in the thirties, in a Siberian concentration camp; of Boris Pasternak, also of Jewish background, who was denounced and vilified and expelled from the Writers' Union after the publication abroad of *Doctor Zhivago;* and of Marina Tsvetaeva, who hanged herself in 1941, two years after returning to her motherland from exile. Akhmatova, Mandelstam, Pasternak, Tsvetaeva — the last great poets of an epoch — are gradually being rehabilitated, but their complete texts are still not available and they have not yet been honored in their own country with adequate biographical or critical studies. Solzhenitsyn, with reference to the bureaucrats, quotes Pushkin: "They are capable of loving only the dead" . . . but even this takes time.

The conviction that time is on their side sustains the artists of Russia. Certainly they are better off than they were in the bloody thirties. The boldest of them do not hesitate to speak with open contempt of their critics, the watchdogs of the party. In fact, I cannot recall a single amiable remark about the state of criticism in the Soviet Union. The more reputation a writer has the more outspoken he can afford to be. An international reputation is the best safeguard of all. Behind the scenes the controversies are incessant and fierce, but only occasionally do they erupt into print, for the party is understandably sensitive about the appearance of the faintest crack in its monolithic façade. According to the rules of the game, the tenets of Leninism are never to be questioned. Stalin can be attacked because his abuse of power is now seen as a corruption and betrayal of the founding principles. The state itself remains an inviolable idea, protected from doubt and dissent by ring upon ring of bureaucrats, armed with considerable authority within their specific sphere of influence and obligated to accept the brunt of blame when things go wrong. The present heads of state within the Kremlin are regarded as basically diffident about cultural matters and more permissive than their predecessors. When writers feel constrained to vent their spleen, they direct it against the intermediary officials in control of publishing and of the Writers' Union, who are generally of an older generation with a vested interest in perpetuating an orthodoxy of style, a conformity of opinion.

At the time of my visit the literary community had not yet recovered from the crisis of February 1966, when Andrei Sinyavsky and Yuli Daniel, after a four-day trial, were sentenced to seven and five years, respectively, at hard labor for secretly publishing abroad, under the pseudonyms of Abram Tertz and Nikolai Arshak, works that were denounced as criminal slanders against the structure of Soviet society. Appalled by the harshness of the sentences, two separate groups of well-known writers and intellectuals petitioned the Kremlin to free Sinyavsky and Daniel. The first petition, demanding outright pardon, had forty signatures; the second, requesting liberty on parole, had sixty-three. Both petitions were summarily rejected. I heard some speculation as to what would have happened if, say, a thousand writers had dared to come to the defense of their colleagues. To organize a protest on such a scale would be a difficult and dangerous undertaking, but it should not be dismissed as a pipe dream.

I was told that Sinyavsky and Daniel were languishing in confinement and that the former was close to a physical breakdown. When I spoke of them sympathetically to a representative of the Moscow Writers' Union, I was rebuked for my concern: "You cannot understand how we feel about those hypocrites. There they sat in the Club day after day, chatting and smiling and pretending to be our friends — and all the time they were smuggling out those vicious attacks on us, on our whole way of life, for the pleasure of foreigners. Their sentences were hard, but they deserved what they got. Americans ought not to use them for propaganda. Don't you have problems enough of your own? The best service you people could do them would be to drop the subject. Your precious pair have a good chance of being released, maybe later in this anniversary year, but only if the pressure lets up."*

Most writers, it should be said, no longer lie in bed fearing a knock at the door. Imprisonment and exile are still within the realm of possibility, to be sure, but they are not the expected lot. Except for the most conspicuous dissidents, punishment is more likely to be devious than dramatic. The writer in Russia today needs, above all, stamina to cope with the petty harassments of the functionaries, their watchful eye, their ever-ready blue pencil, their proprietorship of favors, their privilege of interminably delaying publication. It is to the poet's advantage that poetry is a slippery art, metaphorical and parabolical, difficult to pin down, elusive in its meaning. Not that ambiguity is a perfect shield. The motto on the censor's door could be taken from a nineteenth century satire by Saltykov: "What I do not understand is dangerous for the state." The poet who tries to stay out of trouble by being non-political lays himself open to the charge of being against the state by implication. What gives the poet strength is his knowledge of the historic importance of his role, an importance that even the peasantry acknowledges. As far back as 1847 the radical critic

* Daniel was not released until 1970. Sinyavsky, who was freed a year later, is now teaching at the Sorbonne.

Belinsky, in defying the tyranny of Nicholas I, proclaimed: "The public . . . looks upon Russian writers as its only leaders, defenders, and saviors against Russian autocracy. . . . The title of poet and writer has eclipsed the tinsel of epaulettes and gaudy uniforms."

More than a century later, in 1963, Yevtushenko told the Paris *Express*, in an interview for which he was roundly abused back home: "All the tyrants in Russia have taken the poets as their worst enemies. They feared Pushkin. They trembled before Lermontov. They were afraid of Nekrasov. . . ."

Poets who must wait for years to see their books in print — the excuse is usually the paper shortage — manage to circulate their poems nevertheless. "My typewriter is my publishing house," one poet told me, echoing Akhmatova's quip that "we live in the pre-Gutenberg age." Their word for it is *samizdat.*

It should not be supposed that Soviet poets are filled with seditious thoughts or dreaming of the day when they can pull a Svetlana. On the contrary, they are irrevocably bound to the beauty of their native land and to the marvels of their language. Simply as human beings they are the best advertisements their country could have.

The case of Joseph Brodsky is pertinent. This young Leningrad protégé of Akhmatova is a poet in the metaphysical tradition, a rare breed in Russia. Although his name has become famous throughout the western world, the Russian public has been carefully screened from his verses. In March 1964, after an incredibly stupid and malicious trial that reeked of anti-intellectualism and anti-Semitism, he was condemned to five years' exile in Archangel, in the Arctic circle, as a "social parasite." The ground for this charge was a law that prohibits residence in cities by persons who refuse to do "socially useful labor." Metaphysical poems are obviously of no great use to the Soviet State.

When I arrived in Leningrad early in April 1967, I heard that Brodsky was in town. His friends volunteered to arrange a meeting, but failed to locate him, for he had gone off to Moscow. In my conversations with his associates I sensed two things about Brodsky: that his presence was a dominant one, and that he kept himself scarce.

Back in Moscow a fortnight later, I finally caught up with him at the apartment of one of his friends. Contrary to expectations, he turned out to be a strapping fellow, with penetrating gray eyes, ruddy complexion, sparkling teeth, and a sharp chiseled nose. He struck me as being strong, healthy, extraordinarily self-possessed, virtually indestructible. I was the first American poet, he told me, that he had ever met. He spoke English haltingly, but affirmed that he could read and translate it; and Spanish too. When the conversation became animated, he lapsed into Russian, which his friend translated expertly. We had no official interpreter in attendance.

"My exile was supposed to last for five years," he explained in a matter-of-fact tone. "They sent me to Archangel to work in the fields as an agricultural laborer. In September 1965, after one year and nine months, my sentence was commuted. It was a fruitful experience, and really I enjoyed it. The peasant in whose house I lived treated me as a son. I did not encounter any anti-Semitism. The local officials and indeed the whole community were good to me. I think of those people with love. They were happy to have a poet in their midst and they tried in all possible ways to help me, so that I could write. It was one of my most productive periods."

He talked readily about himself and his work. "I am not a rebel — I am a poet. And I do not write political poems." Among English poets the metaphysicals were closest to him — Donne, Marvell, and Herbert, in that order — along with Blake. Without a moment's hesitation he rattled off the names of his favorite Russian poets of the past hundred years: Annensky, Akhmatova, Klebnikov, Tsvetaeva, Pasternak, Mandelstam, Zabolotsky (another graduate of the concentration camps). He spoke with some admiration of the verse of Alexander Tvardovsky, liberal editor of *Novy Mir,* the leading literary journal, but found it difficult to praise any of his well-known contemporaries. "The ones I like best," he said, "are almost totally obscure."

He expressed himself as optimistic about his future. Two of his poems — short poems, it was true, at a time when nearly all his work ran long — had recently been published in the 1966 *Leningrad Literary Annual,* an anthology of which a

modest issue of 15,000 copies had been printed, at sixty kopecks (about sixty-five cents) apiece — now a collector's item.
Their acceptance was a good sign, for aside from five or six
children's poems none of his work had previously been found
worthy of publication. Some day, he was convinced, a book of
his poems would be accepted. "The problem with publishing
me here isn't politics, it's conservatism. Publishers are too
conservative to take risks." The unauthorized edition of his
poems that appeared in the States in 1965 did not meet with
his approval, for it included too much of his inferior early
verse. No, he wasn't a member of the Writers' Union — he
would have to wait for recognition till he published a book.
But meanwhile — this he announced with a show of pride —
he was a member in good standing of the Trade Union of
Writers attached to the Leningrad Publishing House, by
which he was employed as an occasional translator. The reason for his trip to Moscow — he pointed to the knapsack of
books that he had brought with him — was that he wanted to
obtain more translation assignments.

Shaking his hand at the door, I said to him, "You are the
best-looking parasite I ever saw." He laughed easily, without
embarrassment, and dashed back to inscribe a copy of the
Leningrad Annual for me: "From Russia with love — Joseph
Brodsky"*

"Russia" and "love" are words that go easily together. I
remember Voznesensky saying suddenly, in the middle of a
conversation: "I cannot tell you how much I love my country.
Russia! It's a feeling that goes deep inside me: it's at the bottom of everything." And it is a feeling that he shares with his
brothers in poetry. One respects it. One would not have it
otherwise.

"When a man writes," he has said, "he feels his poetic mis-
sion in the world. The task of the Russian poet today is to look
deep inside man. When I read my poetry to a great number of
people, their emotional, almost sensual expression of feeling,
seems to me to reveal the soul of man — now no longer hidden behind closed shutters, but wide open like a woman who
has just been kissed."

* Brodsky left the Soviet Union in June 1972. He is now living in the United
States.

Is such a man to be feared by the Kremlin? Russia is so great that she can afford to let her people utter anything their heart tells them. If a proclamation to that effect were to be issued tomorrow, the spirit of a whole people would be miraculously lightened.

Meanwhile the diehards of an earlier generation continue to spout the shibboleths of Stalinist socialist realism. In Moscow I attended a seminar of the poetry workshop of the famed Gorky Literary Institute, which boasts the distinction of numbering two of the best-known poets of modern Russia, Yevtushenko and Bela Akhmadulina (who was to become his first wife), among its dropouts. The class was conducted on authoritarian principles by the conservative elder poet Sergei V. Smirnov, who delivered for my benefit a fierce tirade against modernism, intellectualism, and "formalism" (the catchall term for writing that does not conform to party standards). He commanded his students — who were drawn from every corner of the Soviet Union, including Dagestan in the North Caucasus, Alta in South Siberia, Rostov-on-Don, and the Urals — to love their country, to write in the vernacular of their region, and to address their poems to the simple folk who were the salt of the earth. Each of fifteen students in turn rose to offer a brief autobiographical statement and to read a sample of his work in the language of his origins, concluding with a translation of his lines into Russian, if needed. The program seemed well rehearsed. Smirnov praised his favorites extravagantly; the comments from the class were desultory. But I had a surprise coming to me. The last poet to show his wares was a foreign scholarship student from Ghana, John Okai by name, who informed me he preferred to write in English and who proceeded to give a magnificent reading of two of his long-cadenced, accumulative poems, that mount excitingly to the beat and smell of Africa. I brought back with me from Moscow a sheaf of his manuscripts in the hope of sharing them with American readers.*

Kiev was an altogether different story. There, in the heart of the Ukraine, I attended a meeting of the poetry workshop

* Okai's *The Oath of the Fontomfrom and Other Poems* was published here in 1971 by Simon and Schuster.

sponsored by the Literary Society of the Workers of the October District. The class consisted of approximately twenty workers and students of the district, mostly in their young twenties, who met regularly in a clubhouse in a park, not far from the filled-in ravine of dreadful fame called Babi Yar. I had groaned at the prospect of listening for a whole evening to the effusions of a group of indoctrinated apprentices; and my worst expectations were fulfilled when the first student, a gangling youth, read in a high-pitched nasal voice a pair of ghastly odes entitled respectively "Lenin" and "Motherland."

To my amazement the whole class, joined by the mentor, Anatoli Getman, a local poet in his forties, denounced the verses in scathing terms as sentimental and banal. As one student phrased it, addressing the writer, "We know you're patriotic, Vasili, but so are we all. Why don't you just take it for granted and try harder to write some decent poems?" My provisional interpreter, one of the members of the class, slipped me a descriptive note about the unfortunate versifier. It read: "Unqualified worker."

Then a student of twenty, a chunky peasant type in a green sweater, rose to recite his piece. The title was "Mandelstam," a poem of praise. Though the lines came to me haltingly, in an on-the-spot translation from the Ukrainian, I felt intuitively that they caught some of the Mandelstamian essence. After a moment's hush a tall bespectacled boy of serious mien ("mechanic: Jewish") raised his hand. "I have no criticism to offer. Mandelstam is my hero. I love any poem that reminds me of him." His own poem, which he read in Russian, instead of the Ukrainian of his classmates, was an involuted elegy, with metaphysical overtones, for his father. And so the evening continued, for well over three hours, at a level of performance, including the critical discussion, that would have graced most college seminars in the States.

The final half-hour was consumed by the reading of a drab prose documentary on the brutalities of the Fascist invaders during the Great Patriotic War. The class could hardly wait for the middle-aged author, the oldest member of the group — I suspected he was a ringer, introduced for the occasion — to finish his toneless report. The *coup de grâce* was delivered by the student who had written the poem dedicated to Mandelstam. "We're sick to death of that kind of stuff," he flatly pronounced. "It's a bore. What we need is prose writers like Updike and Joyce!"

A few years ago John Updike was one of my predecessors in the cultural exchange program, and clearly his visit made a dent. His *Centaur* and Salinger's *Catcher in the Rye*, both of which have been translated, are the American novels that have created the greatest stir in the Russian literary community since Hemingway.* Among modern American poets most educated Russians are familiar with the work of Frost, Sandburg, and Langston Hughes — but mostly Frost, whose solidity and moral substance appeal to them. There is considerable curiosity about Ginsberg and Ferlinghetti, who are believed to represent American youth, but no wide acquaintance with their writings. While I was in Moscow four poems by Robert Lowell appeared in the excellent world-ranging magazine *Inostrannaya Literatura (Foreign Literature)*, translated by Andrei Sergeyev, who has also translated Frost. I discovered that the justly famous Russian hospitality extends even to the act of translation, for during my visit several of my poems were translated by a battery of leading poets into Russian, Ukrainian, and Georgian. Among the poet-translators who participated with me in unprecedented joint public readings were Voznesensky, Akhmadulina, and Ivan Drach, the fine young Ukrainian poet.

The demand for foreign literature, particularly American literature, is extraordinary, but the record of translations is spotty, since the editorial decisions of the state-controlled publishing houses are subject to the vagaries of bureaucratic taste, with its Puritanical as well as its political biases. Four-letter words and erotic details are strictly taboo; asterisks are overworked. For varying reasons writers of world stature, such as Kafka, T. S. Eliot, Pound, Proust, and Joyce, have been prevented for decades from contaminating the Russian mind except in small, carefully selected doses. But they are not without admirers. In Tbilisi I was entertained by an exceptionally cosmopolitan professor of literature, with an extensive private

* In the seventies Kurt Vonnegut became a favorite.

collection of books in English, mostly acquired during his travels abroad, who was engaged in the monumental task of translating Joyce's *Ulysses* into Georgian — of all languages! — even though he had no assurance that his life-work would ever be published.

Students of foreign literature at the universities are impressive in their command of English and disarming in their curiosity about American writers and writing. At the Kiev State Institute for Foreign Languages four hundred young men and women thronged the auditorium to listen to my informal talk and reading. When I inquired whether an interpreter was needed, they insisted proudly that they could understand me without assistance, and in the question period that followed they proved that they were right. Mostly they wanted to know who were the young writers coming up in America. What Russian writers were known to Americans? How did I appraise Solzhenitsyn, Voznesensky, Yevtushenko? What did I think of the "Beatniks"? How did one become a poet in America, or live as one? As usual, I ended by reading some of my versions of Voznesensky, Mandelstam, and Akhmatova, to whose names and lines they responded with enthusiasm.

On a few occasions students asked me to comment on John Steinbeck's letters from Vietnam justifying our military intervention — a tactful way of sounding out my views. I welcomed the opportunity to explain that Steinbeck did not speak for American writers and intellectuals in general and most specifically not for me. When I openly speculated why nobody approached me directly on the question of Vietnam, I was told that it was taken for granted that a poet would not be in favor of dropping napalm on babies. Steinbeck's position worried them because of his popularity in the Soviet Union, where he himself was recalled by many as a bluff and open person, "a really good American." In the minds of most Russians he was still the progressive young author of that world-famous novel of social protest, *Grapes of Wrath*. How then could he support a war of brutal imperialist aggression?

America is so important to the Russians that they do not know how to be detached about us. "Everything that you Americans do or say concerns us," said one poet. "After all, there are only two powers, two cultures, in the twentieth century worth talking about: the U.S.S.R. and the U.S.A." Russian writers and artists realize that their fates are curiously bound to American foreign policy, since their hopes for a gradual relaxation of state controls rest on the easing of tension between the two countries. As long as war clouds the landscape, the cultural exchange program will continue to be kicked around by the politicians, and the censors will find renewed justification for suppressing dangerous thoughts. An American writer in Russia senses that he is the bearer of good news by the very fact of his presence. The affection with which he is greeted is so overwhelming that part of it must be attributed to his involuntary performance in the role of messenger.

Three scenes, out of a multitude, repeat themselves in my mind, as though they had something important to convey on the import of my journey:

1. I am standing on a mountaintop in the Caucasus, beside the ruins of an ancient basilica, with Maurice and Nico, two new Georgian friends. From a thermos bag they produce a chilled bottle of champagne and a single glass, from which we sip in turn. The Georgian bubbly is a bit sweet, not first-rate, but potable. We drink to poetry, to fraternity, to peace, to Soviet-American friendship. After the last round I smash the glass by flinging it down the rocky mountainside towards the deep gorge where two rivers loop together in a blue confluence.

2. The Voznesenskys are giving a dinner party for me at their Moscow apartment, to which they have invited fifteen or twenty of their friends, including the novelist Aksyonov, the poets Bulat Okudzhava and Semyon Kirsanov with their attractive wives; and the artist Ernst Neizvestny. I lose count of the courses, but the hors d'oeuvres and the salads are particularly delicious, and the generous potions of vodka, wine, and cognac are invitations to euphoria. Dark-skinned Okudzhava, who is of Georgian and Armenian descent, sings his famous satirical "Song About an American Soldier," to the accompaniment of his guitar. Some of the guests join in the chorus; others, like myself, merely pound out the beat to the catchy tune. Kirsanov, who is of an older generation, clever and

comic and steeped in pathos, follows with a husky rendition of a "Thieves' Song" out of the Odessa ghetto, from which he stems. The toasts are eloquent and easy, in the familiar pattern: to the guest of honor, to poetry, to fraternity, to peace, to Soviet-American friendship. At my turn I struggle to my feet and say, with one of the group interpreting me phrase by phrase:

"I knew that I would find here, in Andrei's and Zoya's company, a room full of charming and gifted people, congenial and convivial souls. But let me confess to you that I was shocked to come upon evidence, down in the main lobby, that you are not so gentle as you seem. There, posted on the elevator shaft, I read your ultimatum, the one that is headed, WAR ON THE COCKROACH!, and that describes, like a veritable *Mein Kampf*, your campaign of extermination. What have you poets and artists got against the cockroach? Don't you realize that he is the most tenacious and adaptable of earth's creatures, the one above all who has mastered the art of survival on land and on sea, at any altitude, in the city and in the country, in the tropics and in the Arctic circle? Chase him, step on him, smash him, poison him, and he still endures. After the final holocaust, when every human being has been blasted into dust, who will scuttle from the rubble but our old brown-backed friend? So let us all rise now and pay tribute to the Noble and Indestructible Cockroach! Long may he live!" The table rocks with laughter. They are used to parabolic speech. All the glasses clink.

3. Bela Akhmadulina has arranged a surprise for me on my last night in Moscow. Outspoken, sloe-eyed, vibrant Bela, in her early thirties, with her high Tartar cheekbones and copper-colored bangs, has a tremendous following among students and fellow-poets, despite the slim body of her published work. Apart from the romantic legend attached to her, beginning with the lyrics written to her by her former husband Yevtushenko, she is rated by many as the outstanding lyric poet writing in Russia today. The news that she will share the platform with me on my valedictory appearance is sufficient to fill to overflowing the old auditorium in the "downtown" quarters of the University of Moscow. Every seat in the hall and

balcony is occupied, and there are students sitting in the aisles. It is my biggest audience. Bela, who has been trained as an actress, introduces me extravagantly and gives a dramatic reading of a poem of mine, "By Lamplight," that she has somehow translated despite her ignorance of English, and even amplified, since her version runs twice as long as the original. ("I guess I got carried away," she admits to me a bit sheepishly.) I follow with my translation of Voznesensky's rollicking celebration of her — "You are a goddess!" — together with a rather free and hasty version of one of her recent poems, "Little Planes," a characteristically naked and yet ambiguous lyric. For the rest of the evening we alternate in reading our own work. At the conclusion Bela kisses me onstage, the students rush forward to the platform and serenade me by clapping in unison, while a fresh-faced young girl tosses me a bouquet, to which a note in English is pinned that reads: "From Russian forest we bring you this bunch of wild flowers to thank you for your poems."

On Translating Akhmatova

> Bless thee, Bottom! bless thee! thou art translated.
> — *A Midsummer-Night's Dream*

Pasternak was once rebuked by a pedant who came to his door bearing a long list of the poet's mistakes in translating *Hamlet*. The complaint was greeted with laughter and a shrug: "What difference does it make? Shakespeare and I — we're both geniuses, aren't we?" As if to justify his arrogance, Pasternak's *Hamlet* is today considered one of the glories of Russian literature. My Russian friend who passed the anecdote on to me was unable to recall the visiting critic's name.

The poet as translator lives with a paradox. His work must not read like a translation; conversely, it is not an exercise of the free imagination. One voice enjoins him: "Respect the text!" The other simultaneously pleads with him: "Make it new!" He resembles the citizen in Kafka's aphorism who is fettered to two chains, one attached to earth, the other to

Based on my prefatory note to *Poems of Akhmatova,* by Stanley Kunitz with Max Hayward, Atlantic–Little, Brown, 1973. A version of these remarks appears in *Translation 73,* a collection of papers delivered at Columbia University (March 30, 1973) on the present state of literary translation.

heaven. If he heads for earth, his heavenly chain throttles him; if he heads for heaven, his earthly chain pulls him back. And yet, as Kafka says, "All the possibilities are his, and he feels it; more, he actually refuses to account for the deadlock by an error in the original fettering." While academicians insist that poetry is untranslatable, poets continue to produce their translations — never in greater proliferation or diversity than now.

The easiest poets to translate are the odd and flashy ones, particularly those who revel in linguistic display. The translator of Akhmatova, like the translator of Pushkin, is presented with no idiosyncrasy of surface or of syntax to simplify his task. Her poems exist in the purity and exactness of their diction, the authority of their tone, the subtlety of their rhythmic modulations, the integrity of their form. These are inherent elements of the poetry itself, not to be confused with readily imitable "effects." The only way to translate Akhmatova is by writing well. A hard practice!

Akhmatova's early poems, like those of most young poets, tend to deal with the vagaries of love, breathtaking now and then for their dramatic point and reckless candor. It has been said that she derived not so much from other poets as from the great Russian novelists of the nineteenth century. She herself enters into her poems like a character in a work of fiction, or in a play. On New Year's Day, 1913, when she was twenty-three, she broke a poem open with an expostulation that the guardians of the State were later to use against her: "We're all drunkards here, and harlots:/ how wretched we are together!" On the next New Year's Day she wrote, in bravura novelistic style:

> "What do you want?" I asked.
> "To be with you in hell," he said.
> I laughed: "It's plain you mean
> to have us both destroyed."
>
> He lifted his thin hand
> and lightly stroked the flowers:
> "Tell me how men kiss you,
> tell me how you kiss."

This was the period of her brilliant, if disastrous, first marriage, when husband and wife were the toast of the Bohemian set of St. Petersburg, he as Gumi-lev (Gumi-lion) and she as Gumi-lvitsa (Gumi-lioness). Her slender grace and aristocratic aquiline profile were as celebrated as her verses. Though in the post-Revolutionary years that followed she was to meet with terrible misfortunes; endure the indignities of poverty, official contempt, and silence; and suffer the death or exile of those dearest to her, she remained proud and spirited. Even in her last days, after her "rehabilitation"— sleazy bureaucratic euphemism! — she refused to wear the geriatric mask of complacence. In delirium she wrote:

> *Herewith I solemnly renounce my hoard*
> *of earthly goods, whatever counts as chattel.*
> *The genius and guardian angel of this place*
> *has changed to an old tree-stump in the water.*

Tragedy did not wither her: it crowned her with majesty. Her life, in Keats's phrase, became "a continual allegory," its strands interwoven with the story of a people. Indeed, her poems can be read in sequence as a twentieth century Russian chronicle. The only way to arrange them is in chronological order, while attempting to cover the breadth of her themes and of her expressiveness, which ranges, in Andrei Sinyavsky's words, "from a barely audible whisper to fiery oratory, from modestly lowered eyes to thunder and lightning."

I wish I were a better linguist than I am, but in default of that aptitude I count myself lucky in my partnership with Max Hayward. Akhmatova herself translated with outside help from a number of languages, including Chinese, Korean, Ancient Egyptian, Bengali, Armenian, Georgian, and Yiddish. Translator-poets in the past have consulted linguists as a matter of course, without feeling the need for acknowledging the assistance they received. The modern tendency, reflecting the dynamics of our curiosity about other cultures, is to facilitate and formalize the collaboration between poet and scholar. Largely owing to such combinations of skills, all literatures, however minor or esoteric, are at the point of becoming world literature. If, on occasion, I have rather boldly rendered a line or a phrase, it has always been on aesthetic grounds, never because I felt that my information was unreliable. Intuition is a blessing, but it is better to combine it with clarity of understanding.

In certain quarters the "literal version" of a poem is held sacred, though the term is definitely a misnomer. As Arthur Waley noted: "There are seldom sentences that have word-to-word equivalents in another language. It becomes a question of choosing between various approximations." Translation is a sum of approximations, but not all approximations are equal. Russian word order, for example, says: "As if I my own sobs/ out of another's hands were drinking." One has to rearrange the passage to make it sound idiomatic, and one may even have to sharpen the detail to make it work in English, but one is not at liberty to indulge in willful invention. The so-called literal version is already a radical reconstitution of the verbal ingredients of a poem into another linguistic system — at the expense of its secret life, its interconnecting psychic tissue, its complex harmonies.

Here is an early poem of Akhmatova's, written in the year following her marriage to the poet Gumilev — a very simple poem, perhaps the best kind to use for illustration. If you follow the original text word by word, this is how it reads:

> *He liked three things in the world:*
> *at evening mass singing, white peacocks*
> *and worn-out maps of America.*
> *Didn't like it when cry children,*
> *didn't like tea with raspberry jam,*
> *and female hysterics.*
> *But I was his wife.*

Despite its modesty, the Russian text has its charm and its music, which the slavish transcription forfeits completely. Whatever liberties one takes in translation are determined by the effort to recreate the intrinsic virtues of the source:

> *Three things enchanted him:*
> *white peacocks, evensong,*
> *and faded maps of America.*
> *He couldn't stand bawling brats,*
> *or raspberry jam with his tea,*
> *or womanish hysteria.*
> *. . . And he was tied to me.*

My deviations from the literal are for the sake of prosodic harmony, naturalness of diction, and brightness of tone. The poem in English is based on the irregular trimeters of the original, and it suggests the rhyming pattern without copying it exactly.

"Lot's Wife" is one of Akhmatova's most celebrated poems, often quoted by Russian poets and often imitated too. The theme seems to fascinate them, for fairly obvious reasons.

> *And the just man trailed God's shining agent,*
> *over a black mountain, in his giant track,*
> *while a restless voice kept harrying his woman:*
> *"It's not too late, you can still look back*
>
> *at the red towers of your native Sodom,*
> *the square where once you sang, the spinning-shed,*
> *at the empty windows set in the tall house*
> *where sons and daughters blessed your marriage-bed."*
>
> *A single glance: a sudden dart of pain*
> *stitching her eyes before she made a sound . . .*
> *Her body flaked into transparent salt,*
> *and her swift legs rooted to the ground.*
>
> *Who will grieve for this woman? Does she not seem*
> *too insignificant for our concern?*
> *Yet in my heart I never will deny her,*
> *who suffered death because she chose to turn.*

After Richard Wilbur and I discovered that we had been separately struggling with translations of "Lot's Wife," we compared our versions. Both of us acknowledged that it was the last stanza in particular that had given us a bad time. "Literally" it reads:

> *Who woman this weep for will?*
> *Not least does she not seem of losses?*
> *Only heart my never will forget*
> *Woman who gave life for one single peep.*

The sentiment is noble, but the sound in English is ridiculous. The problem each of us had faced was how to restore the dignity and style that had been lost in transit. Wilbur's fine translation concludes:

> *Who would waste tears upon her? Is she not*
> *The least of our losses, this unhappy wife?*
> *Yet in my heart she will not be forgot*
> *Who, for a single glance, gave up her life.*

Technically Wilbur's considerable achievement is to duplicate the original ABAB rhyme scheme (*not, wife, forgot, life*) without wrenching the sense, whereas I have only the second and fourth lines rhyming to suggest the contours of Akhmatova's measured quatrains. My impression, however, is that Wilbur has had to sacrifice, for the sake of his rhymes, more than they are worth. In a poem of his own I doubt that he would say, "Yet in my heart she will not be forgot/ Who, for a single glance, gave up her life." Nobody speaks like that, but the constrictions of the pattern did not leave him sufficient room in which to naturalize his diction.

In one of my many discarded versions of the stanza I wrote:

> *Who will grieve for this woman? Does she not seem*
> *the very least of losses in our book?*
> *Yet in my heart I never will forget her,*
> *who died in payment for a backward look.*

Perhaps I felt that the force of "backward look" had already been dissipated in the first stanza, and perhaps my ear resisted the terminal clink of the rhyme, but I can see now that those abandoned lines have the advantage of greater fidelity to the text and ease of movement. I may have made the wrong choice. In any event, I doubt that I have finished tinkering with "Lot's Wife."

The object is to produce an analogous poem in English out of available signs and sounds, a new poem sprung from the matrix of the old, drenched in memories of its former existence, capable of reviving its singular pleasures. The Russian poet Nikolai Zabolotsky had another figure for the process. He said it was like building a new city out of the ruins of the old.

Akhmatova is usually described as a formal poet, but in her later years she wrote more and more freely. Some of her poems, particularly the dramatic lyrics that developed out of her histrionic temperament, are so classically joined that they cannot be translated effectively without a considerable reconstruction of their architecture; others are much more fluid in their making. To insist on a universally rigid duplication of metrical or rhyming patterns is arbitrary and pointless, at any rate, since the effects are embedded in the language of origin and are not mechanically transferable to another language. Instead of rhyme our ear is often better pleased by an instrumentation of off-rhyme, assonance, consonance, and other linkages. Prosody is not founded on law, but on the way we speak, the way we breathe. In this connection Osip Mandelstam's widow offers a pertinent commentary:

In the period when I lived with Akhmatova, I was able to watch her at work as well, but she was much less "open" about it than M., and I was not always even aware that she was "composing." She was, in general, much more withdrawn and reserved than M. and I was always struck by her self-control as a woman — it was almost a kind of asceticism. She did not even allow her lips to move, as M. did so openly, but rather, I think, pressed them tighter as she composed her poems, and her mouth became set in an even sadder way. M. once said to me before I had met Akhmatova — and repeated to me many times afterward — that looking at these lips you could hear her voice, that her poetry was made of it and was inseparable from it. Her contemporaries — he continued — who had heard this voice were richer than future generations who would not be able to hear it."

It may be some comfort to reflect that poets are not easily silenced, even in death. As Akhmatova herself wrote, towards the end, "On paths of air I seem to overhear/ two friends, two voices, talking in their turn." Despite the passage of time, the ranks of listeners grow, and the names of Akhmatova and Pasternak and Mandelstam are familiar even on foreign tongues. Some of us are moved to record what we have heard, and to try to give it back in the language that we love.

Translation is usually regarded as a secondary act of creation. One has only to cite the King James Bible, Sir Thomas Malory's *Morte d'Arthur*, Chapman's *Homer*, Dryden's *Aeneid*, Fitzgerald's *Rubáiyát*, and for modern instances the poems of Pound and Waley, to demonstrate the fallacy of this view. Poets are attracted to translation because it is a way of paying their debt to the tradition, of restoring life to shades, of widening the company of their peers. It is also a means of self-renewal, of entering the skin and adventuring through the body of another's imagination. In the act of translation one becomes more like that other, and is fortified by that other's power.

Poet and State

> Geniuses are like a storm; they come up against the
> wind; terrify men; clean the atmosphere.
>
> — Søren Kierkegaard

> "It is impossible to remake the country." Quite so,
> but it is not impossible to remake the country in the
> *imagination.* . . . I want to place a value on everything I
> touch. . . .
>
> — William Carlos Williams

I begin with a parable. When Andrei Voznesensky was a
young man, he aspired to be an architect. One day a terrible
thing happened. The Moscow Architectural Institute, where
he was enrolled, went up in smoke, abruptly terminating his
studies. Voznesensky celebrated the event in a poem that
created something of a sensation. My version of it reads:

> *Fire in the Architectural Institute!*
> *through all the rooms and over the blueprints*
> *like an amnesty through the jails . . .*
> *Fire! Fire!*
>
> *High on the sleepy façade*
> *shamelessly, mischievously*
> *like a red-assed baboon*
> *a window skitters.*

Based on a lecture delivered at the Cooper Union School of Art and Architecture, New York, April 22, 1970.

We'd already written our theses,
the time had come for us to defend them.
They're crackling away in a sealed cupboard:
all those bad reports on me!

The drafting paper is wounded,
it's a red fall of leaves;
my drawing boards are burning,
whole cities are burning.

Five summers and five winters shoot up in flames
like a jar of kerosene.
Karen, my pet,
Oi! we're on fire!

Farewell architecture:
it's down to a cinder
for all those cowsheds decorated with cupids
and those rec halls in rococo!

O youth, phoenix, ninny,
your dissertation is hot stuff,
flirting its little red skirt now,
flaunting its little red tongue.

Farewell life in the sticks!
Life is a series of burned-out sites.
Nobody escapes the bonfire:
if you live — you burn.

But tomorrow, out of these ashes,
more poisonous than a bee
your compass point will dart
to sting you in the finger.

Everything's gone up in smoke,
and there's no end of people sighing.
It's the end?
              It's only the beginning.
*Let's go to the movies!**

---

* From *Antiworlds*, by Andrei Voznesensky, edited by Patricia Blake and Max Hayward, Basic Books, New York, 1966, p. 57.

Why is the poet so in love with that fire? A good citizen should deplore the destruction of property, especially of state property. The poet is drawn to that fire because it reveals itself to him as a metaphor for rage, for a passion burning beyond control, for a new and beautiful disorder that will make a shambles of the old Establishment. Those flames are fanned by a fresh wind blowing through the mind. In this poem, early in his career, Voznesensky affiliates himself with the great art of the West, which persists in opposing the solitary conscience to the overwhelming power of the corporate state.

So too, but with an opposite emphasis, the central theme of both Greek and Elizabethan tragedy is the irreconcilable conflict between individual will, passion, or genius and the dictates of a higher authority, whether sacred or secular. Shakespeare's major tragedies characteristically show us a state in the throes of convulsion induced by human weakness or error in high places. Those whose behavior threatens the security or stability of the kingdom must be beaten down. The stage is piled high with their corpses. In the end, when the turmoil has subsided, the new emblem of authority — Fortinbras or his equivalent — appears on the scene, to a flourish of trumpets. By the sacrifice of the hubristic ego, order has been restored.

The connection between good government and right words — of which poetry is the paradigm — has several facets. Confucius was once asked what he would do first if it were left for him to administer a country. As recorded in the *Analects*, the Master said: "It would certainly be to correct language." His listeners were surprised. "Surely," they said, "this has nothing to do with the matter. Why should language be corrected?" The Master's answer was: "If language is not correct, then what is said is not what is meant; if what is said is not meant, then what ought to be done remains undone; if this remains undone, morals and arts will deteriorate; if morals and arts deteriorate, justice will go astray; if justice goes astray, the people will stand in helpless confusion. Hence there must be no arbitrariness in what is said. This matters above everything."

Plato, on the other hand, felt that the right words for the poet might be the wrong words for the state. In justifying his proposal to expel "the makers" from his ideal Republic, he specifies that he has nothing against poets who know their place and are content to exercise their craft by writing hymns to the gods and praises of famous men. The poets to guard against are those who nourish the passions and desires. These are the sons of Dionysus, the god of wine and ecstasy, as opposed to the rulers of the state, who are sons of Apollo, a relatively moderate divinity. And he asks, in effect, the same sort of question that has issued from the vicinity of the White House in modern times: "How can you hope to preserve law and order if you permit these enemies of reason and decorum to run wild in the streets and disturb the population with their obscenities? Sometimes they get drunk. Sometimes they even get inspired. The reckless god turns them on."

I must have had Plato's animadversions in mind when I wrote in a poem some years ago, before the cracks in the public marble became visible:

> Perhaps there's too much order in this world.
> The poets love to haul disorder in,
> Braiding their wrists with her long mistress hair.

But that is only part of the picture, and I am ready to concede that in certain of his aspects the poet — including the Shakespearian archetype — is a fairly conservative fellow, who has earned whatever grants and honors the establishment chooses to heap on him. For one thing, no matter how inconoclastic he may profess to be, he realizes that he comes of a long line, and that his art is the momentary product of an ancient tradition, which will ultimately claim his words, if they have enough juice in them, and pass them on to the next generation.

Indeed, the poet is a Confucian of a sort, for he reveres his ancestors and acknowledges his debt to them. If, through personal or cultural privation, he is uncertain of his ancestors, he will spend his life, if need be, in search of them. Long before Frantz Fanon advised "the wretched of the earth" that if they were to have a future they must first create a past, poets were busy with their myth-making. And the posterity that poets keep in mind, and for which some of them foolishly write, is one that understands their language and inherits their values.

Form itself may be construed as a means of diverting subversive energies into productive channels. Even a rejection of "the System" gets incorporated into a system. If the poet celebrates, according to his temper, the life of the senses; if his mind is enchanted by the splendor and purity of forms; if he loves, in Keats's phrase, "the principle of beauty in all things," he serves to make existence more tolerable for others. At the least he is "the solitary who makes others less alone."

Since the poet's defense of order is unwitting and disguised, he should not expect to be thanked for it. I can recall how shocked I was early in my teaching experience, when the president of a girls' college told me that my course in "Creative Writing" — obnoxious term! — was exerting a pernicious influence on his charges. "All it does," he said, "is stir up the little bitches." I could not in good conscience reply that I was instructing them in an art designed to comfort, tranquilize, or console. Certainly the modern poets I cherish most are disturbing spirits: they do not come to coo.

The revolutionary is concerned with changing others; the poet wants to change himself. This does not make him less of a radical force. I recall Christopher Caudwell's shrewd observation, in *Illusion and Reality*, that the poet in his search for perfection inadvertently keeps alive the image of an ideal condition. In particular, the Romantic poet is inspired by love for a lost Eden, or for a Paradise not yet made. And a curious circumstance explains why the guardians of the state are right not to put their trust in him. Those kingdoms of his imagination become the reality of others. The news that breaks from them foments discontent with things as they are.

Hypothetically the state approximates the condition of the poem in its ability to maintain a precarious balance of order and freedom, tradition and change, tension and release. "The art of a free society," wrote Alfred North Whitehead, "consists, first, in the maintenance of the symbolic code; and secondly, in fearlessness of revision . . . . Those societies which cannot combine reverence to their symbols with freedom of revision must simultaneously decay." In Whitehead's formula, politics and poetry are made subject to the same law. Their vigor depends on an unremitting reciprocity between pastness and possibility. When the connecting syntax breaks down, the poles fly apart. Tradition deteriorates into orthodoxy or conformity, possibility into futurism or novelty.

The mind lives by its contradictions. And the poetic imagination must oppose any form of oppression, including the oppression of the mind by a single idea. Petty bureaucrats, party hacks, poetasters, all those who have failed, in Chekhov's phrase, to squeeze the serf out of their veins, can be counted on to do the oppressor's dirty work for him.

In a revolutionary period the activists are understandably disappointed in artists who do not overtly serve their movement. The Irish fighters for freedom despised Yeats for his failure to give them his unqualified support, not realizing that it was he who would immortalize their names and their cause:

> *I write it out in verse —*
> *MacDonagh and MacBride*
> *And Connolly and Pearse*
> *Now and in time to be,*
> *Wherever green is worn,*
> *Are changed, changed utterly:*
> *A terrible beauty is born.*

I can recall how vehemently the theologians of the left denounced American writers in the thirties who refrained from producing agitprop tracts. Those who were most abusive were the very ones who later felt that they had been betrayed by their dogma. Some of them turned eventually into reactionary scolds. The Weathermen of the sixties — idealists, most of them, intoxicated by their faith in the holiness of violence — were, in their turn, incapable of grasping that a society bereft of the graces and values that the arts perpetuate would not be a society worth inheriting.

I think of the poet as the representative free man of our time. Since the Industrial Revolution anyone who works for himself and alone has become a rarity. The writer is more different from others than ever because of his immediate, whole, and solitary relation to his work in the midst of a society where men labor in packs or gangs and are productive only in bits and pieces. Among writers the poet is freer than his brothers the novelist and playwright, because his work, unlike theirs, is practically worthless as a commodity. He is less subject than they to the pressure to modify the quality of his work in order to produce an entertainment. Nothing he can do will make his labor profitable. He might as well yield to the beautiful temptation to strive towards the purity of an absolute art. How much more fortunate he is than the contemporary painter or sculptor, whose work has become preeminently a thing to be bought and sold on the auction block at the whim of hustling speculators and custodians!

The modern crisis in poetry is older than most of us think. It goes back in time to a pair of related phenomena, the triumph of reason and the Industrial Revolution. With the Enlightenment, when rationalism became king, the church could no longer offer itself as a chalice in which to pour the wine of transcendence. Art divined itself as a substitute for religion, whereby men could satisfy their old need to belong to eternity as well as to time. The Industrial Revolution threatened people by proposing to turn them into wage-slaves — which indeed it did! It threatened the natural universe, that broad perspective of images, by polluting the landscape, by defiling Eden. Into the gardens of the West crept Satan, in the form of the wily entrepreneur. This is what the English poets at the dawn of the nineteenth century were trying to say, with varying degrees of awareness of what it was that alarmed them. "We have given our hearts away, a sordid boon!" cried Wordsworth. Blake, whose voice gets clearer every year, cursed the "dark Satanic Mills" and promised not to "cease from Mental Fight/ . . . Till we have built Jerusalem/ In England's green and pleasant Land." In Victorian England, when the battle was all but lost, the Jesuit Hopkins, who still clung to his faith that "nature is never spent;/ There lives the dearest freshness deep down things," protested, for an audience not yet born:

Generations have trod, have trod, have trod;
And all is seared with trade; bleared, smeared with toil;
And wears man's smudge and shares man's smell; the soil
Is bare now, nor can foot feel, being shod.

The poet knows that his roots, the roots of being, strike deep into the biosphere; that the entire living creation is sacred to him; that whoever cuts him off from his source withers him; that whoever despoils, defoliates, hates, kills, is his enemy. In Blake's lacerating words: "Each outcry of the hunted hare/ A fibre from the brain doth tear." Coleridge felt man's inhumanity so strongly that he risked blemishing his masterpiece by appending to it a moral tag: "He prayeth well who loveth well/ Both Man and bird and beast."

The God whom Coleridge invokes is the God "of all things, both great and small." But in the distribution of souls the Church subscribes to a restrictive covenant. The prime offense of Christianity against nature is that it has concerned itself with the salvation of man at the expense of all other creatures. Only now is it becoming evident that a gospel confined to the human parish — and in practice to only a fraction of its inhabitants — is a prescription for annihilation.

"A conversation about trees is almost a crime," wrote Bertolt Brecht, "because it involves keeping silent about so many misdeeds" — as if to imply, by his unfortunate example, that there are no sins against nature worth talking about. Even a Communist genius can fall into Christian error. And why not? Marxist dogma is no less man-centered than its adversary.

The frontier where man must defend his life, the principle of life itself, is at the very edge of creation, where existence and non-existence are scarcely distinguishable, where we confront the anonymous and minimal, among the plankton and protozoa. Man will perish unless he learns that the web of the universe is a continuous tissue. Touch it at any point, and the whole web shudders.

The arts, like that web, comprise a far-flung network, a psychic membrane, along whose filaments communication is almost instantaneous. All arts, all artists, are somehow connected. Cézanne paints a new picture in his studio in Aix. Overnight, through the rest of France, thousands of paintings begin to fall off the walls. And all at once poets, waking, look out of their windows at a landscape that they had never seen before. One of them, inventor of the color of vowels, announces: *"Il faut être absolument moderne."* It keeps happening all the time.

The poet knows that revolutions of sensibility are not won at the barricades. He also knows that there is no way in which he can escape history, even if he should want to. Stephen Dedalus's arrogant cry, *"Non serviam,"* still echoes in his ear, flattering his conviction that genius does not stoop to causes. At the same time he realizes that the hour is late now, and that some refusals are no longer permitted him, lest he wither at the heart. "The writer's function," said Camus in his acceptance of the Nobel Prize, "is not without arduous duties. By definition, he cannot serve those who make history; he must serve those who are subject to it." To whom can one pledge one's allegiance except to the victims?

A generation ago it was possible — though I still find it hardly credible — to be both a reactionary and a poet, even a major poet. Yeats adored the aristocracy; Eliot was a snob and sometimes worse; Stevens in some of his letters sounds like a proto-Bircher; and we all know the sad truth about Pound. But I do not go to them for their politics. And besides, if I try hard enough, I can rationalize their defections. These were the last voices of an élitist society — though Pound's case was complicated by an odd infusion of populism. The fruits of Progress dismayed them. They saw a world cheapened and brutalized. So they fought, each in his own way, to preserve a kind of life that was sweeter and nobler to them than the new barbarism that threatened to engulf them.

If poetry teaches us anything about our feelings, it must be that we can have several feelings about the same thing at the same time. These feelings are not necessarily compatible; and if we try to solidify them into a certainty, they become other feelings. When I think of Ezra Pound, I do not try to ignore the shameful fugue of his Fascism and anti-Semitism; but I also remember his generosity to other poets, the wide range of his sympathy and intelligence, his lovely gift for friendship, his seminal influence, and — above all — those poems of his, defying an age that "demanded an image of its accelerated grimace":

> *There died a myriad,*
> *And of the best, among them,*

> *For an old bitch gone in the teeth,*
> *For a botched civilization.*
>
> *Charm, smiling at the good mouth,*
> *Quick eyes gone under earth's lid,*
>
> *For two gross of broken statues,*
> *For a few thousand battered books.*

I value that man in the act of writing that poem.

In a politicized world the labels we pin on people — Communist or Fascist, Democrat or Republican, liberal or conservative — are thought to betoken constant and irrevocable values, of paramount significance. Most of us believe that the shape of the future will be determined politically. When priorities are discussed, it is usually assumed that art is somehow "less relevant" than politics, though both are structures concerned with the quality of life — politics for the short term, art for the long. In Russia, where poets are subject to political censorship, they are regarded as heroes; in our own country, where they write what they please, they are generally treated, outside of academic circles, with indifference, and not infrequently with contempt. Even so fine a critical intellect as Edmund Wilson could ask, "Does it really constitute a career for a man to do nothing but write lyric poetry?" To put me in my place I keep a copy of that impolite query on my desk. But I am fortified by an impolite retort, which I will not repeat here.

Thomas Mann once remarked that history might have been changed if Karl Marx had read the poet Friedrich Hölderlin — Hellenist, enthusiast, pantheist, and madman. The notion of such a pairing is infinitely provocative. I could wish that Nixon had been capable of reading Berryman's *Dream Songs*. But that would be like hoping for him to recover a childhood he lost or never owned. Can any American politician since Lincoln be said to have possessed the quality that Yeats defined as "radical innocence," a root-purity of wonder?

Among poets the exaltation of the innocents springs from their kinship with the natural life force. A patch of bluebells brought Hopkins "news of God." The effort of a plant cutting to sprout led Roethke to exclaim: "What saint strained so much,/ Rose on such lopped limbs to a new life?" Pasternak's dear friend, the poet Marina Tsvetaeva, said of him: "He anticipated Adam, and was still living in the fourth day of creation." Even the Revolution, she noted, entered his consciousness "like everything in his life, through nature. In the summer of 1917, he kept in step with it: he listened." What was he listening for? For whatever the roots could tell him of life, of hope, of rebirth. As Anna Akhmatova wrote in a poem about him: "It means he is tiptoeing over pine needles,/ So as not to startle the light sleep of space." And the last stanza of her tribute begins: "He has been rewarded by a kind of eternal childhood."

Not all the great writers of the century have been so fortunate. Neither Joyce, nor Proust, nor Eliot, nor Frost, nor Stevens — I could name others — can be said to have cultivated their humanity, to have fulfilled themselves outside their art. Pasternak, as he says in one of his poems, remained "alive to the very end."

Among modern American poets I think of William Carlos Williams as belonging to that blessed category. Who else had enough love and life and buoyancy in him to write?:

> *He has on*
> *an old light grey Fedora*
> *She a black Beret*

> *He a dirty sweater*
> *She an old blue coat*
> *that fits her tight*

> *Grey flapping pants*
> *Red skirt and*
> *broken down black pumps*

> *Fat Lost Ambling*
> *nowhere through*
> *the upper town they kick*

their way through
heaps of fallen maple leaves

still green — and
crisp as dollar bills
Nothing to do. Hot cha!*

Of Pasternak and Williams it can be said that they did more than merely care about their art: they cared about others. If they were ruthless on occasion in friendship or love, they were consistently more ruthless with themselves. For these reasons their work gives off a special kind of radiance.

To preserve that shining innocence, that irrepressible élan, and yet to know evil, to be the steady vessel of a rage — how many are great enough for such a task? No bolder challenge confronts the modern artist than to stay healthy in a sick world. Humanity these days, in the view of Claude Lévi-Strauss, recalls the behavior of maggots in a sack of flour. "When the population of these worms increases," he observes, "even before they meet, before they become conscious of one another, they secrete certain toxins that kill at a distance — that is, they poison the flour they are in, and they die." And he presents the ominous drama inside that self-contaminated bag of maggots as a metaphor for the human predicament.

The conscience of the artist constrains him to remain sensitive to the psychological and moral toxins that mankind secretes. He does so at the risk of sounding like a redundant alarm bell. One of the dangers of poetry, certainly, is grandiosity. Let us not deceive ourselves: a poet isn't going to change the world with even the most powerful of his poems. The best he can reasonably hope for is to conquer a piece of himself. Wallace Stevens said, in a modest tone of voice, that poetry was a way of getting the day in order.

* "Late for Summer Weather," in *The Complete Collected Poems of William Carlos Williams 1906–1938*, New Directions, 1938, p. 214.

The Modernity of Keats

A fine writer is the most genuine Being in the
World.

To consider the life of John Keats is to recall his own prophetic comment: "A Man's life of any worth is a continual allegory." He belongs almost as much to legend as he does to the
history of literature. More than anybody else he is responsible
for the modern image of the Romantic poet. It is not an image
that he inherited; it is, rather, an image that he created in his
works and days, out of the ardent beauty of his character, the
"fine excess" of his imagination, the cruel brevity of his span.
Modern readers do not need to be told to admire John Keats:
whether they know it or not, he has already entered into their
dreams, he is a portion of their hopes, he lives in their desires.
As Shelley wrote in "Adonais," his elegy on the death of
Keats: "He is a presence to be felt and known in darkness and
in light. . . . He is a portion of the loveliness which once he
made more lovely."

From a talk given at the School of Visual Arts, New York City. Some of the
material derives from my introduction to *Poems of John Keats,* edited by me
for Thomas Y. Crowell Company, New York, 1964.

That is one way of approaching the study of John Keats and, given the occasion, it is a perfectly suitable way, but considering that he has been dead a century and a half and that his fame in that interval has suffered no diminishing — quite the contrary — I feel that it would be an act of self-indulgence to deliver yet another eulogy. I propose instead to do something quite modest and practical — that is, to look at some of Keats's representative work with a rather cold and watchful eye, the kind of eye that poets tend to turn on other people's poems. That is not quite so simple an undertaking as it may sound. We do not clearly focus on the poets of the past, for we regard them through the eyeball of an ancestral giant who has already thumbed their pages, underscored their most sentimental passages, memorized their worst lines; and this Cyclopean organ, with its superfluity of moisture, can scarcely be termed an ideal instrument of perception. If I can get the focus reasonably right, perhaps I can begin to understand why, ever since the idolatry of my youth, from which I had to fight myself free, I have been impelled to return intermittently to the pages of Keats as to a battlefield in the history of one man's taste, over which have raged certain small but savage wars.

Keats did not go to college. His entire schooling in the liberal arts consisted of seven years at a small academy in the country village of Enfield, some ten miles from London. Shortly before his fifteenth birthday he was taken out of school by his guardian, Richard Abbey, and apprenticed to a surgeon and apothecary. To be a surgeon at that time was to be something less than a physician, of whom professional study at a university was required: the surgeon performed practical services, such as setting bones and pulling teeth, and administered drugs and advice in simple cases. Keats completed his medical training at Guy's Hospital in the slums of London, just south of London Bridge. The dressing of infected wounds was one of his principal activities. In July 1816, he received his license to practice as apothecary and surgeon as soon as he became twenty-one. By the date of his birthday next autumn, he had made a different kind of commitment which seems to have deprived the world, in consequence, of an indifferent surgeon.

Now the wheel of life — and of death — began to turn for him at a dizzying and frightful speed. Though his creative flight had scarcely begun, he had less than five years left in which to draw breath on this planet, actually only three years of productivity, after which he would be far too exhausted by illness to task himself further.

Contrary to the general impression, he was by no means precocious. His first verses were imitative and fumbling. I have had dozens of students in my own classes who were better poets at twenty than was Keats. Unfortunately, their rate of development did not match his. Here is a sonnet, one of three on the perennially teasing subject of Woman, that Keats wrote in his twentieth year and which he valued enough to include in his 1817 volume:

> *Ah! who can e'er forget so fair a being?*
> *Who can forget her half retiring sweets?*
> *God! she is like a milk-white lamb that bleats*
> *For man's protection. Surely the All-seeing,*
> *Who joys to see us with his gifts agreeing,*
> *Will never give him pinions, who intreats*
> *Such innocence to ruin, — who vilely cheats*
> *A dove-like bosom. In truth there is no freeing*
> *One's thoughts from such a beauty; when I hear*
> *A lay that once I saw her hand awake,*
> *Her form seems floating palpable, and near;*
> *Had I e'er seen her from an arbour take*
> *A dewy flower, oft would that hand appear*
> *And o'er my eyes the trembling moisture shake.*

Such versifying is more than merely bad, in its sentimentality and banality: it is totally without promise, unredeemed by a single just phrase or epithet, untouched by any feeling for the sonnet structure. It seems incredible that this same callow young man, by October of the following year, should have produced, in a two-hour fit of improvisation, the resplendent sonnet "On First Looking into Chapman's Homer." In the Chapman sonnet: "Much have I travell'd in the realms of gold, And many goodly states and kingdoms seen . . ." Keats anticipated the kind of poem, without fully realizing it, that has as its matter the experience of poetry. He externalized his matter by treating art as though it were landscape — "Then felt I like some watcher of the skies/ When a new planet swims into his ken;/ Or like stout Cortez when with eagle eyes/ He star'd at the Pacific" — a strategy that was to culminate in Yeats's symbolic voyage to Byzantium.

In Keats's two longish discursive poems of the same year, 1816, both of them dealing with nature and art, his landscape is quite conventionally descriptive, closer to the past than to the modern spirit in its insistence on the edifying and inspirational function of Nature. I quote from "I Stood Tip-Toe":

> *For what has made the sage or poet write*
> *But the fair paradise of Nature's light?*
> *In the calm grandeur of a sober line*
> *We see the waving of the mountain pine;*
> *And when a tale is beautifully staid,*
> *We feel the safety of a hawthorn glade:*
> *When it is moving on luxurious wings,*
> *The soul is lost in pleasant smotherings.*

In those smotherings the influence of his friend Leigh Hunt is palpable. At one point we stop to watch the swarms of silver-bellied minnows "staying their wavy bodies 'gainst the streams," but little else is observed with sufficient closeness to arrest our attention. "Sleep and Poetry" opens with an air of bluff cuteness and breaks on a note of mild hysteria as the poet contemplates, on bended knees, his awful task. In both poems the poet is a peripatetic whose journey to and through a landscape results in an increment of pleasure and of creative power. The relationship is one of cause and effect. Having "stood tip-toe upon a little hill" and permitted himself "to peer about upon variety," he is soon ready to announce:

> *I was light-hearted,*
> *And many pleasures to my vision started;*
> *So I straightway began to pluck a posey*
> *Of luxuries bright, milky, soft and rosy.*

In "Sleep and Poetry" he sees Nature as "an eternal book/ Whence I may copy many a lovely saying/ About the leaves and flowers." Nature and daydreams lead to a healthy conclusion: "And up I rose refresh'd, and glad, and gay,/ Resolving to begin that very day/ These lines. . . ." In the same fashion, more than a decade earlier, Wordsworth had been refreshed by the daffodils:

> For oft, when on my couch I lie
> In vacant or in pensive mood,
> They flash upon that inward eye
> Which is the bliss of solitude;
> And then my heart with pleasure fills,
> And dances with the daffodils.

Wordsworth was able to express a more complex and profound response to the natural universe in several of his major meditations, best crystallized in the familiar lines from "Tintern Abbey":

> For I have learned
> To look on nature, not as in the hour
> Of thoughtless youth; but hearing oftentimes
> The still, sad music of humanity, . . .
> And I have felt
> A presence that disturbs me with the joy
> Of elevated thoughts; a sense sublime
> Of something far more deeply interfused,
> Whose dwelling is the light of setting suns,
> And the blue sky, and in the mind of man:
> A motion and a spirit, that impels
> All thinking things, all objects of all thought,
> And rolls through all things.

Coleridge, in his Dejection ode, made a philosophic summation of this theory of interpenetration:

> O Wordsworth! We receive but what we give
> And in our life alone does Nature live.

"Thy soul," he was to write later of his friend, "received/ The light reflected, as a light bestowed." But it remained for Keats to transcend abstraction and didacticism and to embody this consubstantial experience in his art.

Before I discuss the transcendent odes, however, I want to offer some incidental observations. First, let me comment on three imperfect sonnets written late in 1816, at about the time of his twenty-first birthday. The least of these, from which Robert Frost must have derived one of his most famous closures, begins:

> Keen, fitful gusts are whisp'ring here and there
> Among the bushes half leafless, and dry;
> The stars look very cold about the sky,
> And I have many miles on foot to fare.

I note the metrical lapse — exceptional for Keats, with his fine ear — in the second line, and the adverbial stuffing in the third; but my positive reason for quoting the passage is to illustrate the effort that Keats was making at that time to achieve a tone of direct, familiar address, an effort that could still fall into such embarrassments as, "For I am brimful of the friendliness/ That in a little cottage I have found." Naturally, the cottage belonged to Leigh Hunt. The "Sonnet Written in Disgust of Vulgar Superstition" is chiefly notable for its theme, Keats's disaffection with religion in general and with Christianity in particular. "The church bells," he tells us, "toll a melancholy round"; "the sermon has a horrid sound"; "surely the mind of man is closely bound in some black spell." What consoles him, even as he feels "a chill as from a tomb," is that this vulgar superstition is dying out and that "fresh flowers will grow, and many glories of immortal stamp" — in other words, that religion will be replaced by nature and by art.

On the next to the last day of 1816 Keats improvised, on a challenge, his sonnet "On the Grasshopper and Cricket," beginning luckily, "The poetry of earth is never dead," and ending:

> On a lone winter evening, when the frost
> Has wrought a silence, from the stove there shrills

The Cricket's song, in warmth increasing ever,
And seems to one in drowsiness half lost,
The Grasshopper's among some grassy hills.

A text in prosody could be based on the auditory counterpoint between the heavy sleeping vowels of the next-to-last line — "And seems to one in drowsiness half lost" — and the diminishing consonantal chirp of the last — "The Grasshopper's among some grassy hills."

Saintsbury said that Keats was the first poet in English to make deliberate and constant use of assonance in English, and though my inclination is always to challenge such dicta — what of Shakespeare, who anticipated everything, and Milton, who was one of the most conscious of musicians? — he is certainly more right than he is wrong. By 1818, according to Keats's friend Benjamin Bailey, he had fully developed his prosodic system. "One of his favorite topics of discourse," recalled Bailey, "was the principle of Melody in Verse, upon which he had his own notions, particularly in the management of open & close vowels. . . . Keats's theory was, that the vowels should be so managed as not to clash one with another so as to mar the melody, — & yet that they should be interchanged, like differing notes of music to prevent monotony." In this respect Keats is certainly a forerunner of Symbolist theory.

I do not have the time to dwell on Keats's straight narrative poems, and even if I did I doubt that I should be able to incorporate them usefully in this discussion. There is practically no narrative poetry today. By the end of the nineteenth century the novelists had preempted the narrative art and though some poets may have thought at first that they had a grievance, they did not know how lucky they were to be relieved of the necessity of telling a story. Since the twenties, in fact, the novelists have been trying to do the same, competing with one another in the amount of narrative of which they can divest themselves. All the arts join in testifying that the order that interests the modern imagination is not a sequential order.

Nevertheless, it will be helpful to us in our discussion not to lose complete sight of Keats's chronology. The reviews that greeted *Endymion* in the spring of 1818 were brutally unkind. Though Keats was hurt by the ridicule, he was by no means crushed. After all, he had been the first to recognize that it was a flawed performance. To his brother George he wrote quietly, firmly: "This is a mere matter of the moment — I think I shall be among the English Poets after my death." His even bolder gesture was to begin work on *Hyperion,* which, despite its unfinished state — perhaps because of it — retains an air of noble grandeur. There had been something boyish and appealing, despite the reviewers, about *Endymion;* the imagination responsible for *Hyperion* has severity and magnitude — it is, above all, manly. By an effort of his will, directed against his own nature, Keats has put himself momentarily in command of an epic voice, in the high Miltonic style:

> *Deep in the shady sadness of a vale*
> *Far sunken from the healthy breath of morn,*
> *Far from the fiery noon, and eve's one star,*
> *Sat gray-hair'd Saturn, quiet as a stone,*
> *Still as the silence round about his lair;*
> *Forest on forest hung about his head*
> *Like cloud on cloud. No stir of air was there,*
> *Not so much life as on a summer's day*
> *Robs not one light seed from the feather'd grass,*
> *But where the dead leaf fell, there did it rest.*

Occasionally another pitch of voice interrupts the measured flow — a voice fierce, private, immediate:

> *. . . I am gone*
> *Away from my own bosom: I have left*
> *My strong identity, my real self.*

As Keats was to put it in a letter, this was "the true voice of feeling," as opposed to what he termed, however unjustly, "the false beauty proceeding from art." These distinctions are precisely the ones that have agitated the most seminal poet-critics since his day.

The idea of a poem on the fall of the Titans, with Apollo the

God of light and song as its hero, had occurred to him while he was still grinding away at *Endymion*. In the actual writing he became absorbed in the tragic fate of Hyperion, the older god of the Sun, whom Apollo dethrones. The theme offered certain parallels with Keats's own sense of his plight as a poet of the new age (Apollo) striving to achieve a work of the original imagination, while at the same time stirred by the power and magnitude of his divinely gifted predecessor (Hyperion).

Two cataclysmic events shook Keats at the end of 1818: "poor Tom" died on the first of December; by Christmas, John had fallen wildly in love with Fanny Brawne. As the letters testify, the only love for a woman that could be meaningful, or even possible, for him was a passion that matched in intensity his consuming love for poetry. These two loves were not at peace with each other; on the contrary, they fought for possession of him. He was already agitated by the loss of his brother and beginning to be worried about his own health, specifically about a chronic "sore throat" that he could not shake off. Furthermore, his mind was in a constant fever of creation. At this point Keats had just turned twenty-three; Fanny was a young charmer of eighteen.

In the history of English poetry Keats's next year (1819) must be counted among the miracles. In January he wrote "The Eve of St. Agnes" over a period of nine or ten days. April saw the birth, in a single session, of "La Belle Dame sans Merci." The real explosion came in May, when (ignoring lesser poems) three of the finest odes in the language ("Nightingale," "Grecian Urn," and "Melancholy") were completed within fifteen days. During the summer he worked on "Lamia" and "The Fall of Hyperion." The last of the odes, "To Autumn," unique in its music and its majesty, was written on a Sunday in September. Two days later he abandoned his exalted second try at the Hyperion myth, recast in the form of a dream. And that was about it. The rest was a dwindling and a torment.

In the odes all of Keats's ambitions, gropings, self-examinations, and experiments pay off. The odes constitute our bridge to the world of Elizabethan genius, but they are by no means a throwback to that world or an imitation of it. I quarrel with Ezra Pound's left-handed compliment — that "Keats very probably made the last profitable rehash of Elizabethanism." It is true that the odes are not the cantos, but neither are they "The Shepheardes Calender."

In three years Keats has come a long way from the time of the Daffodil-bit, from Tip-toe time when his look at the scenery left him "light-hearted,/ And many pleasures to [his] vision started."

> *My heart aches, and a drowsy numbness pains*
> *My sense, as though of hemlock I had drunk,*
> *Or emptied some dull opiate to the drains*
> *One minute past, and Lethe-wards had sunk:*
> *'Tis not through envy of thy happy lot,*
> *But being too happy in thine happiness,—*
> *That thou, light-winged Dryad of the trees,*
> *In some melodious plot*
> *Of beechen green, and shadows numberless,*
> *Singest of summer in full-throated ease.*

That full-throated melody from his "Ode to a Nightingale" is the music of metamorphosis, but not metamorphosis in the classical or Renaissance sense. The change that occurs is in the state of being: observer altering into the thing observed.

> *Adieu! adieu! thy plaintive anthem fades*
> *Past the near meadows, over the still stream,*
> *Up the hill-side; and now 'tis buried deep*
> *In the next valley-glades:*
> *Was it a vision, or a waking dream,*
> *Fled is that music: — Do I wake or sleep?*

In his sonnet "On the Grasshopper and Cricket" Keats had practiced that same effect of distancing. There it was anecdotal, here it is intrinsic and substantive. Subject and Object, Here and There have become movable counters. Mind and Nature have chosen each other as partners in a dance. The Nobel Prize physicist of our century who wrote, "We are both spectators and actors in the great drama of existence," could have been writing a commentary on the odes.

The paradox implicit in "Ode on a Grecian Urn" rests on the distinction between the mind of the observer, moving on the flood of time, with truth as its object, and the figures on the vase, caught in the timeless world of art, who have no function, indeed no existence, except in so far as they embody a concept of Beauty. How shall the one know the other? How can these two worlds be reconciled? Keats raises the magnificent questions that had not been asked before, but he has no strategy for answering them except to pretend momentarily that the figures are human, involved in the drama of life and death. Eventually he arrives at an impasse: "Thou, silent form, dost tease us out of thought/ As doth eternity," eternity being unknowable. The aphoristic conclusion is too glib to be persuasive, despite the ardent efforts of the Keatsians to redeem it. No matter how you read, " 'Beauty is truth, truth beauty,' — that is all/ Ye know on earth, and all ye need to know," the lines have a thematic and didactic smack to them. Keats has a finer aesthetic perception in one of his letters when he refers to the reality of ethereal things, and names them: "such as existences of Sun Moon & Stars and passages of Shakespeare," or when, on another occasion, he asserts, "The Imagination may be compared to Adam's dream — he awoke and found it truth."

The last and finest of the odes, "To Autumn," requires little commentary. It needs to be heard. On the surface it is a fairly simple descriptive piece, but all the description has been transformed into process, all the content devoured by the form.

"To Autumn" is the consummation of Keats's art. It represents the triumph of the poet's mind over the matter of the poem, the dissolution of the subject-object relationship, the unification of the field of experience. The meaning of the poem is that it exists: it does not need to try to say anything. I think of it as all music, but I am grateful that it stays language. Many poems, like the medlar pear, get rotten before they are ripe; this one stays golden and does not turn.

Keats knew that his kind of poet, recognizable by mobility of mind and fluidity of identity, by the sacrifice of self, had to be distinguished from what he called "the Wordsworthian or egotistical sublime." He wanted to get away from fixity; in the beginning, perhaps, from the fixity of his inferior social status; eventually, from the fixity of the opinionated man, and from the fixity of his own selfhood. The power of the intuitive life, of the liberated imagination, he defined as Negative Capability only because it resisted the temptation to do something — something positive — about everything, out of its preference for being everything about something. In his own words, "the poetical Character . . . has no self — it is everything and nothing — It has no character — it enjoys light and shade; it lives in gusto, be it foul or fair, high or low, rich or poor, mean or elevated — It has as much delight in conceiving an Iago as an Imogen. What shocks the virtuous philosopher, delights the chameleon Poet." The kind of mind he admired was one so volatile that it contained no obstruction in the shape of ideas. "Every point of thought," he wrote, "is the centre of an intellectual world. The two uppermost thoughts in a man's mind are the two poles of his world — he revolves on them; and everything is Southward or Northward to him through their means — we take but three steps from feathers to iron."

In the medieval world art served the Church; during the Renaissance it celebrated the glory of man and of the State that translated the glory into power; in the modern world, which begins with a pair of Revolutions (French and Industrial) art emerges as a new kind of priesthood, secular, self-ordained, designed to please neither State nor Church, making no concessions even to its own congregation. In Keats's words: "I never wrote one single Line of Poetry with the least shadow of public thought."

After the Enlightenment, which culminated in the eighteenth century with the triumph of Reason and of Reason's sisters, Skepticism and Empiricism, the organized church was no longer capable of serving as an outlet for Man's transcendental yearnings. Art, which had always previously deferred to the sovereignty of extrinsic power, separated itself from the stream of progress, from the establishment, from institutional sanctions, from mundane values, and became a vessel of purification, a sacramental action.

Even today we find that supreme rationalist Jean-Paul

Sartre confessing in his autobiography, significantly entitled *Words*, that for most of his life literature has been for him a quasi-mystical expression. Words were his prayer and his penance; names were more real than things; the only priesthood that tempted him was the priesthood of literature, complete with its magic roots and ritual satisfactions, its sacramental equivalents of communion, mediation, atonement. This is "squalid nonsense" to him now, but even in the act of announcing his liberation, as an atheist, from all illusions, including the illusion of the Word, he cannot free himself from the language of the people of the Book: "I have renounced my vocation, but I have not unfrocked myself. I still write. What else can I do?"

Keats, who was a poet — unlike Sartre — would have had no difficulty in understanding the philosopher's dilemma. Others before him had celebrated the beauty of earth, the might of man, and the majesty of God, but Keats did something else that makes all the difference: he aspired to live his life as though it were a poem, not ascetically, but in the full sensuous bloom of youth, and he sought a language that would incarnate the poetry of his blood. With Keats the ordeal of the life becomes sacred for poetry. "I am certain of nothing," he could say, "but the holiness of the Heart's affections and the truth of Imagination." In his early "Sleep and Poetry" he had prayed for time in which to serve out his novitiate:

> *O for ten years, that I may overwhelm*
> *Myself in poesy; so I may do the deed*
> *That my own soul has to itself decreed.*

Three years later, with the taste of death already in his mouth, he was to spill the bitter cup onto the unfinished pages of "The Fall of Hyperion":

> *What benefit canst thou do, or all thy tribe,*
> *To the great world? Thou art a dreaming thing,*
> *A fever of thy self . . .*
> *Only the dreamer venoms all his days,*
> *Bearing more woe than all his sins deserve.*

Keats was not one to confuse idle reverie and polite versifying with the vocation for which he sweated in "the vale of soul-making," the existential trial. Even in the anguish of his desolation he took pains to elucidate a fine distinction:

> *The poet and the dreamer are distinct,*
> *Diverse, sheer opposite, antipodes.*

It is gratifying to follow Keats in the development of his technical skills, but we do him a disservice if we fail to understand that for him technique was not an aggregate of mechanical skills, but a form of spiritual testimony, the sign of the inviolable Self consolidated against the enemies within and without that would disperse it. Blake, before Keats, had been interested in changing other people's lives; he had been less interested in changing his own. After Keats, who did not live to exhaust the possibility of his changes, and after Baudelaire and Rimbaud, who fought at the gates of modern art, we no longer look for poets in country vicarages and overstuffed salons. We find them, rather, in the thick of life, at every intersection where values and meanings cross; caught in the eternal traffic between self and universe; alert to take spontaneous advantage of every opportunity for choice, to respond energetically, as the planet turns on its axis, to the slightest shift in equilibrium. For these poets "the morality of the right sensation," in Wallace Stevens's phrase, has displaced the paraphernalia of the Christian ethos. The purity is in being true, if only for an instant of awareness, when language makes its clean cut along the grain of being. "Why did I laugh tonight?" is the way Keats begins one of his imperfect poems, too heavily burdened with the load of his mortality; and five generations away the unmasked desperation in that cry still troubles us:

> *Why did I laugh to-night? No voice will tell:*
> *No God, no Demon of severe response,*
> *Deigns to reply from heaven or from Hell.*
> *Then to my human heart I turn at once.*
> *Heart! Thou and I are here sad and alone;*
> *Say, wherefore did I laugh? O mortal pain!*

The last serious lines that Keats wrote were found scrawled on the manuscript of an abortive comic poem. They constitute only a fragment, but these days we are half in love with fragments, and this one is of more interest than most because, in its dramatic immediacy and directness of feeling, it points the way to a kind of poetry that some among us are still trying to write:

> *This living hand, now warm and capable*
> *Of earnest grasping, would, if it were cold*
> *And in the icy silence of the tomb,*
> *So haunt thy days and chill thy dreaming nights*
> *That thou wouldst wish thine own heart dry of blood*
> *So in my veins red life might stream again,*
> *And thou be conscience-calmed — see here it is —*
> *I hold it towards you.*

The spontaneity of Keats's mind is present in almost everything he touched. Some of the random speculations in his engrossing letters, such as those on the reality of the imagination, the "disinterested" nature of the poetic character, Negative Capability, the beauty of the instinctive act, the ordeal of "soul-making," have withstood the attrition of the years, to endure as critical and philosophical touchstones. In the poems themselves his concern with sound and texture, his restless pursuit of a style, the energy of his language, his effort to "load every rift" with ore, his universal empathy, his concentration on the poetic act mark him as forerunner of much that we categorize as "modern" in poetry. By being what he was he brought Shakespeare and the mystery of Shakespearian vision closer to us; in his own fluid identity, he embodied the meaning of Romantic genius; he gave witness to the possibility of a life of poetry that impinges on the heroic.

2

Four for Roethke

*You objects that call from diffusion my
    meanings and give them shape!
You light that wraps me and all things in
    delicate equable showers!
You paths worn in the irregular hollows by
    the roadsides!
I believe you are latent with unseen
    existences. . . .*

— Walt Whitman

Rather abide at the center of your
being; for the more you leave it, the
less you learn.

— Lao-tzu

Remembering Roethke
(1908–1963)

The poet of my generation who meant most to me, in his person and in his art, was Theodore Roethke. To say, in fact, "poet of my generation" is to name him. Immediately after Frost and Eliot and Pound and Cummings and Hart Crane and Stevens and William Carlos Williams, it was difficult to be taken seriously as a new American poet; for the title to "the new poetry" was in the possession of a dynasty of extraordinary gifts and powers, not the least of which was its stubborn capacity for survival. When Roethke was a schoolboy in Michigan in the twenties, these poets had already "arrived." For a long time, in the general view, they remained the rebels and inventors.

Roethke took his own work seriously indeed. Lashed by his competitive and compulsive temper, he committed himself fully to the exhausting struggle for recognition — a desperately intimate struggle that left its mark on him. Only a few

The original version of this reminiscence appeared in the *New York Review of Books*, October 17, 1963.

years before his death, he could refer to himself sardonically as "the oldest younger poet in the U.S.A."

More than a third of a century has passed since he blew into my life like the "big wind" of one of his poems. I was living in the Delaware Valley then. He came, unannounced, downriver from Lafayette College, where he was instructor in English and — more satisfying to his pride — tennis coach. My recollection is of a traditionally battered jalopy from which a perfectly tremendous raccoon coat emerged, with my first book of poems tucked under its left paw. The introductory mumble that followed could be construed as a compliment. Then he stood, embarrassed and inarticulate, in my doorway, waiting to gauge the extent of my hospitality. The image that never left me was of a blond, smooth, shambling giant, irrevocably Teutonic, with a cold pudding of a face, somehow contradicted by the sullen downturn of the mouth and the pale furious eyes: a countenance ready to be touched by time, waiting to be transfigured, with a few subtle lines, into a tragic mask. He had come to talk about poetry, and talk we did over a jug grandly and vehemently all through the night. There were occasions in the years that followed when I could swear that I hadn't been to bed since.

Our evenings in the years that followed seemed to move inexorably towards a moment of trial for both of us when he would fumble for the crinkled manuscript in his pocket and present it for approval. During the reading of his poem he waited in an attitude of excruciating tension and suspicion. If the praise failed to meet his expectation, he would grow violently defensive or lapse into a hostile silence. Nevertheless, he was by no means impervious to criticism or to suggestions. When I proposed *Open House* as the title for his first book of poems (1941), he not only adopted it gratefully but proceeded to write the title-poem that still stands at the head of his collected verse:

> *My secrets cry aloud.*
> *I have no need for tongue.*
> *My heart keeps open house,*
> *My doors are widely swung.*

An epic of the eyes
My love, with no disguise.

On another country visit, in the following decade, he asked me long after midnight to read something choice to him. I picked up Sir John Davies's neglected Elizabethan masterpiece *Orchestra*, a poem that he had somehow never chanced on despite his omnivorous appetite for verse, and I can still recall the excitement with which he responded to the clear-voiced music.

From that encounter, combined with his deep attachment to the best of Yeats — it was beat, above all, that enchanted him — he composed the memorable sequence *Four for Sir John Davies*, which was to set the cadence for a whole new cycle of later poems:

> *Is that dance slowing in the mind of man*
> *That made him think the universe could hum?*
> *The great wheel turns its axle when it can;*
> *I need a place to sing, and dancing-room,*
> *And I have made a promise to my ears*
> *I'll sing and whistle romping with the bears.*

Roethke was not easy on his friends, but neither was he easy on himself. In the proper season, when conversation became dangerous, we would fight it out on the courts for what we liked to boast, with a bow to Joyce, was the lawn tennyson championship of the poetic world. For all his six-foot-three, two-hundred-plus-pound bulk and his lumbering gait, he was amazingly nimble on his feet and ruthless at the kill, with a smashing service and a thunderous forehand drive. The daemon in him played the game just as it wrote the poems. Whatever he did was an aspect of the same insatiable will to conquer self and art and others. He could not bear to lose. If you managed to beat him by cunning and luck, you could not expect to be congratulated by him: he was more likely to smash his racket across his knees. After the steady deterioration of his body had forced him to abandon the game — his knees in particular gave out — he retreated into croquet and badminton, which he played with the same rapture and *Schrecklichkeit*.

As a young man he felt humiliated and disgraced by the periodic mental breakdowns that were to afflict him all his life. There were outbreaks and absences and silences that he had to cover up, partly because he realized what a threat they offered to his survival in the academic world. He was one of the supreme teachers of poetry, but not until he came — after Bennington — to the University of Washington in 1947 did he have any assurance of tenure.

By the time of his arrival in Seattle, Roethke had found the means of transforming his ordeal into language. Eventually, he more than half believed that the springs of his disorder, his manic-depressive cycles, were inseparable from the sources of his art, and he could brag of belonging to the brotherhood of mad poets that includes William Blake, John Clare, and Christopher Smart, with each of whom he was able to identify himself as "lost." His affection for Dylan Thomas had much the same base; but on the other hand, some of his longest friendships, including those with Louise Bogan and W. H. Auden, signified his unswerving admiration for those who stood in his mind as representatives of a sacred discipline.

The book of Roethke's that I continue to think of as the great one is *The Lost Son*, published in 1948. Reviewing it for *Poetry*, I commented on one of his remarkable gifts, that of the compassionate flow of self into the things of his experience. His poems become what they love. No other modern poet seems so directly tuned to the natural universe: his disturbance was in being human. The life in his poems emerges out of stones and swamps, tries on leaves and wings, struggles towards the divine. "Brooding on God," he wrote near the end, "I may become a man." The soul trapped in his ursine frame gathered to itself a host of "lovely diminutives." This florist's son never really departed from the moist, fecund world of his father's greenhouse in Saginaw.

In 1953 Roethke married one of his former Bennington students, Beatrice O'Connell, in celebration of whose beauty he produced a spate of love poems, including the sportive one that begins, "I knew a woman, lovely in her bones." During the weekend visit after their wedding, when he was in a manic phase, he wrote for me in longhand an account of himself that I still have in my possession. One passage reads:

I have tried to transmute and purify my "life," the sense of being defiled by it, in both small and formal and somewhat blunt short poems and, latterly, in longer poems which try in their rhythm to catch the very movement of the mind itself, to trace the spiritual history of a protagonist (not "I," personally), of all haunted and harried men; to make in this series (now probably finished) a true and not arbitrary order which will permit many ranges of feelings, including humor.

Roethke's humor was no gentle, prattling thing. After all, one does not go to the axe to learn about politeness. He found his own ribaldry side-splitting and was convinced that nobody since Edward Lear had composed such hilarious rhymes for children. It was during the wedding visit that he proposed to demonstrate his comic genius by entertaining my three-year-old daughter with a recitation of his nonsense verse. His first selection was a quatrain entitled "The Cow." Dancing around her, thumping out the beat, illustrating the action with appropriate gestures, he roared the lines:

> *There Once was a Cow with a Double Udder.*
> *When I think of it now, I just have to Shudder!*
> *She was too much for One, you can bet your Life:*
> *She had to be Milked by a Man and His Wife.*

The result might have been anticipated. Gretchen burst into tears and tried to hide under the sofa.*

* This episode is translated into one of my poems, "Journal for My Daughter" (*The Testing-Tree*, Atlantic–Little, Brown, 1971, p. 5):

> *There was a big blond uncle-bear,*
> *wounded, smoke-eyed, wild,*
> *who shambled from the west*
> *with his bags full of havoc.*
> *He spoke the bears' grunt-language,*
> *waving his paws*
> *and rocking on his legs.*
> *Both of us were drunk,*
> *slapping each other on the back,*
> *sweaty with genius.*
> *He spouted his nonsense-rhymes,*
> *roaring like a behemoth.*
> *You crawled under the sofa.*

He found it possible, increasingly, to incorporate a wild sort of laughter into his flights. "I count myself among the happy poets," he would say, knowing that the laughter and the fierceness and the terror were indivisible. In "this matter of making noise that rhymes" — his phrase — he dared to seek a combination of vulgarity and nobility, and he put his stamp on the mixture.

In the spring of 1960, Roethke gave his last reading in New York at the Poetry Center, where I introduced him. He had a high fever, and backstage he was jittery, sweating copiously as he guzzled champagne — "bubbly," he called it. On stage, for the first portion of his program he clowned and hammed incorrigibly, weaving, gyrating, dancing, shrugging his shoulders, muttering to himself intermittently, and now and then making curiously flipper-like or foetal gestures with his hands. But gradually, as the evening wore on, he settled into a straight dramatic style that was enormously effective and moving. When he came to his new "mad" sequence, headed by the poem that begins, "In a dark time the eye begins to see," his voice rang out with such an overwhelming roll of noble anguish that many in the audience wept.

As we filed out of the hall, a friend remarked on Roethke's strange affinity to that other lost and violent spirit, Jackson Pollock. "How true!" I thought. And I heard myself repeating a tender and rather enigmatic phrase that the painter Franz Kline had suggested for Pollock's epitaph: "He divined himself."

News of the Root

I study the lives on a leaf; the little
Sleepers, numb nudgers in cold dimensions,
Beetles in caves, newts, stone-deaf fishes,
Lice tethered to long limp subterranean weeds,
Squirmers in bogs,
And bacterial creepers . . .

With *The Lost Son,* Theodore Roethke confirms what some of us have long suspected: that he stands among the original and powerful contemporary poets. In this remarkable collection he undertakes a passionate and relentless exploration of the sources of a life. The two major sections consist of a sequence of thirteen short poems that might be described, roughly, as botanical studies, and a quartet of long poems that are the record of a psychic adventure, the poet's quest of himself. For critical purposes the book needs to be examined as a whole: almost everything in it proliferates from a single root-cluster of images.

A greenhouse is the country of Roethke's childhood, the inevitable place of his return. This world under glass where, as a boy, small among "the lovely diminutives," he grubbed, weeded, pruned, transplanted, is bound in with his family, for whom it was, presumably, an economic as well as a physical

A review of *The Lost Son and Other Poems,* by Theodore Roethke, originally published in *Poetry,* January 1949.

center of gravity. In one of his most successful poems, which illustrates the naked precision and force of his vocabulary, he celebrates the ordeal of the greenhouse in the big wind, when he stayed with it all night, stuffing the holes with burlap. To him the structure, as will be seen, is not a *thing*; it has gender and personality; on this specific occasion it excites his admiration — he speaks of it *con amore*:

> *But she rode it out,*
> *That old rose-house,*
> *She hove into the teeth of it,*
> *The core and pith of that ugly storm*
>
> .   .   .   .   .   .
>
> *She sailed into the calm morning,*
> *Carrying her full cargo of roses.*

The horticultural aspects of Roethke's work should be clearly defined. What absorbs his attention is not the intricate tracery of a leaf or the blazonry of the completed flower, but the stretching and reaching of a plant, its green force, its invincible Becoming.

> *This urge, wrestle, resurrection of dry sticks,*
> *Cut stems struggling to put down feet,*
> *What saint strained so much,*
> *Rose on such lopped limbs to a new life?*

I do not wish to give the impression that Roethke's greenhouse world is rosy, innocent, optimistic. On the contrary, it swarms with malevolent forces. It is a place of scums, mildews, and smuts; of slug-soft stems; of obscenely lolling forms; a place moist and rank ("what a congress of stinks!"), engulfing, horribly fecund. The delicate slips keep coaxing up water; the sprouts break out, slippery as fish. Suddenly we are under ground, under water, in a grave, in a womb, in the deep ponds of the subconscious; plunged like Caliban into our creature-self; enduring the foetal throes. Underness is everywhere:

Came to lakes; came to dead water,
Ponds with moss and leaves floating,
Planks sunk in the sand.

. . . . . .

Nothing would sleep in that cellar, dank as a ditch.

. . . . . .

What fish-ways you have, littlest flowers.

. . . . . .

Where do the roots go?
  Look down under the leaves.

. . . . . .

The dark flows on itself. A dead mouth sings
  under an old tree.

. . . . . .

Last night I slept in the pits of a tongue.

As Roethke, with an almost nightmarish compulsiveness, makes his descent into the mythic regions of Father Fear and Mother Mildew, a furious energy activates his language; his metaphors whirl alive, sucking epithets into their centers of disturbance from the periphery of the phrase; his rhythms wrench themselves out of the fixed patterns of his earlier style and become protean, incantatory, organic; what will not submit itself to him he takes by storm, if he cannot take it by magic. The child encountered "under the concrete benches, Hacking at black hairy roots, — Those lewd monkey-tails hanging from drainholes," might serve as an image of the poet himself at his creative labor.

The ferocity of Roethke's imagination makes most contemporary poetry seem pale and tepid in contrast. Even his wit is murderous. He does not strain for cleverness, but he can achieve a concentration of phrase that is as brilliant as it is violent: "Dogs of the groin barked and howled" . . . "You will find no comfort here, In the Kingdom of bang and blab" . . . "I have married my hands to perpetual agitation, I run, I run to the whistle of money." His imagination is predominantly tactile and auditory (subject at times to the vice of echolalia). He is so aware of the transformations of the self that much of his imagery is palpably metamorphic: "This wind gives me scales, Have mercy, gristle" . . . "Call off the dogs, my paws are gone." At this depth of sensibility, far below the level of the rational, language itself breaks down, reverting to a kind of inspired nonsense, expressive of the childhood of the race as well as of the individual:

> Rich me cherries a fondling's kiss,
> The summer bumps of ha:
> Hand me a feather, I'll fan you warm,
> I'm happy with my paws.

Roethke's first volume, *Open House* (1941), was praised, deservedly, for its lyric resourcefulness, its technical proficiency, its ordered sensibility. The present collection, by virtue of its indomitable creativeness and audacity, includes much more chaos in its cosmos; it is difficult, heroic, moving, and profoundly disquieting. What Roethke brings us in these pages is news of the root, of the minimal, of the primordial. The sub-human is given tongue; and the tongue proclaims the agony of coming alive, the painful miracle of growth. Here is a poetry born of the maelstrom. It would seem that Roethke has reached the limits of exploration in this direction, that the next step beyond must be either silence or gibberish. Yet the daemon is with him, and there is no telling what surprises await us. I find it significant and highly encouraging that the volume ends triumphantly, luminously, with a thrust upward into "the whole air," into the "pierce of angels":

> To follow the drops sliding from a lifted oar,
> Held up, while the rower breathes, and the small boat
>   drifts quietly shoreward;
> To know that light falls and fills, often without our
>   knowing,
> As an opaque vase fills to the brim from a quick pouring,
> Fills and trembles at the edge yet does not flow over,
> Still holding and feeding the stem of the contained flower.

The Taste of Self

I

In a dark time, the eye begins to see:
I meet my shadow in the deepening shade;
I hear my echo in the echoing wood,
A lord of nature weeping to a tree.
I live between the heron and the wren,
Beasts of the hill and serpents of the den.

II

What's madness but nobility of soul
At odds with circumstance? The day's on fire!
I know the purity of pure despair,
My shadow pinned against a sweating wall.
That place among the rocks — is it a cave
Or winding path? The edge is what I have.

III

A steady storm of correspondences! —
A night flowing with birds, a ragged moon,
And in broad day the midnight come again!
A man goes far to find out what he is —
Death of the self in a long tearless night,
All natural shapes blazing unnatural light.

IV

Dark, dark my light, and darker my desire.
My soul, like some heat-maddened fly,
Keeps buzzing at the sill. Which I is I?
A fallen man, I climb out of my fear.
The mind enters itself, and God the mind,
And one is One, free in the tearing wind. *

* "In a Dark Time," by Theodore Roethke, as first published in *The New Yorker*, January 16, 1960; included in Roethke's *Collected Poems*, Doubleday, 1966, with minor variations.

Written for *The Contemporary Poet as Artist and Critic,* edited by Anthony Ostroff (Little, Brown, 1964); originally published in *New World Writing* No. 19 (Lippincott, 1961).

"Searching nature," noted Gerard Manley Hopkins in 1880, "I taste *self* but at one tankard, that of my own being." Comparably, Theodore Roethke searches for a language, a lyric process, in and through a world of multiple appearances, to convey the sensation of the torment of identity. Logic told Hopkins that he was doomed to fail in his effort to distill "this taste of myself, of *I* and *me* above and in all things, which is more distinctive than the taste of ale or alum, more distinctive than the smell of walnutleaf or camphor, and is incommunicable by any means to another man (as when I was a child I used to ask myself: What must it be to be someone else?)." But logic did not prevent him from writing "in blood" the sonnet beginning "I wake and feel the fell of dark, not day," with its harrowing lines from the far side of anguish, "I am gall, I am heartburn. God's most deep decree/ Bitter would have me taste: my taste was me." In Roethke the self is divided, and the hostile parts are seen as voraciously cannibalistic: "My meat eats me."

Like much of Roethke's later work, "In a Dark Time" is marked by a style of oracular abstraction. The vocabulary is plain, predominantly monosyllabic; the pentameters are strictly measured and often balanced; the stanzaic units, with their formalized combination of true and off-rhyme, adhere to a tight pattern. If these fiercely won controls were to break down at any point, the whole poem would collapse in a cry, a tremendous outpouring of wordless agitation.

With lesser poets we are inclined to stay in the poem itself, as in a closed society that satisfies our public needs. Roethke belongs to that superior order of poets who will not let us rest in any one of their poems, who keep driving us back through the whole body of their work to that live cluster of images, ideas, memories, and obsessions that constitutes the individuating source of the creative personality, the nib of art, the very selfhood of the imagination. In my reading of "In a Dark Time" I shall try to indicate, selectively, how its configurations are illuminated by the totality of the poet's vision and intuition.

Stanza I

The poem begins with a paradox, the first of a series of seeming contradictions to establish the dialectic of the structure. The "dark time," like Hopkins's "fell of dark," bespeaks the night of spiritual desolation, that *noche obscura del alma,* in which, according to the testimony of the mystics, the soul is tortured by the thought "that God has abandoned it ... that He cast it away into darkness as an abominable thing," in the classic description by St. John of the Cross. "The shadow of death and the pains and torments of hell are most acutely felt, that is, the sense of being without God. . . . All this and even more the soul feels now, for a fearful apprehension has come upon it that thus it will be with it for ever." Such desolation is not an obsolescent state, nor one reserved only for the religious. Modern philosophy and psychiatry have been much concerned with the condition of anxiety, defined by Dr. Rollo May as "the subjective state of the individual's becoming aware that his existence can become destroyed, that he can lose himself and his world, that he can become nothing." In simpler terms, "anxiety is the experience of the threat of imminent non-being."

Roethke's first words inform us that the speaker has already entered into his land of desolation. If a poem is to be made, which is tantamount to saying if a spirit is to be saved, it will only be by a turning to the light, by a slow recognition of the beloved diurnal forms. As is true of Roethke's major sequence, *Praise to the End,* the archetypal journey of the poem is from darkness into light, from blindness into vision, from death into life. The emergent landscape is already familiar to us: "Eternity howls in the last crags,/ The field is no longer simple:/ It's a soul's crossing time." We have listened before to this poet's invocation of the creatures of earth that arose out of the original deep and that alone can show him the way back to the baptismal source: "Wherefore, O birds and small fish, surround me./ Lave me, ultimate waters."

His first encounters, as he struggles to recover his identity, are not with things in themselves or even with himself as object, but with shadow and echo, the evidences at one remove of his existence. "Once I could touch my shadow, and be happy." In his need for self-esteem he describes himself as a lord, though only "a lord of nature weeping to a tree": he is not ready for the world of human sympathy. His place is in the lower order of creation, in the kingdom where he is most at home. One of Roethke's earliest poems celebrated the heron, not as the philosopher bird, in the manner of Yeats, but as the antic lord of his observed amphibian environment. The leg on which the heron balances in the marsh is his visible connection with the primordial element. As for wrens, they are forever flitting through Roethke's poems in the guise of the most blessed and light-hearted of God's creatures, free as they almost are of the gross burden of corporeality. "The small" are associated with beginnings; they invariably excite the poet's tenderness or his joy, not always unalloyed with dread. The implicit question in this passage is spelt out in another poem:

> *Where was I going? Where?*
> *What was I running from?*
> *To these I cried my life —*
> *The loved fox, and the wren.*

Roethke's quadrupeds, except for those who live in holes, such as the bear and the fox, are not usually "loved"; most of the time they appear as rabid and predatory, "dogs of the groin," the running pack of sex. Reptiles are either overtly phallic or emblematic of "pure, sensuous form."

Stanza II

As if in reply to an accusing voice, the poet launches into an impassioned self-justification. The world may call him mad, but it is only because he refuses to compromise with the world that he suffers this sacred disorder. Madness knows an ecstasy, a burning revelation, that is denied to reason. "Reason? That dreary shed, that hutch for grubby schoolboys!" In his ordeal of despair and terror he has faced the absolute. "Who else sweats light from a stone?" "Tell me, body without skin, does a fish sweat?" the momentary clarity of vision, born of the authenticity of suffering, fades. "That place among the rocks" would seem to be suggested by the "sweating wall" in the previous line. In one sense it is Golgotha, the place of suffering; in another, it is a place beyond, but dimly apprehended, as through a clouded window — a habitation fit for one who identifies himself with the "beasts of the hill." Is it a promise of rest, of hiding, of Being? Or of departure, journeying, Becoming? Caves and nests, in Roethke, are womb images, representing the sub-world of intuition and the unconscious. Conversely, the "winding path" signifies the world of one's unfolding fate, realizable only in terms of action. The "edge" that the poet lays claim to, in an abrupt return of certainty, is expounded in another context:

I was always one for being alone,
Seeking in my own way, eternal purpose;
At the edge of the field waiting for the pure moment . . .

If I read Roethke aright, he is differentiating between the spiritual life, which is achievable through discipline, prayer, and revelation, and "the life within," which is the soul locked inside the cabinet of flesh, the cave, and not locked in alone, but with the central devouring worm. Hell is the trap where one is forever tasting oneself. To be saved one must undertake in the dark the long journey from flesh, that is, from the country of one's birth and bondage, that bloody incestuous ground, to the other side of the field, or to the appalling height, the jumping-off place, where the clean light falls on everything one has learned to love. Is this a parable for art? Blake tells us that "the road of excess leads to the palace of wisdom," and, again, that "improvement makes straight roads; but the roads without improvement are roads of Genius." There is a kind of poetry that, in its creative excess, insists on pushing itself to the edge of the absurd, as to the edge of a cliff, at which point only two eventualities remain conceivable: disaster or miracle. The real and beautiful absurdity, as every artist knows, is that the miracle sometimes occurs.

Stanza III

The voice is one of growing assurance, as the things of this world emerge more and more sharply, not only in their bold lineaments but in their metaphorical radiations as well. No contemporary poet can use the word "correspondences" without harking back to Baudelaire and his Symbolist heirs. For Roethke, nature is the wayward source of joys and illuminations, the great mother of secrets, from whom they must be wooed or pried, out of urgent necessity, and at any cost.

> *Sing, sing, you symbols! All simple creatures,*
> *All small shapes, willow-shy,*
> *In the obscure haze, sing!*
>
> *The moon, a pure Islamic shape, looked down.*
> *The light air slowed: It was not night or day.*
> *All natural shapes became symbolical.*

At the visionary climax of the poem, under the transformations of the cloud-torn moon, the air becomes electric with the agitated flight of birds. Everything is in motion, plunged beyond the syntax of time, to the brink of incoherence, where there are no divisions between night and day, reason and unreason, ecstasy and despair. The steadying thought is that "a man goes far to find out what he is"; in other words, that the life justifies the journey to "the edge." Elsewhere, in a variant of this maxim, Roethke has written, "I learn by going where I have to go." The last two lines of the stanza are a triumphant collocation of the spiritual and phenomenal levels of this total experience: the self dying, the world revealed. Past pity for himself and past tears, our "lord of nature weeping to a tree" hardens to a man arrived "in a long tearless night." The light that he sees blazing from "all natural shapes" is termed "unnatural," largely in the sense of "supernatural," transcending nature, but certainly also with the force of an epithet transferred from witness to object. Roethke has answered for himself the question that he posed in an earlier poem:

> *Before the moon draws back,*
> *Dare I blaze like a tree?*

The answer may well be: Yes, by becoming a tree.

Stanza IV

As the transcendent moment fades, the poet returns to the prison-house of his senses. The slow rhythm, the massed percussive effects suggest the heaviness of his tread, the weight of his body. He can scarcely untrack himself from the word "dark." Where once he wrote, "The dark has its own light," he now asserts the countertruth. In the blindness of desire is the deepest dark. Even the soul is seen as contemptible, an insect frenzied with heat (desire) that keeps batting itself at the window of perception, trying to get out.

> *In the slow coming-out of sleep,*
> *On the sill of the eyes, something flutters,*
> *A thing we feel at evening, and by doors,*
> *Or when we stand at the edge of a thicket. . . .*

The true ancestor of this ominous apparition can be found in "The Lost Son":

> *Sat in an empty house*
> *Watching shadows crawl,*
> *Scratching.*
> *There was one fly.*

As Hopkins when a child puzzled, "What must it be to be someone else?," Roethke inquires, pressing the same question of identity, "How can I find myself in the confusion of my separate and divided selves?" What desolates him is the thought that he has no true identity, and what makes him whole again is the recognition and confession that he is "a fallen man," whose quintessential taste is that of being lost. To embrace this knowledge is to overcome the dread of non-being, is to be redeemed or, so to speak, reborn. In the final couplet the separation between mind and God is dissolved in the mystery of interpenetration. Having found the divinity in himself, man is free — free to fly, like the birds of the preceding stanza — in the chancy wind that will leave him "torn and most whole."

"In a Dark Time" recalls the lamentation that more than a century ago John Clare wrote in madness, beginning "I am: yet what I am none cares or knows." The parallelism extends to the sestet structure as well as to the theme, whose history of explicit formulation runs back through Descartes and Iago to the eternal Yahwe's "I am that I am." Roethke's poem seems to me more solid, more profound, more terrible than Clare's, altogether finer, but I must grant that it is curiously less affecting, perhaps for the simple reason that it is less naïve, more ambitious. Amid so much nobility and injured pride one longs for the artless human touch. At his infrequent best when Clare writes, "I am the self-consumer of my woes"; when he speaks of living "like vapours tost/ Into the nothingness of scorn and noise"; when he deplores "the vast shipwreck of my life's esteems," we cannot doubt that he is eating dust; his long sigh overrides the beat and surges through to the final word. Roethke's admirable restraints on his cold rage have not permitted him the liberty of a sustained action. Each self-enclosed stanza is conceived as a separate stage for which new scenery must be set up for a repetition of the drama of rebirth. Only an extraordinary creative energy, such as is manifestly present here, could set the stages rolling like a procession of pageants in a medieval mystery. Roethke succeeds, for me, in effecting this illusion through three complete stanzas of mounting intensity and almost halfway through the fourth, where I stumble on his rhetorical question. The fussy grammar of "Which I is I?" is only part of the trouble; I am more concerned with the clinically analytic tone, which jars on the ear that has been listening to a stranger music. Furthermore, I am not wholly persuaded by the final couplet, superbly turned as it is. It may be my own deficiency that leads me to resist whatever seems to smack of conventional piety, but I cannot agree that anything in the poem prepares me for so pat a resolution. The "natural" climax remains, marvelous though unresolved, in Stanza III.

Despite its flaw, "In a Dark Time" asserts its power by the traces of agitation it leaves in its wake. Few poems offer such eloquent testimony to the capacity of the human spirit to renew itself by immersion in the destructive element.

Poet of Transformations

> Behold, I show you a mystery; we shall not all sleep,
> but we shall all be changed.
>
> — I Corinthians XV.51

In the myth of Proteus we are told that at midday he rose from the flood and slept in the shadow of the rocks of the coast. Around him lay the monsters of the deep, whom he was charged with tending. He was famous for his gift of prophecy, but it was a painful art, which he was reluctant to employ. The only way anyone could compel him to foretell the future was by pouncing on him while he slept in the open. It was in order to escape the necessity of prophesying that he changed his shape, from lion to serpent to panther to swine to running water to fire to leafy tree — a series of transformations that corresponds with the seasons of the sacred king in his passage from birth to death. If he saw that his struggles were useless, he resumed his ordinary appearance, spoke the truth and plunged back into the sea.

A lifework that embodied the metamorphic principle was abruptly terminated on August 1, 1963, when Theodore

Originally published in *The New Republic*, January 23, 1965.

Roethke died, in his fifty-fifth year, while swimming at Bainbridge Island, Washington. He was the first American bardic poet since Whitman who did not spill out in prolix and shapeless vulgarity, for he had cunning to match his daemonic energy and he had schooled himself so well in the formal disciplines that he could turn even his stammerings into art. If the transformations of his experience resist division into mineral, vegetable, and animal categories, it is because the levels are continually overlapped, intervolved, in the manifold tissue. Roethke's imagination is populated with shapeshifters, who turn into the protagonists of his poems. Most of these protagonists are aspects of the poet's own being, driven to know itself and yet appalled by the terrible necessity of self-knowledge; assuming every possible shape in order to find the self and to escape the finding; dreading above all the state of annihilation, the threat of non-being; and half-yearning at the last for the oblivion of eternity, the union of the whole spirit with the spirit of the whole universe.

Roethke's first book, *Open House* (1941), despite its technical resourcefulness in the deft probings for a style, provided only a few intimations of what was to develop into his characteristic idiom. The title poem, in its oracular end-stopping and its transparency of language, can serve as prologue to the entire work:

> *My truths are all foreknown,*
> *This anguish self-revealed. . . .*
>
> *Myself is what I wear:*
> *I keep the spirit spare.*

Perhaps the finest poem in this first volume is "Night Journey," in which the poet, telling of a train ride back to his native Michigan, announces his lifelong loyalty to what he never tired of describing, even if somewhat sardonically on occasion, as the American heartland. The poem opens:

> *Now as the train bears west,*
> *Its rhythm rocks the earth . . .*

— how important that verb of rocking is to become! — and it
ends:

> *I stay up half the night*
> *To see the land I love.*

The middle of the poem is occupied by a quatrain that
prefigures one of his typical patterns of response:

> *Full on my neck I feel*
> *The straining at a curve;*
> *My muscles move with steel,*
> *I wake in every nerve.*

Some thirty years later — he seemed never to forget an experience — in the first of his "Meditations of an Old Woman,"
the old woman being presumably his mother when she is not
Roethke himself, he was to offer, through the medium of her
voice recalling a bus ride through western country, a recapitu-
lation of that same sensation: "taking the curves." His imagination was not conceptual but kinesthetic, stimulated by
nerve-ends and muscles, and even in its wildest flights local-
izing the tension when the curve is taken. This is precisely
what Gerard Manley Hopkins meant when, in one of his
letters, he spoke of the "isolation of the hip area." The
metamorphosis of the body begins in the isolation of the part.

Another poem in *Open House*, entitled "The Bat," concludes:

> *For something is amiss or out of place*
> *When mice with wings can wear a human face.*

It took time for Roethke to learn how full the world is of such
apparitions . . . and worse!

The confirmation that he was in full possession of his art and
of his vision came seven years later, with the publication of
The Lost Son (1948), whose opening sequence of "greenhouse
poems" recaptures a significant portion of his inheritance.
Roethke was born, of Teutonic stock, in Saginaw, Michigan, in

1908. The world of his childhood was a world of spacious commercial greenhouses, the capital of his florist father's dominion. Greenhouse: "my symbol for the whole of life, a womb, a heaven-on-earth," was Roethke's revealing later gloss. In its moist fecundity, its rank sweats and enclosure, the greenhouse certainly suggests a womb, an inexhaustible mother. If it stands as well for a heaven-on-earth, it is a strange kind of heaven, with its scums and mildews and smuts, its lewd monkey-tail roots, its snaky shoots. The boy of the poems is both fascinated and repelled by the avidity of the life-principle, by the bulbs that break out of boxes "hunting for chinks in the dark." He himself endures the agony of birth, with "this urge, wrestle, resurrection of dry sticks, cut stems struggling to put down feet." "What saint," he asks, "strained so much, rose on such lopped limbs to a new life?" This transparent womb is a place of adventures, fears, temptations, where the orchids are "so many devouring infants!":

> They lean over the path,
> Adder-mouthed,
> Swaying close to the face,
> Coming out, soft and deceptive,
> Limp and damp, delicate as a young bird's tongue.

When he goes out to the swampland to gather moss for lining cemetery baskets, he learns of the sin committed *contra naturam*, the desecration against the whole scheme of life, as if he had "disturbed some rhythm, old and of vast importance, by pulling off flesh from the living planet" — his own flesh. And he encounters death in a thousand rotting faces — all of them his own — as at the mouldy hecatomb he contemplates death crowning death, in a dump of vegetation . . . "over the dying, the newly dead."

The poet's green, rich world of childhood was self-contained, complete in itself. Mother waited there: she was all flowering. When father entered, that principle of authority, he was announced by pipe-knock and the cry, "Ordnung! Ordnung!" So much wilderness! and all of it under glass, organized, controlled. For the rest of his life Roethke was to seek a

house for his spirit that would be as green, as various, as ordered. And he was often to despair of finding it. In one of his
last poems, "Otto," named after his father, he concludes:

> *The long pipes knocked: it was the end of night.*
> *I'd stand upon my bed, a sleepless child*
> *Watching the waking of my father's world —*
> *O world so far way! O my lost world!*

Roethke's passionate and near-microscopic scrutiny of the
chemistry of growth extended beyond "the lives on a leaf" to
the world of what he termed "the minimal," the very least of
creation — bacteria, aphids, newts, tadpoles. These are creatures still moist with the waters of the beginning. At or below
the threshold of the visible they correspond to that darting,
multitudinous life of the mind under the floor of the rational,
in the wet of the subconscious.

Roethke's immersion is these waters led to his most heroic
enterprise, the sequence of interior monologues which he ini-
tiated with the title poem of *The Lost Son,* which he continued in *Praise to the End* (1951), and which he persisted up
to the last in returning to, through a variety of modifications
and developments. "Each poem," he once wrote, "is complete
in itself; yet each in a sense is a stage in a kind of struggle out
of the slime; part of a slow spiritual progress; an effort to be
born, and later, to become something more." The method is
associational rather than logical, with frequent time shifts in
and out of childhood, in and out of primitive states of consciousness and even the synesthesia of infancy. Motifs are
introduced as in music, with the themes often developing con-
trapuntally. Rhythmically he was after "the spring and rush of
the child," he said . . . "and Gammer Gurton's concision:
mütterkin's wisdom." There are throwbacks to the literature
of the folk, to counting rhymes and play songs, to Mother
Goose, to the songs and rants of Elizabethan and Jacobean
literature, to the Old Testament, the visions of Blake and the
rhapsodies of Christopher Smart. But the poems, original and
incomparable, belong to the poet and not to his sources.

The protagonist, who recurrently undertakes the dark

journey into his own underworld, is engaged in a quest for spiritual identity. The quest is simultaneously a flight, for he is being pursued by the man he has become, implacable, lost, soiled, confused. In order to find himself he must lose himself by reexperiencing all the stages of his growth, by reenacting all the transmutations of his being from seed-time to maturity. We must remember that it is the poet himself who plays all the parts. He is Proteus and all the forms of Proteus — flower, fish, reptile, amphibian, bird, dog, etc. — and he is the adversary who hides among the rocks to pounce on Proteus, never letting go his hold, while the old man of the sea writhes through his many shapes until, exhausted by the struggle, he consents to prophesy in the *claritas* of his found identity.

Curiously enough — for I am sure it was not a conscious application — Roethke recapitulated the distinctive elements of this Protean imagery in a prose commentary that appeared in 1950. "Some of these pieces," he wrote in *Mid-Century American Poets,* referring to his sequence of monologues, "begin in the mire; as if man is no more than a shape writhing from the old rock." His annotation of a line of his from "Praise to the End" — "I've crawled from the mire, alert as a saint or a dog"— reads: "Except for the saint, everything else is dog, fish, minnow, bird, etc., and the euphoric ride resolves itself into a death-wish."

Roethke's explanation of his "cyclic" method of narration, a method that depends on periodic recessions of the movement instead of advances in a straight line, seems to me particularly noteworthy. "I believe," he wrote, "that to go forward as a spiritual man it is necessary first to go back. Any history of the psyche (or allegorical journey) is bound to be a succession of experiences, similar yet dissimilar. There is a perpetual slipping-back, then a going forward; but there is *some* 'progress.'"

This comment can be linked with several others by Roethke that I have already quoted: references to "the struggle out of the slime," the beginning "in the mire." I think also of his unforgettably defiant affirmation: "In spite of all the muck and welter, the dark, the *dreck* of these poems, I count myself among the happy poets."

In combination these passages point straight to the door of Dr. Jung or to the door of Jung's disciple Maud Bodkin, whose *Archetypal Patterns in Poetry* was familiar to Roethke. In Jung's discussion of Progression and Regression as fundamental concepts of the libido-theory in his *Contributions to Analytical Psychology,* he describes progression as "the daily advance of the process of psychological adaptation," which at certain times fails. Then "the vital feeling" disappears; there is a damming-up of energy, of libido. At such times neurotic symptoms are observed, and repressed contents appear, of inferior and unadapted character. "Slime out of the depths," he calls such contents — but slime that contains not only "objectionable animal tendencies, but also germs of new possibilities of life." Before "a renewal of life" can come about, there must be an acceptance of the possibilities that lie in the unconscious contents of the mind "activated through regression . . . and disfigured by the slime of the deep."

This principle is reflected in the myth of "the night journey under the sea," as in the Book of Jonah, or in the voyage of The Ancient Mariner, and is related to dozens of myths, in the rebirth archetype, that tell of the descent of the hero into the underworld and of his eventual return back to the light. The monologues of Roethke follow the pattern of progression and regression and belong unmistakably to the rebirth archetype.

In the opening section of "The Lost Son," for example, the hallucinated protagonist, regressing metamorphically, sinks down to an animistic level, begging from the sub-human some clue as to the meaning of his existence:

> At Woodlawn I heard the dead cry:
> I was lulled by the slamming of iron,
> A slow drip over stones,
> Toads brooding in wells.
> All the leaves stuck out their tongues;
> I shook the softening chalk of my bones,
> Saying,
> Snail, snail, glister me forward,
> Bird, soft-sigh me home.
> Worm, be with me.
> This is my hard time.

At the close of the same poem, which remains for me the finest of the monologues, the protagonist, turned human and adult again, is granted his moment of epiphany; but he is not ready yet to apprehend it wholly; he must wait:

> *It was beginning winter,*
> *The light moved slowly over the frozen field,*
> *Over the dry seed-crowns,*
> *The beautiful surviving bones*
> *Swinging in the wind.*
>
> *Light traveled over the field;*
> *Stayed.*
> *The weeds stopped swinging.*
> *The mind moved, not alone,*
> *Through the clear air, in the silence.*
>
> > *Was it light?*
> > *Was it light within?*
> > *Was it light within light?*
> > *Stillness becoming alive,*
> > *Yet still?*
> >
> > *A lively understandable spirit*
> > *Once entertained you.*
> > *It will come again.*
> > *Be still.*
> > *Wait.*

The love poems that followed early in the 1950's — Roethke was forty-four when he married — were a distinct departure from the painful excavations of the monologues and in some respects a return to the strict stanzaic forms of his earliest work. They were daring and buoyant, not only in their explicit sensuality, their "lewd music," but in the poet's open and arrogant usurpation of the Yeatsian beat and, to a degree, of the Yeatsian mantle:

> *I take this cadence from a man named Yeats;*
> *I take it, and I give it back again. . . .*

By this time Roethke had the authority, the self-assurance, indeed the euphoria — "I am most immoderately married" — to carry it off.

Even when he had been involved with the *dreck* of the monologues, he was able, in sudden ecstatic seizures of clarity, to proclaim "a condition of joy." Moreover, he had been delighted at the opportunity that the free and open form gave him to introduce juicy little bits of humor, mostly puns and mangled bawdry and indelicate innuendoes. He had also written some rather ferocious nonsense verse for children. Now he achieved something much more difficult and marvelous: a passionate love poetry that yet included the comic, as in "I Knew a Woman," with its dazzling first stanza:

> I knew a woman, lovely in her bones,
> When small birds sighed, she would sigh back at them;
> Ah, when she moved, she moved more ways than one.
> The shapes a bright container can contain!
> Of her choice virtues only gods should speak,
> Or English poets who grew up on Greek
> (I'd have them sing in chorus, cheek to cheek).

Inevitably the beloved is a shapeshifter, like the poet himself. "Slow, slow as a fish she came." Or again, "She came toward me in the flowing air, a shape of change." "No mineral man," he praises her as dove, as lily, as rose, as leaf, even as "the oyster's weeping foot." And he asks himself, half fearfully: "Is she what I become? Is this my final Face?"

At the human level this tendency of his to become the other is an extension of that Negative Capability, as defined by Keats, which first manifested itself in the Roethke greenhouse. A man of this nature, said Keats, "is capable of being in uncertainties, mysteries, doubt, without any irritable reaching after fact and reason . . . he has no identity — he is continually in for and filling some other body." In "The Dying Man" Roethke assumes the character of the poet Yeats; in "Meditations of an Old Woman," he writes as though he were his mother; in several late poems he adopts the role and voice of his beloved.

The love poems gradually dissolve into the death poems.

Could the flesh be transcended, as he had at first supposed, till passion burned with a spiritual light? Could his several selves perish in love's fire and be reborn as one? Could the dear and beautiful one lead him, as Dante taught, to the very footstool of God? In "The Dying Man" he proposes a dark answer: "All sensual love's but dancing on the grave." Roethke thought of himself as one with the dying Yeats: "I am that final thing, a man learning to sing."

The five-fold "Meditations of an Old Woman" that concludes Roethke's selective volume, *Words for the Wind* (1958), is almost wholly preoccupied with thoughts of death and with the search for God. He had started writing the sequence almost immediately after the death of his mother in 1955. Here he returns to the cyclic method of the earlier monologues. In the First Meditation the Old Woman introduces the theme of journeying. All journeys, she reflects, are the same, a movement forward after a few wavers, and then a slipping backward, "backward in time." Once more we recognize the Jungian pattern of progression and regression embodied in the work. The journeys and the five meditations as a whole are conceived in a kind of rocking motion, and indeed the verb "to rock" — consistently one of the poet's key verbs of motion — figures prominently in the text. The rocking is from the cradle toward death:

> *The body, delighting in thresholds,*
> *Rocks in and out of itself. . . .*

An image of transformations. And toward the close:

> *To try to become like God*
> *Is far from becoming God.*
> *O, but I seek and care!*
>
> *I rock in my own dark,*
> *Thinking, God has need of me.*
> *The dead love the unborn.*

A few weeks before his death Roethke completed his arrangement of some fifty new poems, published under the title *The Far Field*. The range and power of this posthumous volume have yet to be fully grasped or interpreted. Among its contents are two major sequences, *The North American Sequence,* consisting of six long meditations on the American landscape and on death . . . on dying into America, so to speak; and a group of twelve shorter, more formal lyrics, under the generic heading "Sequence, Sometimes Metaphysical," bearing witness to a state of spiritual crisis, the dance of the soul around the exhausted flesh and toward the divine fire.

"How to transcend this spiritual emptiness?" he cries in "The Longing," which opens the North American sequence. The self, retracing its transformations, seeks refuge in a lower order of being:

> *And the spirit fails to move forward,*
> *But shrinks into a half-life, less than itself,*
> *Falls back, a slug, a loose worm*
> *Ready for any crevice,*
> *An eyeless starer.*

He longs "for the imperishable quiet at the heart of form."

In a sense he has completed his dark journey, but he has not yet found either his oblivion or his immortality. He yearns for the past which will also be future. The American earth calls to him, and he responds by struggling out of his lethargy: "I am coming!" he seems to be saying, "but wait a minute. I have something left to do. I belong to the wilderness. I will yet speak in tongues."

I have left the body of the whale, but the mouth of the night is still wide;
On the Bullhead, in the Dakotas, where the eagles eat well,
In the country of few lakes, in the tall buffalo grass at the base of the clay buttes,
In the summer heat, I can smell the dead buffalo,
The stench of their damp fur drying in the sun,
The buffalo chips drying.

Old men should be explorers?
I'll be an Indian.
Ogallala?
Iroquois.

That diminishing coda is a miracle of compression and connotation.

In "The Far Field," the fifth poem of the North American sequence and the title poem of the collection, Roethke speaks of his journeying, as his mother did in the earlier Meditations:

I dream of journeys repeatedly:
Of flying like a bat deep into a narrowing tunnel,
Of driving alone, without luggage, out a long peninsula,
The road lined with snow-laden second growth,
A fine dry snow ticking the windshield,
Alternate snow and sleet, no oncoming traffic,
And no lights behind, in the blurred side-mirror,
The road changing from glazed tarface to a rubble of stone,
Ending at last in a hopeless sand-rut,
Where the car stalls,
Churning in a snowdrift
Until the headlights darken.

As always, in these soliloquies, the poet sinks through various levels of time and of existence. There was a field once where he found death in the shape of a rat, along with other creatures shot by the nightwatchman or mutilated by the mower; but he found life, too, in the spontaneous agitations of the birds, "a twittering restless cloud." And he tries to relive his selfhood back to its mindless source, so that he may be born again, meanwhile proclaiming his faith in the inexorable wheel of metamorphosis:

I'll return again,
As a snake or a raucous bird,
Or, with luck, as a lion.

Sometimes the faith wavers. In "The Abyss," a poem outside

the North American sequence, he inquires, "Do we move toward God, or merely another condition?" ... "I rock between dark and dark."

But if the shapeshifter for a moment despairs of his identity, he still has strength and will enough to drag himself over the threshold of annihilation.

> *A fallen man, I climb out of my fear.*
> *The mind enters itself, and God the mind,*
> *And one is One, free in the tearing wind.*

I do not always believe in these ecstatic resolutions — they sometimes seem a cry of need rather than of revelation — but I am always moved by the presence of the need and by the desperation of the voice.

"Brooding on God, I may become a man," writes Roethke in "The Marrow," a poem at once dreadful and profound, electric and shuddering:

> *Godhead above my God, are you there still?*
> *To sleep is all my life. In sleep's half-death,*
> *My body alters, altering the soul*
> *That once could melt the dark with its small breath.*
> *Lord, hear me out, and hear me out this day:*
> *From me to Thee's a long and terrible way.*
>
> *I was flung back from suffering and love*
> *When light divided on a storm-tossed tree;*
> *Yea, I have slain my will, and still I live:*
> *I would be near; I shut my eyes to see;*
> *I bleed my bones, their marrow to bestow*
> *Upon that God who knows what I would know.*

Such furious intensity exacts a price. The selves of the poet could be fused only by the exertion of a tremendous pressure. If only he could be content to name the objects that he loved and not be driven to convert them into symbols — that painful ritual.

In "The Far Field," where he evokes his own valedictory

image, Whitman is with him, and Prospero, and — in the shift-
ing light Proteus, the old man of the sea, fatigued by his
changes:

> *An old man with his feet before the fire,*
> *In robes of green, in garments of adieu.*

The lines that follow have a touch of prophecy in them as the
poet, renewed by the thought of death, leaving his skins behind him, moves out into the life-giving and obliterating
waters:

> *A man faced with his own immensity*
> *Wakes all the waves, all their loose wandering fire.*
> *The murmur of the absolute, the why*
> *Of being born fails on his naked ears.*
> *His spirit moves like monumental wind*
> *That gentles on a sunny blue plateau.*
> *He is the end of things, the final man.*
>
> *All finite things reveal infinitude:*
> *The mountain with its singular bright shade*
> *Like the blue shine on freshly frozen snow,*
> *The after-light upon ice-burdened pines;*
> *Odor of basswood on a mountain slope,*
> *A scent beloved of bees;*
> *Silence of water above a sunken tree:*
> *The pure serene of memory in one man, —*
> *A ripple widening from a single stone*
> *Winding around the waters of the world.*

3

Root Images

> Nature! — she creates ever new forms; what exists has never existed before; what has existed returns not again — everything is new and yet always old. . . . *One obeys her laws even if one resists them.*
>
> — Goethe

> No one can free himself from his childhood without first generously occupying himself with it.
>
> — Carl Jung

Swimming in Lake Chauggogagogman-chauggagogchabuna-gungamaugg

Pre-memory floods the mind
like molten lava on the sands.
— Anna Akhmatova

When I was a boy in Massachusetts one of my favorite haunts was Lake Webster, named from the town of its location. It was a lovely lake, in a then relatively unspoiled country-side, but no lovelier, I suppose, than several other lakes and ponds that I could have frequented nearer my home in Worces-ter. The reason for my preference was that I had made a thrill-ing discovery while browsing among the books of local history in the Worcester Public Library. There I learned that the In-dians who once lived on the shores of Lake Webster had a word of their own for it: *Chauggogagogmanchauggagogcha-bunagungamaugg*. To think that this was reputed to be the longest lake-name in the world! To know, moreover, that this fantastic porridge of syllables made sense, and what delicious sense, signifying: "I-fish-on-my-side, you-fish-on-your-side, nobody-fishes-in-the-middle!" I practiced how to say it, prid-

---

Originally published in *The Christian Science Monitor*, April 26, 1966, under the title "The Poet on His Work — 'Awake After Midnight.'"

ing myself on talking Indian . . . nor to this very day have I forgotten the combination.

To utter that mouthful, to give the lake its secret name, was somehow to possess it, to assert my power over the spot, as by an act of magic. Years later, when I became interested in philology, I read, with a sense of *déjà vu*, the theory that in the beginning of the human adventure a word consisted of a long and elaborate sound or series of sounds associated with the ritual of the tribe and expressed in a chant with appropriate gestures; that into each word-sentence, as in extant primitive languages, a whole complex of thought, emotion and feeling was packed.

One of the familiar grievances of the modern poet is that language gets more and more shabby and debased in everyday usage, until even the great words that men must live by lose their lustre. How to make words potent and magical again, how to restore their lost vitality? A poet is a man who yearns to swim in Lake Chauggogagogmanchauggagogchabuna-gungamaugg, not in Lake Webster. He loves a language that reaches all the way back to its primitive condition. So it is that the words of a poem are full of subterranean electric feelings, pent-up music, sleeping gestures. A poem trembles on the verge of lapsing into music, of breaking into dance: but its virtue lies in resisting the temptation — in remaining language. There is an ideal lyric in my head whose words flow together to form a single word-sentence, an unremitting stream of sound, as in the Indian lake-name; I am not reconciled to the knowledge that I shall never be able to write it.

A good deal of craft goes into the making of a poem, much more than most readers and some writers suspect. Poems are not produced by the will; and craft alone, though it may assure the manufacture of a reasonably competent set of verses, is insufficient for the creation of a poem. How many times have I heard my poet-friends, in the doldrums between poems, despair of the possibility of writing another! Solitude and a fierce attentiveness precede insight, which other ages could call "vision" without embarrassment. "The man wipes his breath from the window pane," wrote Yeats, "and laughs in his

delight at all the varied scene." Or as Blake phrased it earlier:
"If the doors of perception were cleansed, everything would
appear to man as it is, infinite."

The poets whom I most admire look on life with a watchful
and affectionate eye, unfogged by sentimentality. They study
the things of the world, but not from the world's view. One of
their disciplines is to resist the temptation to skim poems off
the top of their minds. Poets need stamina as much as they
need imagination. Indeed, when we speak of the imagination,
we imply an activity of surplus energy . . . energy beyond what
is required for mere survival. An interviewer once asked me a
rather brash question: "What do you consider to be your chief
asset as a poet?" — to which I gave the reply that I thought he
deserved: "My ability to stay awake after midnight." Perhaps
I was more serious than I intended. Certainly the poems of
mine that I am most committed to are those that I recall
fighting for hardest, through the anxious hours, until I managed to come out on the other side of fatigue, where I could
begin to breathe again, as though the air had changed and I
had found my second wind.

One such poem that I can offer, not without trepidation, for
comment is "End of Summer":*

> *An agitation of the air*
> *A perturbation of the light*
> *Admonished me the unloved year*
> *Would turn on its hinge that night.*
>
> *I stood in the disenchanted field*
> *Amid the stubble and the stones,*
> *Amazed, while a small worm lisped to me*
> *The song of my marrow-bones.*
>
> *Blue poured into summer blue,*
> *A hawk broke from his cloudless tower,*
> *The roof of the silo blazed, and I knew*
> *That part of my life was over.*

* *Selected Poems* p. 48.

> *Already the iron door of the north*
> *Clangs open: birds, leaves, snows*
> *Order their populations forth,*
> *And a cruel wind blows.*

I can remember how and where that poem began more than a decade ago. It was an afternoon in late September. I was chopping weeds in the field behind my house in Bucks County, Pennsylvania. Toward sunset I heard a commotion in the sky and looked up, startled to observe wedge after wedge of wild geese honking downriver, with their long necks pointing south. I watched until the sun sank and the air turned chill. Then I put away my garden tools and walked back to the house, shivering with a curious premonition. After dinner I went upstairs to my study and tried until dawn to get the words down on paper. Nothing came that seemed right to me. Five days later I had hundreds of lines, but they still added up to nothing. In the middle of the fifth night I experienced a revelation: what was wrong with my enterprise was that I was attempting to compose a descriptive piece about the migration of the birds, whereas it was the disturbance of the heart that really concerned me and that insisted on a language. At this point I opened the window, as it were, and let the geese fly out. Then the poem came with a rush.

In my first draft the opening lines read:

> *The agitation of the air,*
> *The perturbation of the light. . . .*

I write my poems by speaking them — they are meant to be heard. What I heard displeased my ear because the plethora of "the's" made too thick a sound. The indefinite articles that I introduced in my revision serve to open up the lines and to accelerate the tempo.

In the second stanza the words that interest me most are "amazed" and "lisped." Both of them were afterthoughts. Originally my posture was "surprised," while the invertebrate redundantly "sang" its song. "Amazed" is much more open-mouthed and suspended than "surprised"; moreover, it hooks on to "admonished" and "amid" before it, to "marrow" in the next line, and to "blazed" in the next stanza. At the same time it relieves the passage of a frightful excess of sibilants. As for "lisped," I consider it the perfectly right and proper thing for a small worm to do.

The image of the roof of the silo flashing back the sunlight suggests an epiphany to me, the precise moment of illumination. Actually, I had no silo on my place in the Delaware Valley: it forced itself into my poem, to erupt as the climax of a progression, out of another landscape that had once been dear to me, and I recognized instantaneously that it came with the imprimatur of psychological truth.

In the final stanza the opening of "the iron door of the north" releases the arctic blast before which, in sequence, are driven "birds, leaves, snows," three variants of migration. After the fact I am aware that here the sounds become harsher, as the rhythm is sprung and the strong stressing hammered out. In my own reading of the poem I give the concluding syllable an almost painful protraction, as though the wind would never stop blowing.

Earlier I said that I had let the geese fly out of the poem. Was I mistaken? It occurs to me now that their ghosts are present, their wings keep beating, from the first word to the last in "End of Summer."

The Worcester Poets

An old rhyme goes:

> *Seven cities warred for Homer being dead,*
> *Who living had no roof to shroud his head.*

Michael True is to be congratulated for refusing to emulate the delinquent scribes of Chios, Smyrna, Colophon, Ithaca, Pylos, Argos and Athens. Because he cares about poetry and because he is a generous man, he has undertaken, in conjunction with the Worcester County Poetry Association, to honor the poets of Worcester while some of us, despite our bad habits, are still alive.

All poets are brothers and sisters under the skin of language, and I have long known that two of my most admired colleagues had at least a birthplace in common with me. Sup-

Originally published as the Foreword to *Worcester Poets: With Notes Toward a Literary History*, by Michael True, The Worcester County Poetry Association, Worcester, Mass., 1972.

pose, I speculate, we had stayed home — what would have become of us? In that parochial climate, given our different backgrounds, would we have managed to find one another? All three of us, curiously, developed an inordinate love of place, but not of *that* place. Elizabeth Bishop's early attachment was to Nova Scotia and, in recent years, to Brazil. I recall her saying once that she was born in Worcester "quite by accident" and did not linger long. Charles Olson identified himself with Gloucester, the half-mythic seaport of his poems. My own preference is for Cape Cod, after years of rural existence in Connecticut and Pennsylvania. New York, where I spend the winter months, is only a habitation, to be endured, not cherished. Elizabeth and Charles were able to forget Worcester; I doubt that I ever shall. Perhaps it scarred me more.

I left in my early twenties. Subsequently, with a gesture of bravura, I wrote of "the youth, the undefeated,"

Whose falcon-heart, winged with the golden shout
  Of morning, sweeps windward from his native city,
  *Crying his father's grief, his mother's doubt.**

Parochialism. Sectarianism. How I loathed them! But not all my disaffection was of specifically local origin. Family misfortunes, the pangs of adolescence, the itch of ambition contributed to my restlessness. I felt like one of the vaguely desperate and ardent characters in Sherwood Anderson's *Winesburg, Ohio* — stories of small-town existence that troubled and inflamed me. More than half a century has passed — can I believe it? — since I sat on the stoop of a friend's house, exclaiming with schoolboy fervor, "I'll remember this book till the day I die."

It would be wrong to suppose that I did nothing but mope and rage through my Worcester life. Without glossing over the frustrations, I can truthfully say that I had my joys . . . marvels too . . . ecstasies.

In my sixth year I heard a preacher in the street prophesying the end of the world. Back home on Green Street — where I lived then with my mother and two older sisters — I climbed to the flat roof of our fourth-story apartment and lay on my

* "The Fitting of the Mask," in *Selected Poems* p. 82.

back, trembling with excitement, till the night came and Halley's Comet swam into view. How could I be mindful of the hysteria below, of the police searching for me in basements and alleys? I must have fallen asleep, for I saw the stars shooting like rockets overhead, in a helter-skelter dance, rearranging themselves until they scribbled a message across the Milky Way. "IT IS I," was what the stars testified. Not everybody's God is such a good grammarian.

As my mother's dress-manufacturing business began to prosper — she must have been one of the first woman executives — we moved to Providence Street. Number 46 is the address that comes to mind. By the time I had reached fourth grade in the school at the foot of the hill, I had already written a collection of tales, mostly about my adventures in the Frozen North. One of my assigned compositions for Miss McGillicuddy began with the smashing sentence: "George Washington was a tall, petite, handsome man." She gave my essay an A-plus and read it annually to my successors, as a sample of immortal prose, well into the next generation. Eventually I was transferred to the school on Ledge Street. Valedictorian at the graduation exercises, I recited Kipling's "Recessional" *con amore* and vowed to follow in his footsteps. Each day I added three new words to my vocabulary and practiced tongue-twisters.

As I look back, I can see how fortunate I was to have gone to Classical High School, where the educational standards were comparable to those of top-flight private schools. I remember with particular affection and gratitude white-haired Mr. Abbott, who introduced me to Caesar's Gallic wars; Margaret Walsh, my Spanish teacher, with whom I fell madly and mutely in love; Perry Howe, coach of the debating and declaiming teams, who helped me to overcome my shyness and taught me the power of the spoken word; and Martin Post, who tossed aside his textbooks, full of moralizing chestnuts, and read us Shakespeare's and Herrick's songs in class. It was he who demonstrated on the piano, long before the word "synaesthesia" gained psychological or aesthetic currency, that sounds have colors. In how many seminars of student poets have I repeated that same thrilling exercise!

At the sepulchral public library on Elm Street, where the floors buckled and the rooms smelled of old books, old wood, and immemorial dust, I borrowed to the limit of five volumes a day from the open shelves and crowded bins. Another sanctuary was the art museum at the far end of town. And still another, of a different sort, was the woods beyond our new stucco house on Woodford Street, where I followed the Indian trails and hunted for arrowheads. Of that house, which still stands; of those trails; of the abandoned quarry, whose sheer rock face I climbed alone, hand over hand, to prove my courage or my foolhardiness; of the breathless games I played in the leafy stillness; of the daydreams of my youth, I have already written in certain of my poems.

I have much, much more to tell, but this is scarcely the proper occasion for spilling everything. On another day, when the wind from the past is right, I must set down, if only as a chapter of Americana, the narrative of my horse-and-buggy adventures, when I was lamplighter on the Quinapoxet roads. But who out there remembers where Quinapoxet is — or was? Who has dipped his hand in the waters of Goose Pond?

Now a sulky weather dogs the heart,
There is no bottom to the day,
The water lily's Chinese stalk
Drags heavy, as the white-lipped boy

Climbs from detritus of his birth,
The rusted hoop, the broken wheels,
The sunken boat of little worth,
Past balconies of limber eels

Until, along that marshy brink,
The springy trails devoid of plan,
He meets his childhood beating back
*To find what furies made him man.**

* "Goose Pond," in *Selected Poems*, p. 56.

Of "Father and Son"

Now in the suburbs and the falling light
I followed him, and now down sandy road
Whiter than bone-dust, through the sweet
Curdle of fields, where the plums
Dropped with their load of ripeness, one by one.
Mile after mile I followed, with skimming feet,
After the secret master of my blood,
Him, steeped in the odor of ponds, whose indomitable love
Kept me in chains. Strode years; stretched into bird;
Raced through the sleeping country where I was young,
The silence unrolling before me as I came,
The night nailed like an orange to my brow.

How should I tell him my fable and the fears,
How bridge the chasm in a casual tone,
Saying, "The house, the stucco one you built,
We lost. Sister married and went from home,
And nothing comes back, it's strange, from where she goes.
I lived on a hill that had too many rooms:
Light we could make, but not enough of warmth,
And when the light failed, I climbed under the hill.
The papers are delivered every day;
I am alone and never shed a tear."

At the water's edge, where the smothering ferns lifted
Their arms, "Father!" I cried, "Return! You know
The way. I'll wipe the mudstains from your clothes;
No trace, I promise, will remain. Instruct
Your son, whirling between two wars,

Written for *The Contemporary Poet as Artist and Critic*, edited by Anthony
Ostroff (Little, Brown, 1964); originally published in *New World Writing* No.
20 (Lippincott, 1962).

In the Gemara of your gentleness,
For I would be a child to those who mourn
And brother to the foundlings of the field
And friend of innocence and all bright eyes.
O teach me how to work and keep me kind."

Among the turtles and the lilies he turned to me
The white ignorant hollow of his face.

Once a poem has been distributed, it is no longer the property of the poet. By the time it is published he has become
somebody else, and part of the change in him must be attributed to his knowledge that he is free from the necessity of
making that poem again. Even if he could! He can try, of
course, to remember who he was and how he felt during the
event, but his memory is not wholly to be trusted, since it is
stained with afterthought and prone to rationalize everything
he has done, particularly when he has done something as un-
reasonable as writing poetry. The poet's professional identity
is elusive even to himself: it is not a fixity to be recaptured, but
rather an accumulation of quite special, often compulsive energies that disappear by flowing into the poem. After the event
poet as well as reader is left with nothing but an arrangement
of words on a page to testify that something more or less un-
usual or valuable has happened. Of "Father and Son" I propose that it is a fairly representative poem of mine — representative at least of one dominant strain in my work — and, so far
as I can tell, of no special difficulty.

It is only other people's poems that have ever seemed to me
obscure. The manifold tissue of experience, in Whitehead's
phrase, with which one is concerned presents itself with a
bewildering density, an overlay of episodes and images, both
public and private. What makes art possible is that one is also,
at the same time, a bundle of simplicities. But modern criticism is frightened of these simplicities. The hard and inescapable phenomenon to be faced is that we are living and
dying at once. My commitment is to report the dialogue.

"Father and Son" was born of a dream and much of the
dream-work has passed into the poem. I wrote it on the eve of
World War II, so that there is a touch of prophecy in the phrase

"whirling between two wars." Most of the landscape goes back to my boyhood in Worcester, where we lived (in a stucco house) at the edge of the city, but "the sweet curdle of fields" must have originated in the milky, sometimes clotted night-mists of the Delaware Valley, where I was resident at the time. I do not propose to launch into a full-scale autobiography here, but I am ready to say that all the essential details of the poem are true, as true as dreams are, with characteristic fusions, substitutions, and dislocations. The sister who died and the big house on the hill were not invented for the occasion; they belong to that part of my life which I keep trying to rework into legend. The line "I lived on a hill that had too many rooms" is a distant echo of the Gospel pronouncement, "In my Father's house are many mansions."

One of the oddities of poetry is the symbolic extensibility of plain facts. A literalist might say, of the nineteenth line, that I was referring, on the one hand, to the mechanics of generating electricity with a Kohler engine ("light we could make") and, on the other, to the lack of central heating in a country house ("but not enough of warmth"). In a sense I was! To seize on what is literal in a poem, what relates to ordinary human experience, is the first task of criticism. "And when the light failed, I climbed under the hill" — is a gloss required? If so, I should direct the reader to Blake's tremendous lines, from which I must have made an unconscious borrowing:

> Tho' thou art worshipped by the Names Divine
> Of Jesus and Jehovah, thou art still
> The Son of Morn in weary Night's decline,
> The lost Traveller's Dream under the hill.

The pond of "Father and Son" is linked with the "Goose Pond" that provides a title for another of my poems.* It was a small, reputedly bottomless waterhole that I frequented in Quinapoxet, outside Worcester, and my memory of it is alive with snakes and pickerel and snapping turtles and pond lilies (no, not turtledoves and definitely not literary lilies). A boy had drowned in it, and the legend went that his body had

* *Selected Poems*, quoted on p. 121, this volume.

never been recovered, My companion, who could shoot down squirrels from the trees and birds on the wing and split a water-snake in two at a hundred yards, grew up to kill his wife and her lover, perhaps with the same gun. But that, I suppose, is another story. Somewhere fact ends and myth begins, but I could not begin to determine the boundary line. As far as I am concerned, the pond in Quinapoxet, Poe's "dank tarn of Auber," and the mere in which Beowulf fights for his life with Grendel and the water-hag are one and the same. It is the pond where I am never surprised to find demons, murderers, parents, poets. Did my father really die there? No, he never even saw it; and I was the one who came closest to drowning.

Nobody, alas, seems to like my line "The night nailed like an orange to my brow," but I have lived with it too long to think of changing a word. What is so outlandish about it? Throughout the poem the moon, though never named, is fiercely burning . . . shining in the bone-dust and the mist, reflected at the last in "the white ignorant hollow" of the father's face. Most of us must have known breathless nights, so heavy and close that the moon has walked with us. To suffer this night of the moon so intensely is to be impaled by it. To one who says flatly, "Oranges are not nailed," my flat answer is, "In this poem they are." The reader cannot be expected to know that when I was six years old, running barefoot, I stepped on a nail that protruded — God knows how — through a rotten peach and hobbled home with that impossible fruit hammered to my flesh. When I was fourteen or fifteen, I discovered Tennyson and I can still recall how enchanted I was with the sensuous mystery of the opening lines:

> With blackest moss the flower-plots
> Were thickly crusted, one and all:
> The rusted nails fell from the knots
> That held the peach to the garden-wall.

Though Tennyson was thinking of a peach *tree*, no doubt espaliered, it was years before I stumbled on that realization. Nail and fruit, then, have a long history of association in my mind, and the image that eventually sealed their connection has nothing to do with ornament or fancy, but is an emanation of my felt truth. Such moments in a poem, evident only by the pressure building behind them, can never fully explain themselves, but the poet must take his risk with them as an article of faith. In the end, for whatever it may be worth, they constitute his signature.

"Father and Son" was conceived as a dramatic lyric, with some kinship to the dramatic monologue. The divisions of the poem are not to be construed as stanzas, but as narrative blocks or paragraphs, each with its distinctive rhythm of action, and the indicated pauses are meaningful in the reading and the interpretation. The fourth and final division consists of the last two lines, which should be set off from the rest of the poem by a space. Unfortunately, in the layout of my *Selected Poems*, these lines are transposed to the overleaf, so that the break is obscured. Perhaps I magnify the importance of this small detail, but I feel quite certain now, as I examine the comments, that a clearly spaced version is essential for a firm grasp of the structure.

The way that a poem develops is largely out of one's control, since the end is willed by the means, but I sense that my impulse towards a form generally tends to move along the lines of certain ineluctable archetypes, particularly those of death and rebirth, the quest, and the night-journey (or descent into the underworld). In all three patterns — which may be consubstantial — the progress is from a kind of darkness into a kind of light. As I understand the main level of the action, the son in his quest is not looking for pity or pardon. It is to be noted that he makes no confession of sins. The losses that he reviews are those peculiar to the human condition and of special interest to the father, since they involve property and family. "Instruct me how to live" is the substance of his prayer, but in the irony of circumstance it is addressed to one who is dead and who, furthermore, has destroyed himself. Presumably the son who wants to be saved is unaware of the self-destructive elements in his nature that impel him towards the father; unaware till the very instant when his begetter enters the water and becomes one with it — both source and death-trap. The last two lines, constituting a simultaneous *peripeteia* and *anagnorisis*, reversal and discovery, announce for me the shock of recognition that moves beyond despair. Now that for the first time the father shows his terrible face, the son is delivered from his bondage, from his trance of love and yearning, from his seductive loyalties. His triumph is in what he *sees*. I read the ending on a note of tragic exaltation.

Let me admit that I have written this piece with a measure of reluctance, conscious of promises but fearful of surrendering to the temptation of saying more than I should. With an intimate poem so much of the power is stored in the silences — those spacings between words and lines and thoughts — where the secret battle is being fought. The temptation to fill the spaces with verbalization is real, for the poet who returns to his own work under stress, as when he reads it in public, is engaged in a secondary act of creation, which he is liable to confuse with the first. To reply to criticism at all is to risk sounding more defensive than one has hoped to be. If the poet were a saint, he would remain indifferent to responses, resting in his knowledge that the words of the poem stand forever separate from the words about it, and that he has already had his chance.

4

Studio Life

There will be no portrait left of modern man because he has lost his face and is turning towards the jungle.

— Oskar Kokoschka

The thing that's wrong with modern art right now . . . is the fact that there isn't any longer a strong, powerful academic art worth fighting against. There has to be a rule even if it's a bad one because the evidence of art's power is in breaking down the barriers.

— Pablo Picasso

The Sister Arts

One reason why I stay in New York, though I suspect that it impairs my prospects for longevity, is that so many of my artist friends live here. By and large I prefer the company of painters and sculptors to that of poets, who tend to be rather surly and withdrawn. The romantic impressions that I had of studio life as a boy were, of course, naïve and highly colored, but still they had an element of truth in them. Artists flock to the metropolis mainly because the museums and the galleries and the money are there, but also, I propose, because they are temperamentally gregarious. Every art movement is a testimonial, at bottom, to the vitality of a complex of friendships.

If I should say to a painter that I envy his art because the poet at his desk is never free from mental struggle, whereas the artist finds a measure of satisfaction and release in the sheer physical activity required of him, the rhythm of his

Originally published in *Art in America*, October–November 1965, as an introduction to a portfolio of contemporary poetry, chosen and illustrated by twenty-two American painters, and edited by Francine du Plessix.

body, I know from experience that this compliment will be taken amiss, so that I try, not always successfully, to suppress it. Painters, especially in their youth, have such a good time together that I sometimes wonder why they want poets around at all, but the history of these associations is so redundant in modern times — witness Keats-Haydon, Baudelaire-Delacroix, Rilke-Rodin, Apollinaire-Picasso, Eluard-Picasso, Breton-Aragon, Lorca-Dali, etc. — that it would be difficult to believe that the gratifications are not mutual.

The great lesson that Rilke, with his fragility and neurasthenia, learned from contact with the abounding energy of Rodin was the importance of hard work: *"Il faut toujours travailler."* What artists discover in poets is more tenuous; perhaps it is largely a state of nervosity and awareness, a capacity for being nothing and experiencing everything. The most extraordinary evidence of the natural affinity between poet and painter is the number of creative spirits who have combined in themselves both talents. In the heyday of Surrealism and Dadaism, movements that belonged as much to literature as to art, poet-painters and painter-poets sprang up in Paris by the dozen. Here, where the arts have been more compartmentalized, we can nevertheless identify the painter Marsden Hartley as one who wrote poems, and the poet E. E. Cummings as one who painted pictures. Michelangelo and Blake are the most notable examples of the type, but if we reach back to the eighth century in China we can locate their progenitor in the person of Wang Wei, preeminent among the T'ang poets and father of the southern school of Sung landscape painting, of whom it was said that "his pictures were poems and his poems pictures." The same could apply to Buson who, ten centuries later, flourished in Japan as a master in the *haiku* style.

To Japanese readers the effectiveness of the seventeen-syllabled *haiku* is largely dependent on the silences that surround the images, which are presented sparely, without subjective coloration. Here is my version of a famous one by Buson:

> *On the great bronze bell*
> *At noon a white butterfly*
> *Motionlessly sleeps.*

Stillness on stillness, as the most ephemeral of creatures folds its wings on the temple-bell that waits in readiness to announce the Eternal. In the highly formalized tradition of Japan the painting, or sketch (*haiga*), that serves as a companion piece, is executed in a quick breath, just as the *haiku* was written, and with a minimum of brushwork, allowing for the eloquence of white space in the same way that the poem uses what is left unsaid. A single poetic experience is rendered simultaneously in two media; the same rhythmic life courses through picture and script.

But the Japanese artist is working within the limits of a visual convention, so codified that each line he draws, each area he washes belongs recognizably to pictorial vocabulary. The contemporary western artist, who lacks a comparable convention, is presented with a poem that does not seem to require his services, since it is a self-sufficient form, much more fully articulated than its oriental counterpart. He must not only define the nature of his relationship to the poem and his understanding of it — not always a simple matter, given the complications and contradictions of the poetic voice — but he must also justify his tinkering with it. And — what is most formidable among these challenges — he must invent a style of graphic translation that enables him to register his variable sense of the poem. If he does less than this, he has not done much.

The easiest way out for the artist is to make a literal illustration of the poem. Let the poet speak of a monkey in a banana-tree and, sure enough, there it is drawn by hand for you — whee! that monkey in that banana-tree — on the same or on a facing page, just as in a first-grade primer. What could be more boring?

A more interesting strategy is that of interpretation of the text, the offering of a visual commentary, which in itself constitutes an act of criticism and may even go so far as to supply a counter-statement to the poem. I can conceive, for example, of a drawing or painting derived from the previously quoted *haiku* of Buson that would not even faintly suggest a temple-bell or a butterfly, but that might be born of the mood occasioned by the contemplation of these images. The artist might enjoy the poem and yet not yearn for Nirvana, in which case he might be impelled to break the spell of inaction that gives the lines their enchantment and to set the whole page whirling with his greed for life. Such a response is by no means restricted to the figurative artist. As for those artists who appear, on the surface, to be working abstractly but whose forms somehow manage to suggest landscape or figures descriptive of the poem's content, I am inclined to categorize them as illustrators without conviction. The bolder effect would be to pass beyond illustration and, even, interpretation in order to attempt something more: namely, the re-embodiment of the poem in terms of the graphic imagination. To achieve this end the materials supplied by the poetic imagination, predominantly images and words, must first of all be destroyed or fragmented in the process of experiencing them. Only then, I venture, when images break into line and color and words into calligraphy, can the poem begin to be reconstituted in a different medium.

In his panegyric of Delacroix, Baudelaire noted that it is "one of the characteristic symptoms of the spiritual condition of our age that the arts aspire, if not to take one another's place, at least reciprocally to lend one another new powers." A century later the observation seems much more pertinent than at the time it was made. Painting and sculpture, drama and dance, prose and poetry, in their overlapping and combining, continue to press towards a dissolution of boundaries. And all the arts grow increasingly restless, not only in their impatience with traditional categories, but even more radically in their rejection of a concept of aesthetic limits. At this moment of transit, while the style of an age, or at least of a generation, is evolving, it seems to me imperative that poets and painters should continue their civilized discourse. When the poetic imagination is confined to poetry alone, it runs the risk of withering. Given that circumstance, no art — least of all, painting — could hope to flourish. In Leonardo's words, which need to be restudied, "Painting is a form of poetry made to be seen."

Meditations of a Sitter

Blake said it for me:

O why was I born with a different face?
Why was I not born like the rest of my race?

But is it true we were born with the face we wear after forty?
I think instead, with Rilke, that we go out into the world to
find our face. So many of my generation, the handsomest
among them, have nothing to show for all the dreams and
promise of their youth but a bag of ashes clapped sodden on
their shoulders. Perhaps the supreme triumph of the Industrial Revolution is the mass production in our time of the No-
Face. The more power we pack into our bombs, the more we
seem to drain from the human countenance. Is it not written
that the TV personality — Truly Vapid — shall inherit the

From "Sitting for Rosati the Sculptor," in *Art News*, March 1959, with
photographs by Rudolph Burckhardt of James Rosati's series of clay studies
and the finished bronze head.

earth? The only interesting men's faces I encounter are those of madmen, artists, and saints, but I do not know any saints.

The empty ones are those who do not suffer their selfhood.

Art is born out of need before it becomes choice, out of weakness before it becomes strength. Artists are no better than other people. On the contrary, they know they are worse. The poet is a man who learns he cannot live with the self that was passed out to him by the Grand Commissar at birth. Consequently, he is compelled to create a legendary self, the self of art.

It is only a venial curiosity, tinctured with vanity, that leads me to inquire whether this head by Rosati resembles me. Aesthetically the question is irrelevant. All art, including autobiography as well as portrait sculpture or painting, is a form of fiction. My image of myself could not conceivably correspond with Rosati's image of me. Two sensibilities are forever divided, except in the act of love, by the membrane of the physical universe.

But — the artist is not content to stagnate in the cistern of his own personality. He is continually trying to overflow into other lives, as if his own were not sufficient for him. Such a fountaining requires energy, energy to spare beyond the needs of the life, energy for the wilderness at the edge of the garden, energy for the long nights and the endless conversations, energy "to murder and create."

Poetical character is as much a prerequisite for painters and sculptors as it is for poets themselves. Each art is more like any other art than it is unlike it; that is why cross-pollination between the arts is possible and, indeed, in the great periods, customary. Most of the writers I know, including the best, are ineffably naïve about modern art, as their choice of acquisitions demonstrates. As for painters, I long ago learned to expect nothing but ignorance from them about poetry. But there are signs of change in the wind. One of the most gratifying   d

enriching aspects of life in New York these days is the growing frequency of association between poets and artists. The
latter tell me — how generous they are! — that they have so
much to learn from the poets, but my own conviction runs
that it is they, the artists, who have more to give. How they fill
a room! You can sense they are riding the crest.

Rosati and I have this in common: we were both fiddlers in
our youth and played in orchestras, he with the Pittsburgh
String Symphony, I with the Pierian Sodality at Harvard
under Walter Piston. It was a figure by Donatello at the Car-
negie Museum — sprung out of the mind with so much human
grace and spirit — that made him stop wanting to play other
men's tunes. As for me, one day I read John Donne and locked
my fiddle-case.

Fragment of a conversation: "You don't mind belonging to
the human race when you see a head by Matisse."

According to Rosati, my head (of which he speaks objec-
tively, as though I had delivered it to him on a platter) has two
sides, expressing an essential contradiction. The right side
belongs to fire, the left to earth. A wild cocked eye goes
heaven-hunting, while its heavy-lidded sensual partner
broods at home.

Ideally, the relationship between sitter and artist is a reciprocal one. The sitter inspires the artist; the artist creates the
sitter.

Not without longing, from "the plummet-measured face" of
ancient Greece, bespeaking an art of rational proportion, we
turn our asymmetrical heads, clanging with atonality and off-
rhyme, and listen for what distant drum? In this twentieth
century, mathematical law took the universe by storm, but
abandoned the human figure.

The human head, the human figure always tell a story.
When the story was one the world wanted to hear, art was full
of anecdotes.

Faith died, the soul departed from the body, the rider dismounted from his horse, centaurs and heroes at once became extinct, and the artist yawned at the sight of the human figure.

Give us back the light of the eye!

Prophecy: the figure will return to art when it has a better story to tell. If a new world were to be created tomorrow on another planet, the first pictorial impulse would be to show Adam and Eve in the Garden . . . accompanied, of course, by the Serpent.

Without the Serpent there would have been no art. He taught us Tragic Joy.

Contrary to the general reaction, much contemporary sculpture impresses me as a work of excessive self-denial. Such a devaluation of desire! "The head Sublime, the heart Pathos, the genitals Beauty, the hands & feet Proportion," wrote Blake.

Perhaps, when we talk about sculpture, we tend to overstress the material substance of the art, as though it defined the medium. Actually the ubiquitous element overrides and practically negates the various transformations of matter, whether they be in stone or metal or more pliable stuff. All sculpture is cut out of the ambient air.

If Leonardo was right when he wrote that "painting is a form of poetry made to be seen," then it follows that sculpture is a form of poetry made to be touched.

"I am what I am," cried the block of stone to the sculptor. "Leave me alone!"
"Quiet!" he replied, poising his chisel and hammer. "I am about to free you from weight and measure!"

The Temptations of the Artist

O saisons, ô châteaux!
Quelle âme est sans défauts!

— Arthur Rimbaud

More than others the artist is a child of his age, a vulnerable child, responsive to all the changes of its weather, cheered by its promises, riddled by its doubts, seduced by its fashions, infected by its vices. We are not speaking of demi-gods. Some of the artist's temptations have an ancient lineage, for example sloth, which the monks in their medieval cloisters knew as *acedia*. Or for example pride, inextricable from the pursuit of fame, defined by Milton as "that last infirmity of noble mind." Other temptations are generational, peculiar to the epoch, and in attracting them the artist serves as a kind of lightning rod, electric with the libidinal energies of his time. These latter temptations are the ones that interest me more.

The one certainty about the style of any period is that sooner or later it will change, not necessarily for the better, not necessarily for the worse. In the normal course of events a style tends to flourish until it exhausts its vital impulse. The styles

Originally delivered as the Adolf Ullman Memorial Lecture in the Creative Arts, Brandeis University, May 2, 1968.

of the past usually lasted for a generation or so, sometimes for a century or more, with only slight modifications. No period, to my knowledge, has witnessed such rapid revolutions of taste as our own, such splinterings, fragmentations, explosions. Perhaps the breakdown of the family is a contributing factor. When fathers and sons, not to speak of grandparents, lived under the same roof, they shared a tradition, partaking of it with their daily bread. Now the generations live in separate camps, at odds with each other, with scarcely a language in common. The sons are in a hurry to reject the fathers. Indeed, assassinations are not unheard of.

All of us who have weathered the events of the past few years must have experienced the sensation that history itself is speeding up, as if for a dreadful climax. And history no longer waits for the written word: television manufactures it without stop (except for commercials) to be instantly consumed in our homes. Correlatively the whole machinery of the modern art world — dealers, museums, critics, collectors — is geared for the production of instant art history; and the young artist who is not snatched up and made famous overnight considers himself to be an instant failure.

If he is a clever young man, as he is likely to be, and if he is unresigned to the status of nonentity, he will respond to the pressures of the marketplace by a bold switch of styles or of materials, in order to exhibit something new, something shockingly new, that has some chance of competing for attention with the day's fresh crop of rapes and murders. Later, of course, it will be discovered that Marcel Duchamp was there before him — that mocking prestidigitator, who anticipated everything. The pursuit of novelty is one of the least original and most meretricious of aesthetic strategies. The true original occupies himself for a lifetime with discovering and realizing what is ineluctably his own.

Once at a cocktail party I found myself in conversation with an art critic who asked me what I thought about a young poet whom he had just met in another corner. When I tried to formulate a reasonably intelligent and discreet response, he interrupted me abruptly, saying, "I don't mean is he any good or not. I mean is he *avant-garde*."

The cult of *avant-gardisme* is inseparable from the cult of novelty. As applied today, the term is a complete misnomer, since a true *avant-garde* consists of an audacious handful who stand in an adversary relation to the art establishment and who could not conceivably be confused with it. In the past the critics followed in the wake of the creative spirits, sometimes even a generation later; their task was to interpret and appraise what had happened and to redefine the tradition so as to permit it to incorporate the changes. Today in certain quarters of the American *avant-garde* establishment the critics are more likely than not to take the lead, defining and promoting a style, recruiting disciples and collectors, indicting and even excommunicating artists of another persuasion. History, it has been said, is written by the survivors. A more cynical observation, for any knowledgeable reader of contemporary art criticism, is that it is perpetually being rewritten — in the interests of a school, a style, or sometimes even a carefully nurtured reputation. In this respect the art world is not unique. The new development on the music front, remarked Igor Stravinsky, is the apotheosis of "the critic as hero."

Since the tendency in modernist critical journalism is to divorce art from pleasure, from meaning, and from the moral universe, there is precious little left to expound aside from genealogy and technical data, for which a highly complicated and impressive jargon resembling English has been developed. The art-style in question, regardless of the artists who practice it, remains the trademark of the critic.

It is to the credit of American painting of the fifties, as exemplified in the work of Pallock, de Kooning, Rothko, and dozens of others of that generation — including Guston, Kline, Still, Motherwell, Hofmann, Tworkov, Tomlin, Brooks, Baziotes, Tobey, Stamos, Cavallon, Gottlieb, Reinhardt, etc. — that what it aspired to was an art of lyric or heroic self-assertion.* The works of that generation, individual as they were — and they now look even more various than at the time of their execution — erupted almost simultaneously on to

*In sculpture the creations of Alexander Calder and Louise Bourgeois may be cited as embodying the lyric principle; David Smith and Louise Nevelson, the heroic.

stage center of the international scene by virtue of their bravura and their vital authenticity. Eventually it became the fashion to scorn the "painterly" quality of Abstract Expressionism, along with its subjectivity and its humanistic implications, but it still remains, despite the excesses and redundancies that afflicted it, the most impressive and seminal American art-style of the century.

The work that immediately displaced it in favor, with successive explosions of Pop and Op, already looks dated and banal. Minimal or Primary Art, in its several manifestations, can have a cold purity, but I suspect that it is too reductive to sustain attention for long, even the lasting attention of its engineers. Not having access to the Puritan temperament, I cannot guess what ultimate satisfactions are to be found in an art that is deliberately drained of emotion. With a degree of relish I note that in certain recent productions of this school, despite the stringency of the program, color and sensuous detail manage to creep in. A number of hard-edge, chromatic, and colorfield paintings strike me as agreeably, sometimes brilliantly ornamental, and not much more, regardless of the critical abracadabra that tries to persuade us, in Clement Greenberg's formula, that "the irreducible essence of pictorial art consists in but two constitutive conventions or norms: flatness and the delineation of flatness." It is a source of depression and tedium that so much discussion of contemporary art is carried on in a pedantic and stultifying tone. I prefer to listen to a human accent, such as pleasures my ear when I come across a sentence in a letter by William Butler Yeats, an old man's letter, that goes: "I am still of opinion that only two topics can be of the least interest to a serious and studious mind — sex and the dead."

"Reduce, reduce, reduce was my thought," Duchamp has explained. "In French there is an old expression, *la patte*, meaning the artist's touch, his personal style, his 'paw.' I wanted to get away from *la patte* and from all that retinal painting."* The art that he envisioned was intellectual, mechanical, and dry. "It had to be planned and drawn as an architect would do it." As far back as 1910, according to his

* Calvin Tomkins, *The Bride & the Bachelors*, Viking, 1965.

chronology, he was inveighing against retinal or, as he sometimes called it, "olfactory" art, the work of painters enamored
of the smell of their paints. In contrast, around 1960 I can
recall de Kooning bragging, with a rather charming boyish-
ness, that if you got up close enough to his paintings, by God
you could smell them! Both of them have their triumphs, and
though there is no doubt in my mind as to which is the greater
painter, it can not be denied that the generational triumph, as
of this moment, measured by influence, belongs to the man
who in 1919 embellished a photograph of the Mona Lisa with
a moustache and beard. An analogous act of aesthetic tribute
and desecration was performed by Robert Rauschenberg in
1953 when he erased, for public viewing, a drawing by de
Kooning.

"The kind of talk you heard then in the art world was so
hard to take," Rauschenberg has commented. "It was all about
suffering and self-expression and the State of Things. I just
wasn't interested in that, and I certainly didn't have any interest in trying to improve the world through painting."*

Rauschenberg's comparably brilliant friend and mentor,
John Cage, composer, inventor, philosopher, mycologist, had
had a similar revelation three years earlier, in 1950, when he
discovered that he could draw up a series of large charts for his
rhythmic structures, susceptible in the plotting to the use of
chance. "Until that time," he has said, "my music had been
based on the traditional idea that you had to say something.
The charts gave me my first indication of the possibility of
saying nothing."†

In an informed summary of the state of recent American
painting, the critic Max Kozloff refers to Frank Stella, born in
1936, as "the conscience of his peers," a conscience manifested in "parallel alignments of stripes, executed most often
in metallic colors, separated by the tiniest channels of un-
primed canvas, and contained within frames that varied from
U forms to polygons, the centers most recently holed out."‡ In

* *Ibid.*
† *Ibid.*
‡ Max Kozloff, "The New American Painting," in *The New American Arts*,
edited by Richard Kostelanetz, Collier Books, 1967.

the following paragraph Kozloff warns that "the befuddled spectator" who "tries for conceptual significance" will be "warded off by the painter's purposeful blankness of mind." What puzzles me is how a blank mind can serve as the conscience of a civilization.

In the euphoric spring of Pop Art I recall discussing, with a museum curator, the productions of Andy Warhol, whom he held in high esteem. When I remarked that the work seemed to me empty, he replied, "What's wrong with emptiness?"

I do not mean to give the impression that the art world is a monolithic institution. If there are many who shout the slogan, "Less! Less!" there are others who insist, "More! More!" Among the latter are the exponents of happenings, mixed media, intermedia — the vocabulary is still fluid — who are bored with the traditional forms, restless with limits, determined to liberate the arts out of their separate compartments and to achieve a grand and mass-directed amalgamation. No doubt the energy and enthusiasm of the various groups dedicated to the occupation of the areas between the arts are more notable than their accomplishments, which tend to be messy. Some of their propaganda is as disarming as it is naïve. One comment that I have treasured for more than two years reads: "An Oldenburg Eskimo Pie may look something like an Eskimo Pie, yet it is neither edible nor cold. There is still a great deal to be done in this direction in the way of opening up aesthetically rewarding possibilities."

The new artists like to think of themselves as being intimately linked to the genius of the modern scientific imagination, but it is obvious that they are functioning at a much more superficial level. Their real contact is not with science, in its speculative purity, but with technology, or applied science, the handmaiden of industry, which they are tempted to idolize. If I recall a recent conversation with Kenneth Burke correctly, his useful term for the American worship of technology is *technism*.

The technistic orientation of certain American artists becomes most apparent when we hear them discuss their materials. "Art since the nineteenth century," comments the Minimal artist Robert Morris, "has had a drive to free itself from politics, philosophy, illustration. My pieces are not intended to comment on technology, but they relate to the general technological form that's been evolving for centuries — sheet metal, cut up, folded and fastened into, say, the box-like shapes of refrigerators. Because of its general quality, it has no connotations."* What we are witnessing is the progressive mechanization or, if you will, dehumanization of art, the threat of which has so long tired our attention that we scarcely notice the actual occurrence. Alexei Gan's Constructivist manifesto of 1920, after a considerable hiatus, begins to seem more and more prophetic:

> Art is dead! There is no room for it in the human work apparatus. Work, technique and organization! Let us tear ourselves away from our speculative activity and find the way to real work, applying our knowledge and skills to real, live and expedient work . . . replacing art which by its very nature cannot be disentangled from religion and philosophy and is not capable of pulling itself out of the closed circle of abstract, speculative activity.

In the Soviet artist's dream, which may be moving towards fulfillment, the artist would forsake the studio in order to take his place in the laboratory, workshop or factory.

At its most advanced level constructivist workmanship passes into kinetic art, either motor-driven or electronic, in which the technology is so sophisticated that it is subject to recurrent breakdown and early obsolescence. One art gallery, I am told, which does a booming business in kinetics, offers a six-months' maintenance contract with each piece that it sells. The artist himself does the repair work. It must be assumed that the workmanship is less expert than on a dishwasher, which is usually sold with a year's guarantee.†

Historically, though the arts change they do not improve. Eugene O'Neill is not better than Aeschylus; nobody in our time is likely to supersede Shakespeare or Mozart or Rembrandt — a hard thought to some of us. But an art work whose aesthetic potential is inseparable from its mechanical source

*New York Times, April 28, 1968.
†The gallery in question is now extinct.

of power has become hostage to the idea of progress. Technology is bound to improve. Next year's model will work better. There is no point in pursuing the implications. Already we have seen examples of a plastic, disposable, mass-produced art.

A parallel phenomenon on the road to dehumanization is the art work made by others. The ubiquitous Duchamp led the way some fifty years ago when he instructed his sister Suzanne, in a letter from Buenos Aires, to suspend a textbook in geometry from the balcony of her apartment in order to expose its theorems to the daily ravages of the weather. In 1922 Moholy-Nagy composed five paintings by telephone, dictating the use of standardized colors and graph paper. A young artist recently had a show of "drawings executed by others." Some Primary sculptures, it is no secret, are made at the factory from diagrams or specifications supplied by the artist; at least one famous cube was ordered by the artist over the telephone. And around the corner the computer is waiting.

"I can assure you," says Jean Tinguely, the Swiss motion sculptor, "that once you get rid of the notion of art you acquire a great many wonderful new freedoms." His ramshackle suicide-machine, "Homage to New York," that failed spectacularly to destroy itself in the garden of the Museum of Modern Art in 1960, has succeeded in spawning a numerous progeny of contraptions and breakages that go by the name of Destruction Art. Duchamp's surprisingly sour prophecy, as reported by Calvin Tomkins, is worth noting at this point: "I'll tell you what's going to happen . . . we're all going to drown in a sea of mediocrity. Maybe Tinguely and a few others sense this and are trying to destroy art before it's too late."

Much of modern art represents an attack, conscious or unconscious, on the human personality, an effort to annihilate it, to remove its signature. Perhaps personality is too great a burden to bear in the absence of sanctions and values, in the presence of so many monstrous ills. And perhaps art is too special, too difficult, too absurd to create in a world that must be standardized for the benefit of multiplying consumer populations. Let it become a thing like other things and let it be manufactured on the production line.

Or be satisfied with art as a game. Or define it as "purpose-less play."*

Once Alfred North Whitehead remarked, with a dash of philosophical salt: "Scientists who spend their life with the purpose of proving that it is purposeless constitute an interesting subject of study." Of equal interest must be counted those artists whose life is spent in demonstrating that art is useless.

After a couple of excruciating experiences with poisonous mushrooms, John Cage came out of the woods with a poignant observation: "I became aware that if I approached mushrooms in the spirit of my chance operations" — that is, in the spirit of his art — "I would die shortly."

But doesn't art deserve at least as much respect as one's digestive system?

*Much, but not all, of current [1975] conceptual art can be described as both depersonalized and "purposeless." I count the late Robert Smithson's earthworks among the notable exceptions.

Mark Rothko

Mark Rothko was such a restless and impatient soul. He never could sit through any kind of meeting. The way he squirmed! When I spoke at his funeral service I knew he would be pleased that the ceremony was so brief.

The image I summoned up was from the decade past, a happier decade — already it seems another age, as the ranks of our fellowship thin, year by year. He is wearing his battered black fedora, perched high on the glistening dome of his forehead; somehow an emblematic hat, for things were never quite the same after the wind blew it out of reach one winter evening. His nearsighted eyes behind the thick glasses are liquid with patriarchal affection and solicitude. His mouth is sensuous, quick to tremble with feeling.

"Tovarich!" he cries, with a huge embrace that locks me in, snug against his baronial frame, as if to protect us both against everything fretful, anxious, invidious, the adversaries from whom he would flee at last in search of peace.

Once I told him that he was the last rabbi of Western art.

And that made him smile, which was a relief, since one could never be quite certain when his face would darken.

I think of him as a poet among the painters, a lyric imagination in the dominion of the abstract. The scale of his work is more than a matter of dimension, for I have seen small paintings of his that look monumental. They are the breath of a vision, scarcely more than a breath, an existential stain . . . a glimpse, a memory, perhaps, of an archetypal simplicity and grandeur: "Shapes of things interior to Time, Hewn out of chaos when the Pure was plain." That transcendental quality, his effect of a pulsing spiritual life, of an imminent epiphany, was a secret he did not share with others and maybe only partly understood himself.

5

Tête-à-Tête

The whole work of man really
seems to consist in nothing but
proving to himself every minute that
he is a man and not a piano-key.
— F. M. Dostoievsky

Man can embody truth but he
cannot know it.
— W. B. Yeats

Poet: *"A Slightly Laughable and Glamorous Word":*
A Conversation with Robert Lowell

Robert Lowell speaks with an air of gentle authority. Surprisingly, for a New Englander, his voice has a soft Southern tincture, which may be traced back to his formative years when he modeled himself on the Southerners Allen Tate and John Crowe Ransom. His wife, who supplies another auditory influence, is the Kentucky-born novelist and critic Elizabeth Hardwick,* one of the founding editors of the *New York Review of Books.* Since 1960, when the Lowells braved the shock of transplanting themselves from Boston, they have figured prominently in the literary and intellectual life of New York. With their daughter Harriet, an ebullient seven-year-old, from whose flights of fancy and rhetoric her father has been known to borrow, they occupy a cooperative duplex apartment in mid-Manhattan, off Central Park. The Victorian

* Lowell is now married to Caroline Blackwood. He has been living, for the most part, in England, but returns periodically to the United States in order to conduct a poetry seminar at Harvard.

Originally published in *The New York Times Book Review,* October 4, 1964.

décor, dominated by "an unauthenticated Burne-Jones" hanging above the fireplace, and the majestic proportions of the book-lined living room, with its twenty-foot ceiling, recall the turn of the century, when the building was designed as a luxurious nest of studio apartments for non-struggling artists.

"Our move from Boston to New York gave me a tremendous push," says Lowell. "Boston is all history and recollection; New York is ahead of one. Sympathetic spirits are a rarity elsewhere. Here there is a whole community of the arts, an endlessly stimulating fellowship . . . at times too stimulating. No one is too great for New York, and yet I grant there is something frightening about it."

He is asked to comment on a passage from his remarks at the Boston Arts Festival in 1960, when he was the honored poet: "Writing is neither transport nor a technique. My own owes everything to a few of our poets who have tried to write directly about what mattered to them, and yet to keep faith with their calling's tricky, specialized, unpopular possibilities for good workmanship. When I finished *Life Studies*, I was left hanging on a question mark. I am still hanging there. I don't know whether it is a death-rope or a lifeline."

"Thankfully," he responds with the hint of a smile, "the lifeline seems to me both longer and stronger than I thought at that time."

He notes that he is feeling unusually fit, as his bronzed look confirms, after a summer in Castine, Maine, where the Lowells have an old Colonial house on the Common, a gift from his cousin Harriet Winslow. His weight — he has a tendency to gain — is down to 170 pounds, ideal for his six-foot frame.

"In *Life Studies*," he continues, "I wanted to see how much of my personal story and memories I could get into poetry. To a large extent, it was a technical problem, as most problems in poetry are. But it was also something of a cause: to extend the poem to include, without compromise, what I felt and knew. Afterwards, having done it, I did not have the same necessity. My new book, *For the Union Dead*, is more mixed, and the poems in it are separate entities. I'm after invention rather than memory, and I'd like to achieve some music and elegance and splendor, but not in any programmatic sense. Some of the poems may be close to symbolism. After all, it's a bore to keep putting down just the things you know."

As Lowell talks, slumped in his chair until he is practically sitting on his spine, he knits his brow in the effort to concentrate and stirs an invisible broth with his right index finger. The troubled blue eyes, intense and roving behind the thick glasses, rarely come to rest.

"The kind of poet I am was largely determined by the fact that I grew up in the heyday of the New Criticism, with Eliot's magical scrutiny of the text as a critical example. From the beginning I was preoccupied with technique, fascinated by the past, and tempted by other languages. It is hard for me to imagine a poet not interested in the classics. The task is to get something new into old forms, even at the risk of breaking them.

"So much of the effort of the poem is to arrive at something essentially human, to find the right voice for what we have to say. In life we speak with many false voices; occasionally, if we are lucky, we find a true one in our poems. A poem needs to include a man's contradictions. One side of me, for example, is a conventional liberal, concerned with causes, agitated about peace and justice and equality, as so many people are. My other side is deeply conservative, wanting to get at the roots of things, wanting to slow down the whole modern process of mechanization and dehumanization, knowing that liberalism can be a form of death too. In the writing of a poem all our compulsions and biases should get in, so that finally we don't know what we mean."

The contradictions of which Lowell speaks are present in his face and manner. The sensitive curved mouth contrasts with the jutting, fleshy chin; the nose is small, with wide circular nostrils; he is articulate, informed, and positive, but his gestures are vague and rather endearingly awkward. With his friends he has an air of affectionate dependency, which makes him seem perpetually boyish, despite the forty-seven years, the grizzled hair, the deep parentheses etched at the corners of his mouth. He is knowing about fame and power, but no less knowing about his weaknesses. His ambition and pride are real, but so is his modesty. It would be hard to imagine another poet of comparable stature saying to his interviewer and meaning it, "I should be interviewing you," or prefacing a book of his poems with such a disarmingly candid note as the one that introduces *For the Union Dead:*

> I want to make a few admissions and disclosures. My poems on Hawthorne and Edwards draw heavily on prose sentences by their subjects. "The Scream" owes everything to Elizabeth Bishop's beautiful, calm story, *In the Village.* "The Lesson" picks up a phrase or two from Rafael Alberti. "Returning" was suggested by Giuseppe Ungaretti's "Canzone." "The Public Garden" is a recasting and clarification of an old confusing poem of mine called "David and Bathsheba in the Public Garden." "Beyond the Alps" is the poem I published in *Life Studies,* but with a stanza restored at the suggestion of John Berryman. . . .

He has a great gift for friendship. No one is more generous than Robert Lowell in acknowledging his indebtedness to anybody who has ever helped him with a problem or with a poem.

"The poets who most directly influenced me," he says, "were Allen Tate, Elizabeth Bishop, and William Carlos Williams. An unlikely combination! . . . but you can see that Bishop is a sort of bridge between Tate's formalism and Williams's informal art. For sheer language, Williams beats anybody. And who compares with him for aliveness and keenness of observation? I admire Pound but find it impossible to imitate him. Nor do I know how to use Eliot or Auden — their voice is so personal. Williams can be used, partly because he is somewhat anonymous. His poems are as perfect as anybody's, but they lead one to think of the possibility of writing them in different ways — for example, putting them into rhyme."

Lowell has no secondary skills or hobbies to distract him from his absorption in literature. At 9:30 every morning, when he is in the city, he retires to his separate and private apartment on an upper floor of the building in which he lives. There he spends at least five or six hours reading and writing. He reads only three or four novels a year now, but is quite omnivorous in his capacity for literary periodicals and for books of poetry, criticism, and history. He makes a point of returning regularly to the classics "with the aid of some sort of trot." Recently he has been reading Juvenal and Dante. Some of his scholarship is specifically designed to prepare him for his courses at Harvard, where he teaches two days a week. "I have had the advantage," he reflects, "of an independent income, which made it unnecessary for me to work for a living. I came to teaching voluntarily and quite late, having been unfit for it in my youth."

Lowell occupies himself tirelessly with literary evaluations, comparisons, and ratings. "The modern poem of length that interests me most," he remarks sweepingly, "is Pound's Cantos, the only long poem of the century that really comes off, even with all its flaws. One reason for my sustained interest in it is that it continues to puzzle me. In so many respects Pound remains a pre-Raphaelite figure, filled with nostalgia for the pure song of the troubadours and a lost pre-Renaissance innocence. What saved him as a poet was his bad politics, which got him involved in the contemporary world. The Cantos are not so good as Faulkner, but they are better than Hemingway and better than the work of any other novelist we've had since James. Dreiser's *American Tragedy,* which is comparable in scale, is humanly superior to the Cantos, but technically and stylistically inferior."

His taste for fine prose is as keen as his taste for verse. "As Pound said, poetry ought to be at least as well-written as prose. Furthermore, if you have sufficient control of the measure, you ought to be able to say anything in poetry that you can say in prose. The main difference between prose and poetry is a matter of technique: prose is written in paragraphs, poetry in lines. I am fascinated by the prose grip on things that somehow lets the music in and invites the noble splendor of a formal art. Swinburne's voice is dead because it's all music and no experience. Hardy owed a great deal to Swinburne, as we know from his elegy, but his grasp on reality put him out of Swinburne's class. Both Hardy and John Clare were clumsy but honest craftsmen who sometimes wrote remarkably well. Some of the intricate musical stanzas in Hardy have the solidity of a stone-mason's job. In an anthology that I was reading the other day I came across 'The Frigate Pelican' of Marianne

Moore's with a sense of relief and liberation, not because it wasn't well-made but because it was made differently, outside the groove of conventional poetics. It caused the other poems to wither. I am still tempted by metrical forms and continue to write them on occasion, but I am aware that meter can develop into a kind of paralysis. Sometimes I start regular and end irregular; sometimes the other way around."

With an accelerated stir of his finger, Lowell tries to sum up his argument on the relationship between prose and poetry. "In general, the poets of the last generation have lasted much better than the novelists. By way of illustration, contrast Williams with Thomas Wolfe. Yet the poets need the prose-writers and have a lot to learn from them. The style of a Flaubert or of a Faulkner affects the tradition of poetry as much as it affects the tradition of fiction. An ideal poetic language is more likely to resemble the art of Chekhov than that of Dylan Thomas. Maybe Thomas's language is too sonorous to be at the center of poetry. The best poets have an enormous respect for prose. After all, the great novelists of the nineteenth century make *Idylls of the King* seem frivolous. The supreme epic of the last 150 years is *War and Peace;* of the last fifty years, *Ulysses.*"

The conversation veers to the subject of poetic reputation. Lowell is without doubt the most celebrated poet in English of his generation. Almost from the beginning it seemed that he could do no wrong. Why? After several false starts and a deepening of the furrows in his brow, Lowell proposes a tentative reply:

"I can't really explain why that much attention has been paid to me. Looking back at *Lord Weary's Castle,* for example, my first full-length collection, I see it as out of the mainstream, a rather repellent, odd, symbolic Catholic piece of work. It may be that some people have turned to my poems because of the very things that are wrong with me. I mean the difficulty I have with ordinary living, the impracticability, the myopia. Seeing less than others can be a great strain. One has to learn how to live with one's limitations. I don't like to admit that my gift is for short pieces, but I'm better off knowing it."

The British critic A. Alvarez has paired Lowell with John

Berryman as writers of "poetry of immense skill and intelligence which coped openly with the quick of their experience, experience sometimes on the edge of disintegration and breakdown. . . . Where once Lowell tried to externalize his disturbances theologically in Catholicism and rhetorically in certain mannerisms of language and rhythm, he is now . . . trying to cope with them nakedly, and without evasion."

Lowell does not try to skirt the issue, though it is difficult for him to discuss. "We are more conscious of our wounds," he ruminates, "than the poets before us, but we are not necessarily more wounded. Is Stevens or Eliot or Pound really any sadder at the heart or more vulnerable than Keats or Coleridge? The difference may be that modern art tries more deliberately to save the unsavable by giving it form. I am inclined to argue that it is better to be happy and kind than to be a poet. The truth is that no sort of life seems to preclude poetry. Poetry can come out of utterly miserable or disorderly lives, as in the case of a Rimbaud or a Hart Crane. But to make the poems possible a huge amount of health has to go into the misery."

Lowell finds the sources of his poems, variously, in a theme, an image, a musical phrase, sometimes in a prose passage or in another poem, preferably in a foreign language. The first draft is only a beginning. Only once did he ever complete a poem in a day. That was "The Tenth Muse," a poem about sloth! He makes a practice of showing his original draft to his poet friends, whose criticisms and suggestions he dutifully studies. A poem for him does not, as for Yeats, close shut with a click like a box. It only becomes less blurred. He does not believe in perfectibility. "In a way a poem is never finished. It simply reaches a point where it isn't worth any more alteration, where any further tampering is liable to do more harm than good. There are passages in all my books that make me wince, but I can't do anything with them. The worst grievance is the limitation inherent in any poet's character — the fact that Wordsworth, for example, can't be turned into Falstaff. That central limitation is far more serious than a few bad lines."

At the door, where he offers a warm valedictory hand, Lowell stands for a moment surveying the pantheon of his friends and heroes whose photographs adorn the staircase wall. These cherished countenances, who are very much a part of the Lowell life and household, include — in so far as one remembers — T. S. Eliot, Ezra Pound, William Carlos Williams, Robert Frost, Boris Pasternak, John Crowe Ransom, Edmund Wilson, the Allen Tates, I. A. Richards, William Empson, Randall Jarrell, Flannery O'Connor, and Elizabeth Bishop.

Exhausted as he is, at two in the morning, after more than five vehement hours of conversation, he is loath to let you go until the final resolving word has been spoken.

"You wouldn't write poetry unless you felt it had some chance of lasting. But if you get too concerned about posterity, you're in danger of becoming pompous and fraudulent. The poet needs to keep turning to something immediate and alive . . . something impertinent, engaging, un-Olympian. It's a waste of time to dream about immortality, but it's important to try for a poem that continues to be good, even though you realize that it's somehow a mockery for a poem to last longer than you do.

"You write poetry without hoping to attract too much attention, and it would be foolish to aim for a great audience that doesn't exist. Most people have a contempt for poetry — it's so ineffectual — but there may be some envy mixed up in that reaction. Today 'poet' is a slightly laughable and glamorous word."

"Blood and Poetry Are the Same":
A Conversation with
Andrei Voznesensky

K: Let's begin, Andrei, by talking about your new book, and the direction it signifies for your poetry. The last time I spoke to you about your work was in Moscow in 1967. At that time you thought you would be moving toward a more intimate kind of verse. Has that really been your development, or are you still committed to a public art?

V: Well, you see, Stanley, my new book, *The Shadow of Sound,* came out half a year ago. Suddenly it's not so loud a book as the one before it. I don't recite this poetry at the large readings, only for 1,500 people or less.

K: Because you feel the poems are not really right for big audiences and large halls?

V: I wanted my audience closer: to feel the emotion with me, and to be touched inside and to think. In this book I also

An abridged version of this conversation appeared in the *New York Times Book Review,* April 16, 1972; *Antaeus* published the full text in its Summer 1972 issue.

have some poems which you call "concrete," but I call them "visual poetry." Visual forms with sense inside. It's a poetry without sounds, only visual.

K: Are these abstract patterns? We have a long tradition in English of patterned poetry. George Herbert in the seventeenth century wrote poems in the shape of a cross or an urn, and the theme itself is consistent with the pattern.

V: I'll give you an example. One of my poems is called "Seagull: Bikini of God." We cannot see God, He is not visible, but He is everywhere, He exists, and we can only see His bikini. His bikini is a seagull and it comes to us, we see God come to us, like Jesus walking on the water in the New Testament. Certainly it is a kind of joke — the bikini, it's a little sexy — but there's a sense of something serious too.

K: Sometimes when you talk about poetry, I hear you say things that make me feel you are intrinsically a religious person. And that you are trying to assert some kind of spiritual conviction through your art. Is this true?

V: Indeed it is. But not religious in the orthodox sense. The Bible and the Koran are only metaphors for nature and processes. With our eyes we see only shadows of something called God — not nature, but a metaphysical nature. And the sounds in our different alphabets — Russian, English, Hebrew, Chinese — are only shadows of a sound we don't know.

K: All poets want to believe in a transcendental harmony, a music of the spheres. Our poems can never satisfy us, since they are at best a diminished echo of a song that maybe once or twice in a lifetime we've heard and keep trying to recall. And it occurs to me that your name is relevant. In Russian, Voznesensky has the root-sense of "ascension."

V: It's from my great-grandfather, who was a priest. I must tell you that after *The Shadow of Sound*, which Doubleday will publish, I have a book called *Eye*, which in Russian also means "together" and "conception." Some of my poems, I feel, are very close to your style. And we have spiritual affinities. It doesn't matter whether it's from Russia or the United States — it's just poetry. People need poetry, to save them from becoming robots. That's why they buy our books.

K: They buy more of yours. How many copies of your last book of poems were printed in Russia?

V: A hundred.

K: A hundred thousand . . . the usual size of your editions.

V: It's usual because we have no paper.

K: Russia loves her poets — that's so clear. When the rumor spreads that a new book by a favorite is in stock, people fight to get into the bookstores. Almost overnight there's not a copy left on the shelves, isn't it true? And the government printing house isn't exactly a sentimental institution — what goes out of print stays out of print. My guess is that you could easily sell 500,000 copies of any book of yours.

V: They had 700,000 orders before the book came out!

K: You have been here several times, you have many friends among our poets, you have a sense of our whole cultural mix. I wonder whether you detect any basic difference between the lot of a poet in this country and that of a poet in Russia.

V: It's very strange that the poets of our so-called new wave write in a style like your own generation — hermetic, complicated, formal, quite difficult. Your so-called rebellious poetry is more like the work of earlier Russian poets of the century, in the revolutionary epoch.

K: The sons always reject their fathers. So much depends on who your fathers were.

V: It's really strange. I like your poetry, and many of Auden's poems, and those of your friend Lowell, and Wilbur too . . .

K: Of course we're all very different. And yet I have the feeling that your closest identification is with our Beat Generation.

V: Yes, I love them.

K: And they're *quite* different.

V: I love Robert Bly's works and Allen Ginsberg's *Howl;* I think Corso is very talented. It's the question of a counter-culture, which is different in each country. In Russia now, we're coming close stylistically to Pasternak, Mandelstam, and the early Mayakovsky, when he was using very complicated forms. One thing I like about the Beat Generation is that they have a connection with their audience.

K: How important is audience to a poet? Isn't there a danger of becoming a performer, an entertainer, and in the process losing your secrecy, your innerness, the true source of your power?

V: Yes, there is such a danger. Audiences are sometimes too broad and ignorant — but a poet has to take risks. In Russia we have some poets who wanted above all to please their audiences — and it killed them. A real poet is superior to his audience. You cannot be a clown for the crowd. You write for yourself, and sometimes your words have the power to move others. If popularity is what you want most, you're sure to lose it fast, along with your art — I've seen it happen to some of my friends. Once the crowd knows you're not greater than they, they leave you.

K: I think it was Longinus who taught me that the ideal audience for poetry is composed of layers of generations. Better 1,000 readers in each generation for fifty generations than 50,000 readers all at once. An audience that cuts through time has greater gravitational force.

V: You're right. If a poet is only of his generation, he'll die with his generation. Our greatest poet, Pasternak . . . of which generation was he the voice? — of the revolution, the war years, the post-war years — which? Nobody can pin him down. Each generation takes what it needs from his work.

K: The same holds true for his friend, Anna Akhmatova, whose poems I have just finished translating. Not only is she a witness to all the terrors and marvels of modern Russia — she speaks out of an indomitable *persona*. She is a woman, but more than a woman — a compassionate and proud human being — and those poems stand, in their authenticity, like pillars of stone. No wonder the young in Russia know so many of them by heart. I remember how they kept pulling them out of hiding, from their bureau drawers.

V: Yes, Akhmatova is a beautiful poet, for all ages.

K: Russian poets have always been associated with the assertion of the free spirit, the opposition to tyranny. From the beginning they were in the forefront of the struggle for human rights — that is why they are held in such honor. Tell me, does the Russian poet still have a political function?

V: Certainly. Even so intimate a poet as Akhmatova was a social poet too. What you say is true not only of Russia, but also of Poland and all the eastern European countries. In Poland there is a Street of Two Prophets, where two poets once lived. In my country, Pushkin, Lermontov, Mayakovsky, Pasternak were symbols of the struggle for freedom. Some of them were killed. In Russia blood and poetry are the same. It is not so easy.

K: Pushkin, Lermontov, Mayakovsky all died violent deaths.

V: Yesenin too. I have just written a new poem about Yesenin. After he committed suicide, people came and saw on the walls the marks of his fingernails. In his mind he wanted to die, but in his gut he wanted to live. This is what I wrote about. A terrible picture!

K: In America, as a technological society, dedicated to progress, a theory of obsolescence is built into our culture. Generations come to maturity and then pass in a rush. Every five or ten years, compared with the old tradition of thirty years, there is a new generation, a new fashion, a new style, and this cuts through everything — fashion, politics, poetry. A young man of your age is no longer a youth here; his juniors are already doing something else and keep pushing to displace him. There is tremendous competition for that little space on that small platform. But in

Russia history is moving more slowly. There isn't this acceleration of the tempo: the older poets and the younger poets are really not very different. The younger poets — some of them — may be reverting stylistically to their grandfathers rather than to their fathers, but the continuity is very clear, the tradition is very strong, and that seems to me a central difference between the Russian poet and the American poet. You are more conservative in your art.

V: In Russia poetry is such a serious activity — a matter of blood, as I said — that it is not the fashion to change it lightly. Our people change dress, and right now the young are letting their hair grow long, but poetry doesn't change so fast, because it is not dress, it is not dancing, it is a more important thing.

K: Also it's more official than it is here. The state as the sole publisher in Russia exerts a leveling and restraining pressure, simply out of the conservatism you might expect from any bureaucracy. Suppose you were to commit yourself wholly to concrete verse in its more extravagant forms — who would publish you?

V: New poets come from the stage in Russia, from readings. Before poems are published they become known by being read aloud. Akhmadulina, Yevtushenko, Okudzhava, and myself became known through our readings.

K: Have you been doing much traveling in Russia recently? Where have you read?

V: I spent the summer in Riga — that's Latvia — and read in the hockey stadium, a beautiful sports palace. There were about 8,000 people in the audience. But now I really prefer — perhaps I'm getting older — to read for small, intimate groups, for my friends in a room. That is why I'm sometimes against my friend Yevtushenko; he wants larger and larger audiences, and that is certainly the democratic way, but I want smaller audiences . . . elite, well educated, quiet, and deep. If you need poetry, come. If you need something else, don't. I'm not Elvis Presley, I'm not the Beatles.

K: Everybody in America now knows the way you read a poem, it's famous. How did this style of reading develop? Is it in the Russian tradition? Is it, as I assume, out of Mayakovsky? I heard other Russian poets, writers of lyrics, who spoke their poems the way most Americans do, without theatrics. What about your reading style?

V: First, I would like to say that my style is not an actor's style. Some of us resemble actors, but I don't like actors' readings. I read in the same way I write. I remember the process of creation, and the words flow out from inside me. That is my way. Certainly I have heard how Pasternak read poetry, and the beautiful way Mandelstam read, and Mayakovsky too, but they had their own styles, because they had their own way of writing. Akhmadulina reads another way, Yevtushenko still another. He reads with gestures, with his face . . .

K: But his style, to Americans, sounds very much like your style, because it's a big style, a platform style.

V: I think he reads poetry better than I do. He reads more like an actor. Perhaps it is impossible for a foreigner to hear the differences. He likes to use gestures more than I do. I only use my right hand, and that's for rhythm. He uses his arms, his head, his legs. And it is beautiful the way he does it. But we are not the same. We have very little in common. I like him as another human being. But I don't really remember how I read.

K: In Russia when I asked young writers who were the poets they most admired, they would invariably name Bela Akhmadulina and you. I'm fond of the kind of lyric she writes, subjective and intense, with the most subtle controls. American audiences would be enchanted to hear her. She's a Tartar beauty — high cheekbones, slanted eyes — with an extraordinary voice and presence. She and I did a reading together in Moscow, do you remember? Americans would learn something new about Russian poetry from her. If she comes, I can assure you that she'll have a marvelous reception.

V: I consider her the best living Russian poet. She's great. She sends you her love, I forgot to tell you. Just now she's written a lot of new poems. I've heard from her that she has an invitation from America, and I'm sure she will come. We were together in Riga at the same time. I told her that you had translated a poem of mine dedicated to her, and she recalled that she had read for you a poem dedicated to me.

K: Yes, I translated that one too — "The Little Planes."

V: This summer she sent me a new poem, which I consider one of her best, and not merely because it was dedicated to me. And I wrote another dedicated to her . . .

K: This is like a continuing serial!

V: She has to come here and read, and meet the poets, because the American people have to know what Russia is, and what talented people it has. We have an exposition of our diamonds abroad, and of our cosmonauts, and we should have one of our best Russian poets.

K: Andrei, I don't recall that you've ever discussed your method of composition. Earlier you spoke of the importance of sound to you. Most poets know that sound and sense are tied together. How does this relate to the way you write a poem?

V: I never write by hand. All my works are in my head — I know all my poems by heart. I may be walking down a street or in the woods — perhaps I'm strolling through Rome — and a rhythm starts inside, maybe connected with my breathing, fast or slow. Maybe it's the rhythm of the world, of nature. In Yoga teaching why is breath a rhythm? Because it should be at one with the rhythm of the universe. In my poetry I try to connect my rhythm of breath, or maybe of blood, to the rhythm of the whole universe; to catch this whole rhythm inside me.

K: Do you speak these rhythms aloud?

V: No. Only in my head. Afterwards I come back and have my

friend write them down. Once I have written something, I cannot change it. For me it is finished. It is impossible for me to write a poem over a period of time. I try to begin and stop immediately, to work on a poem for a few hours and then not touch it again. This is because you have one kind of cry today and another tomorrow. One kind of moan now and another kind later. If you write poems over a long period of time they become eclectic, since you change from day to day. I understand Mayakovsky's essay on how to write poetry. He works with notebooks; he puts down maybe fifteen rhymes in a month's time, and then he writes a poem using these rhymes. I think he is great, and this method works for him, but for me it doesn't. If you invent a rhyme today, it is no good tomorrow.

K: Yeats used to work that way too. He would block out a poem, putting the key words down on the page, and the rhyming words, and then he would more or less fill in — which seems an extraordinary way for so great a poet to work. And yet for him it was right, obviously.

V: If the poetry is good, the method is right.

K: For me the poem is always something to be discovered, and you can only discover it by going down into your caves and reaching out for the language, which is forming, crystallizing, but not yet shaped. You don't know what you have until you touch it.

V: Do you write by hand, or in your head?

K: Both. I start by hand, but I don't really take very seriously what I'm writing. I let it flow, so that a lot of language spills onto the page, and I don't know whether it's good or bad. But then I keep rewriting, through countless changes, saying it, chanting it, until a music begins to fill me. Once I hear the beat, I'm in clover. Poems would be easy if our heads weren't so full of the day's clatter. The task is to get through to the other side, where we can hear the deep rhythms that connect us with the stars and the tides.

V: It's a very difficult life, being a poet. Like going to bed on

TV, with everybody looking. Like keeping a diary for the world's eyes. You have to be open for inspection, reveal all the dirty and beautiful things that happen to you. If you hide something, it will kill your poems. Sometimes I think it's too terrible . . . like being in a zoo.

K: But at least, Andrei, we're our own keepers.

6

Works and Lives

The works of the great poets have never yet been read by mankind, for only great poets can read them. They have only been read as the multitude reads the stars, at most astrologically, not astronomically.
— Henry David Thoreau

Art-speech is the only truth. An artist is usually a damned liar, but his art, if it be art, will tell you the truth of his day. . . . And you can please yourself, when you read *The Scarlet Letter*, whether you accept what that sugary, blue-eyed little darling of a Hawthorne has to say for himself, false as all darlings are, or whether you read the impeccable truth of his art-speech.
— D. H. Lawrence

The Vaudeville of the Mind

There are few events more cataclysmic in the life of an introspective young man than his first reading of the philosopher Hume. When Conrad Aiken was a student at Harvard it is probable that he came upon that triumphant passage in the "Treatise of Human Nature" affirming that we are

> ... nothing but a bundle or collection of different perceptions, which succeed each other with an inconceivable rapidity, and are in a perpetual flux and movement. The mind is a kind of theater, where several perceptions successively make their appearance, pass, repass, glide away, and mingle in an infinite variety of postures and situations. . . . The comparison of the

Originally published, as "The Poetry of Conrad Aiken," in *The Nation*, October 14, 1931. The occasion for the essay was the appearance that year of two volumes by Aiken, *The Coming Forth by Day of Osiris Jones* and *Preludes for Memnon*. My following review, "Learned in Violence," dated six years later, complements this study. I feel now much as I did then about Aiken's work. Among his later publications my favorite is *A Letter from Li Po* (1955).

theater must not mislead us. They are the successive perceptions only, that constitute the mind; nor have we the most distant notion of the place where these scenes are represented, or of the materials of which it is composed.

A letter from the poet to Houston Peterson, quoted in the latter's *Melody of Chaos*, reveals Aiken haunted from the inception of his poetic career by the notion of

. . . a single human consciousness as simply a *chorus*: a chorus of voices, influences. As if one's sum total of awareness and identity were merely handed to one progressively and piecemeal by the environment. As if one were a mirror. As if one were a vaudeville stage across which a disjointed and comparatively meaningless series of acts was perpetually passing. This flux being one's being.

Aiken does not trace this picture of the self "to any particular source in his own experience, to any book or person," comments Mr. Peterson, as though to confirm his assumption that the original poet is original philosopher too. I am more inclined to accept the observation of I. A. Richards that one idea — even a borrowed one — is sufficient for the lifetime of a poet. Aiken was fortunate enough to borrow his idea in youth and to find it endlessly viable and fascinating.

The letter that served to elucidate the theory behind his early work, dating from about 1915, is also a perfect synopsis of *The Coming Forth by Day of Osiris Jones*. Deriving its title and some of its substance from the Book of the Dead, in which the deceased is always called Osiris, this technically ingenious work acquaints us with the late Mr. Jones by representing the objects he possessed and admired, the clothes he wore, the rooms he occupied. While Jones is being weighed in the Great Balance, the "things" of his mortal existence become vocal. They accuse him; they ignore him; they babble round him with the malice of unreason. Only his Books, symbolic of memory, defend his soul. The poem is a dramatization, in short, of the consciousness-as-chorus idea; stylistically the most clever and materially the most complete statement of

Aiken's theme. If it appears less suggestive than, say, *Senlin*, and more superficial than, say, *The House of Dust*, the explanation is probably in its concision, its tougher diction, its freedom from mellifluous rhetoric. If it remains a minor performance, it is because of a grave error of proportion: too much trivial detail (Characteristic Comments, Inscriptions in Sundry Places, etc.) not compensated by bulk. You may catalogue flyspecks, metaphysical or otherwise, in a work the size of *Ulysses*, but the Joycean humor is ill-advised in a forty-three-page poem. It takes too long for the details to add up to an emotion.

I have said that *The Coming Forth* is an offshoot of Aiken's old poetic root. Its departure in form, however, makes it something of a sport. I value it more than I should, perhaps, in the catalogue of Aiken's work, because of the gratifying certainty that I shall never confuse it with anything else he has written. All the symphonic poems except *Senlin* — though I know them well — mix in my head, dissolve into a single music. I see a pathetic, rusty-haired little fellow who eternally sits at a window, chin propped up in his hands, sleeves fuzzy at the elbows — eternally sits and dreams through the pane. Somewhere an invisible orchestra begins to play. Out of the crannies of his brain troop "nuns, murderers, and drunkards, saints and sinners, lover and dancing girl and sage and clown." A weird melodrama unfolds. The ghostly mummers, obedient to Hume's explicit stage directions, "pass, repass, glide away, and mingle in an infinite variety of postures and situations." When they are gone, all that remains for the observer is a confused awareness of the major tragedy of minor souls.

> *Is there a horn we should not blow as proudly*
> *For the meanest of us all, who creeps his days*
> *Guarding his heart from blows, to die obscurely?*

Festus, the only one of Aiken's protagonists to attain heroic stature, fled from his own power, crying, "I will not have a god who is myself!" Why does the contemporary soul seek to divide itself among its adventures and possessions? Perhaps to evade the burden of conscience unrelieved by the promise of salvation. Perhaps because in the modern world only sensations and things have value.

One of the characteristics of an integrated poet — for example, Yeats — is that his works complement one another; Aiken's overlap. It is as though he has lacked the patience or the time utterly to drain from his consciousness the acid of his first creative impulse. Of all his long poems only *John Deth* impresses me as being wholly pure in concept, self-bounded in achievement.

The world is his poison; music is his anodyne; the ego is his companion. The study of the ego, in its ecstasies, in its intricate and ambiguous humiliations, is his passion. As for the problem of salvation, it scarcely enters into his lucubrations. He has little faith in grace, except the grace of love; and no faith at all in works. A poem, I should say, interests him less than its creation; suicide, less than despair; murder, less than jealousy; the event, less than the prelude. Hence the title, *Preludes for Memnon*, of his forthcoming volume, a collection (brilliant, on the whole) of sixty-three dramatic-lyric poems. Seeing a leaf fall, the poet meditates on the "wars of atoms in the twig."

> *This is the world; there is no more than this,*
> *The unseen and disastrous prelude, shaking*
> *The trivial act from the terrific action.*
> *Speak: and the ghosts of change, past and to come,*
> *Throng the brief word. The maelstrom has us all.*

A study of the *Preludes* in proof sheets suggests that Aiken is beginning, with romantic bravura, to embrace the maelstrom. He speaks more frequently and familiarly of God than was his wont. "It is to self you come — and that is God," he writes. And again, "No gods abandon us, for we are gods." What will this divinity do with his time?

> *In the beginning, nothing; and in the end,*
> *Nothing; and in between these useless nothings,*
> *Brightness, music, God, one's self. . . . My love,*

Heart that beats for my heart, breast on which I sleep, —
Be brightness, music, God, myself, for me.

In these new lyrics of Aiken one occasionally detects an un-
comfortable straining for effect, a movement toward the monstrous and unforeseen conclusion — or, in its lighter phase,
toward the paradoxical or merely shocking. The ultimate poetic manifestations of a thoroughgoing hedonistic solipsism
might prove, at the least, curious.

Aiken's idealism has one undeniable virtue: it provokes him
ceaselessly to poetry. Fertility may or may not be a sign of
genius. In Aiken's case I do believe it marks him out as pos-
sessing or being possessed by that "queer thing." Continuously present in his work is the sense of musical delight,
which, together with the power of producing it, Coleridge
rightly defined as a gift of imagination, a sign of the poet born,
not made. Aiken's imagination is apparently inexhaustible.

It is commonly said that he is over-facile, and it is true that
he at times deludes himself into the conviction that he is
saying something when he is really saying nothing at all. An
artificer at heart, he will, for the sake of rounding off a phrase,
of arriving at a climax, or even of achieving a rhyme, betray
himself miserably with words. He will stuff a poem with such
cumulated emptiness as:

You in whose smile are the flamings and fadings of suns,
In whose laughter are hidden the secrets of the past,
In whose "yes" are the blue corridors of eternity,
In whose "no" flash the scarlet lightnings of death. . . .

Having learned how simple it is "to invert the world invert-
ing phrases," he is frequently quite content to play with ideas
like the ubiquitous juggler in his poems. Having once written,
"The world is intricate, and we are nothing," he is constrained
to wonder why he might not just as well have said, "The world
is nothing; we are intricate." He will strike off any number of
bad poems in order to forge a good one, and he will publish
them all, being reckless of his talent.

An almost pathologically savage concept of evil is embodied

in his work. It is more than "the sound of breaking" at the center of the world; it is the living world full of decay:

> *Torrents of dead veins, rotted cells,*
> *Tonsils decayed, and fingernails:*
> *Dead hair, dead fur, dead claws, dead skin:*
> *Nostrils and lids; and cauls and veils,*

the "abysmal filth of Nothingness" that the Goya of his crapulous vision beheld pouring from time when the seconds cracked like seeds. A physician's son, Aiken is fully cognizant of the processes of catabolism. He is capable of anatomizing an emotional state with fiendish cruelty.

Nevertheless, there emanates from the body of his work an unmistakable vapor of sentimentalism. Sentimentalism is an easier word to spell than to define, but if you will carefully consider two verses, one reading

> *The melodious mystery of flesh,*

and the other,

> *I had found unmysterious flesh,*

you may agree with me in thinking the one flabbily adolescent in thought and expression, the other hard and mature. The first line is from Aiken's *Senlin*; the second from a lyric by Louise Bogan. Aiken began by being a "soft" poet. His latest work, notably *The Coming Forth*, is considerably harder in texture. This is as much a matter of technique as of substance. In the beginning, persuaded by a musical analogy, he sought to record, as it were, the onomatopoeia of disillusion. In the long symphonic pieces he wished to compose a "music" distinguished by its "elusiveness, its fleetingness, and its richness in the shimmering overtones of hint and suggestion." He melted down the skeleton of syntax and poured it into the rhythm of his mood. Whereas, in the metaphysical poets, one can almost feel the bare delicate bones of grammar under the phrase, Aiken substituted melody for grammar. Time was his style. Whether or not he will ever withdraw from his twilights and fluxes is problematical, although his recent work hints at the possibility. It will not be enough for him merely to woo the pure crystalline beauty of the Uranian* style: he must first tire of the perpetual vaudeville of his brain and drive from the theater his company of jugglers, acrobats, and clowns, leaving himself alone with the alone.

*In a generous and forbearing note Aiken inquired about this allusion. Urania was the muse of astronomy and the Aphrodite of ideal love.

Learned in Violence

Conrad Aiken is not the kind of poet whom our younger school inclines to admire or imitate. His has been a stubborn and, in many ways, heroic journey inward, following the Freudian stream. The political and social forces of our time have failed to touch him at his creative centers, though I do not doubt his intellectual awareness of them. What needs to be kept in mind is that the seemingly inexhaustible fertility of his imagination would seem to indicate that the course he has chosen may be, for him, the proper course. We must not judge a poet by the poetry he does not write.

Aiken's book is subtitled *Preludes to Definition*, but we do not have to wait for his world to be defined: that definition is implicit in every line he writes. His vision is of the shadows in the cave, and the cave itself impalpable as fog; of the swirling of phantoms, the dance of atoms, the blind gusts of desire. "God is your fancy," he writes, "and you are his." What holds

A review of *Time in the Rock: Preludes to Definition*, by Conrad Aiken, originally published in *Poetry*, May 1937.

the dissolving cloud-rack together is memory, the persistence
of mind. Aiken insists that continual resurrection is the condition of life. Man, hero and scapegoat of a thousand deaths,
must not forget what he was, lest he fail to continue to be.

The purpose, meaning, form — even the technique — of
Aiken's poems become clarified for us only as we perceive
them in their true function, as mnemonic exercises. We cannot
understand this desperate clutching at dead roots, stumps,
images, syllables, stones, unless we recognize the terror of the
ego hanging over the abyss of disaster and oblivion, the brink
of the unconscious. These preludes are feasts of remembering,
efforts "to have back"

> *even that simple evening, that simple flight,*
> *the cloud advancing on the wall of night,*
> *the rain advancing on the wall of wind,*
> *the mind advancing on the world of sight.*

Note particularly the supreme idiosyncrasy of Aiken's later
work, the repetitions, the catches. These mnemonic devices
tend to resist the authority of the creative will; they lead to the
tedious abracadabra of automatic writing, such ritualistic pig-
Latin as

> *And in the wide world full of sounds and nothings*
> *of faces and no faces and no sounds*
> *of words and wounds and in the words no world*
> *but only you whose face we cannot fathom*
> *and you whose word is what a word is only.*

Language itself is a perpetual miracle to Aiken: "each single
syllable is ringed with heaven and hell." There is an Indian
sect that holds all manifestations of life, even maggots and
lice, sacred; Aiken's religion of the Word, his fear of mutilat-
ing free verbal associations, is responsible for many of his failures. His best poems in this book are those of controlled word-
play in which he holds fast to a dominating image or concept.
Number XXXVII, with its astonishing "flight of bones"; LXXV
and LXXXV, brutal in self-exposure; XII, the crickets' song,

a tender fancy; and XX, the grave address to "you who love" — these so dexterous, so evocative, so beautifully fluent, are the ripe expressions of an undefeated lyric passion.

Aiken's loss of prestige in recent years is explicable in the light of his complete subjectivity, verging on the madness of solipsism; his prolificness; and the not infrequently absurd excesses of his style. But he has written:

> *O patience, let us be patient and discern*
> *in this lost leaf all that can be discerned;*
> *and let us learn, from this sad violence learn,*
> *all that in midst of violence can be learned.*

And he has written:

> *Lie down: we are absolved: we go from here*
> *to wider emptiness, and such dispersals*
> *of death, and cruelty, and the death of pain,*
> *as no life knew before, or will know after.*

A poet who can achieve time and again such solemn music transcends his defects and limitations. He does not need to worry about being in fashion.

A Lesson from Rilke

At the New York Botanical Garden is a sugar palm that after thirty years under glass has finally begun to blossom. Ninety feet above ground huge tassels are sprouting from the uppermost leaf axils. Soon the tassels will drop off, and the tree, having used up all its starch, will infallibly die. In somewhat the same fashion the nineteenth century idea of genius came to belated maturity during the first quarter of the twentieth. In its magnificent flowering it gave us such writers as Proust and Joyce and Rainer Maria Rilke, superficially dissimilar, but each obsessed with the problem of the artist, each carrying in his consciousness the seeds of death. Proust shut himself up with his asthma and snobbism; Joyce, with his pride; Rilke, with his hurt. They brought to painfully exquisite perfection the life of the nerves, the life of memory. Joyce alone was capable of laughter, Proust of dispassion, Rilke of faith. Monu-

Originally published in *Poetry*, March 1935.

mentality was not in Rilke's scope, but of the three he made the clearest and fullest esthetic statement.

The best of the Austrian poet, who died in 1926, is, of course, in his verses, of which the substance and sensibility, but not the haunting rhythms, the scrupulous texture, are capable of transliteration. Of the four books (the autobiographical *Journal of My Other Self* [in German *Die Aufzeichnungen des Malte Laurids Brigge*], the naïve and tender *Stories of God*, the prose-poem of *The Tale of the Love and Death of Cornet Christopher Rilke*, and *Letters to a Young Poet*) which have been made available here in recent years by the publishing house of W. W. Norton, largely through the devotion of his translator, M. D. Herter Norton, by far the most important is *The Journal of My Other Self* (1903–1910), a book of impressions, sensations, fevers, and memories, occasioned by his residence in Paris, where he was secretary to Rodin; a book so sensitive it might have been written with the tips of his nerves; a transparent record of

> the almost immeasurable: the rise of half a degree in a feeling; the angle of refraction, read off at close quarters, in a will depressed by an almost infinitesimal weight; the slight cloudiness in a drop of desire, and the well-nigh imperceptible change of color in an atom of confidence.

Rilke excites one most when he treats of the terrible, the grotesque, the lacerations and the frets. Less original and arresting are his too highly colored recalls of childhood, his traffic with the supernatural, his religious and metaphysical speculations. This is the sort of observation that no one else has ever made with such acuteness and profundity:

> There are quantities of people, but there are even more faces, for each person has several. There are some who wear the same face for years: naturally it wears out; it gets dirty; it splits at the folds; it stretches, like gloves one has worn on a journey. These are thrifty, simple folk; they do not change their face; they never even have it cleaned. . . . There are others who change their faces in uncannily rapid succession, and wear them out. At first they think they have enough to last them forever; but they have scarcely reached forty when behold, they have come to the last of

them. This, naturally, leads to tragedy. They are not accustomed to being frugal with faces. Their last is worn through in a week, has holes in it, and in many places is as thin as paper; and then gradually the lining — the no-face comes through, and they go about with that.

One of Rilke's primary ideas, elaborated in *The Journal*, is that of the proper death: the need of dying one's own death, of carrying that death within one like the kernel of a fruit, of exhausting all the forces, accidents, and implications of one's destiny. "Let life happen to you . . . life is right," is another statement of this dominating concept. The hero of his most popular work, *The Tale of the Love and Death of Cornet Christopher Rilke*, whose loving and dying are performed with equal munificence of spirit and finality, upholds like a flag the virtues that the poet most admired. Though Rilke at times experienced poverty, sickness, neglect, and despair, he never forsook his class. His pride in his noble ancestry is always apparent; the praise of martial glory (though he had gone through hell at military school and was to visit it again) is often on his lips; one of his chief sorrows is his rootlessness. "What sort of a life is it really," he cried, "without a house, without inherited possessions, without dogs?"

God was very close to him: in every clean and shining object; even, despite his aristocratic leanings, in ordinary things with humble uses. The finest of his *Stories of God* tells of a group of children who decide that God is something that one can take in one's hand and put in one's pocket and carry about with one all day: God, in short, is a thimble, which each of them has in turn for a day. Sometimes in the midst of their play one of them calls out, "Who has God now?" Rilke never made a satisfactory answer to that question. (Questions were always dearer to him than answers.) It is true that he could point to the thimble, but at the same time he was intensely aware that the finger throbbed and was sore. He might complain, yet he dared not judge.

This, then, is to Thy liking, in this dost Thou take pleasure: that we should learn to endure all and not judge. What are the grievous things, and what the gracious? Thou alone knowest.

Some years later, after the bitterness of Europe had stained his heart and he could hardly bear to write again, Rilke flung at himself these implacable words: "Not to understand: yes, that was my sole occupation."

Yet how hard he had tried. With what patience, conscience, and devotion he had applied himself to the discipline of life and art. In the beginning he had been so humbly confident of the way. Together with all the inheritors of the romantic concept of genius, he had professed that the work of art is "of an infinite loneliness"; the artist, a unique and solitary being; the soul of the artist, pierced with swords; the duty of the artist, to go down into the deeps of his own affliction and there probe, with patient zeal, the fungi and the wounds. His advice to "the young poet" had been solemn and precise:

> Love your solitude and bear the suffering it causes you with sweet-sounding lamentation.
>
> It is good to be solitary, for solitude is difficult; that something is hard must be a reason the more for us to do it.
>
> The only courage that is demanded of us: to have courage for the most extraordinary, the most singular, and the most inexplicable that we may encounter.

But today we are not so sure about the nobility of "sweet-sounding lamentation"; we begin to suspect that the apotheosis of the difficult must make a dulcet sound in the ears of those who have the cunning or the strength to transfer their share of the burden and discomfort of the race to the backs of others; we find that the courage we most need is not "for the most extraordinary, the most singular, and the most inexplicable," but for the most common.

These notes began with a reference to the maturation of the sugar palm at the Botanical Garden. Let me add now that when a new generation springs from its seed, there will be two things to remember about the parent growth, two equally important things: first, that it blossomed; second, that it died.

The Single Conscience

The prophets and the priests are traditional enemies. In her exposition of "the ideas that have made modern literature" Mary Colum attempts to effect an armed truce — but only a truce — by proposing a division of responsibilities and powers between the practicers of art and the preceptors of ethics. Contending that morals are fundamentally "at loggerheads with art," she endows the human race with two main consciences, the ethical and the aesthetic, and asks us to resign ourselves to their incompatibility.

> Morals are the fruit of the ethical conscience, art of the aesthetic conscience; each has its own rules, and while in actual practice neither ethics nor art can be at all times judged exclusively by its separate laws, just as nothing in life can be so judged, it is the

Originally published in *Poetry*, May 1938, as a statement of exception to the doctrine of "the two consciences" propounded in Chapter 7 of *From These Roots: The Ideas That Have Made Modern Literature*, by Mary M. Colum, Scribner's, New York.

desire of every artist that his work should be judged purely by aesthetic laws.

In such a Scholastic dichotomy the artist is set, we may say, in the kingdom of nature, with "life" as his subject, and told that he is free to act. But this freedom has its limits, for there is another and greater kingdom — more populous, in any case, since art is "produced for a minority" — and in this outer kingdom of grace or moral law man must accept what God or the State reveals. Mrs. Colum wants to be fair to the citizens of both kingdoms. She concedes the right of the artist "to work according to the eternal laws of his art." On the other hand: "If the artist has a right to choose any material he wishes and the right to employ every means he can to make a lasting thing and defend it, the public also has the same right to defend what it has made, its rules and regulations for the convenient conduct of life." In this statement I am struck by the curious opposition of "artist" to "public" — as though the creative person existed outside the human race and were engaged in a professional conspiracy to destroy it. What seems to me even more astonishing is the picture of the institutions of authority fighting, with their backs to the wall, against the embattled artists. Pity the poor, helpless, innocent State and her unfortunate sister, the Church, who have nothing to defend themselves with against the poets except wealth and power, the police, the military, the courts, the concentration camps, and, if need be, the gun! (The State, of course, feels no compunction about applying these same instruments of persuasion to the Church, when conflicting interests supervene to inhibit their sisterly affection.)

I cannot applaud the justness or moderation or even the intelligence of an assertion that "no public or law ought, in a civilized country, to have the right to suppress or destroy a work of art, although it has the right to censure and condemn it, or even, in cases, to limit its circulation." If it is conceded that artists must eat, whoever condones the restriction of their market (because "the public" is displeased) extenuates the not very mild or benignant process of starving them out.

To grant authority to the ethical conscience over the aesthetic, no matter with what appeal for sweet reasonableness in action, is to accept the constitution and by-laws of the Society for the Suppression of Vice, to justify the anticultural ruffianism of local demagogues, to invite the disaster that has befallen art in the totalitarian states.

The theory of the two consciences is not only inexpedient, but also in flat contradiction of the evidence. Above the level of the balladist, and not infrequently at that level, the poet is confronted by the ineluctable necessity of making moral judgments. The ethical significance is not always so conspicuous as in the work of Dante, Goethe, Milton, Tolstoy, and Thomas Mann, but, however elusive, it is always there, the twin threads of good and evil running through the fabric. Mrs. Colum praises, elsewhere in her book, Coleridge's theory of the imagination. But Coleridge would have been horrified at the divorce of the imagination from moral imperatives. "No man," he wrote, "was ever yet a great poet, without being at the same time a profound philosopher." An imagination that is not healthy enough to assimilate ethical laws is too much of a weakling to face the rigors of poetry. The artist is everything that he can experience. Society responds to him, and a sympathetic, mutually enriching relation is achieved, when the communal life approximates in variousness and intensity the experience of its artists.

One of the reasons why modern poetry has appeared so obscure, cold, and baffling to the population is that it represents a multiplicity of phenomena and psychological adventure that can seem only eccentric to men in the grip of a routine that limits and conditions their spiritual as well as their physical reflexes. In his *Men of Mathematics* E. T. Bell remarks of Archimedes: "This is one of his titles to a modern mind: *he used anything and everything that suggested itself as a weapon to attack his problems.*" Of the truly contemporary poet — and it is necessary to be contemporary before one can be classic — it may be said that he incarnates and expresses the wild audacity of the modern mind. In this connection Thomas Mann writes:

Art, above all things, belongs in the sphere of the venturesome, the daring. It forever reaches out to extremes and never lacks that "touch of audacity" without which, according to Goethe, "no

talent is conceivable." Art abhors the mediocre, as it abhors the
cheap cliché, the trivial, the insipid and the base. . . .

An act of the imagination, the transmutation of the infinite
particulars of experience into finite form, is the most complete
operation of the mind, when it functions as "the organ of civilization." Nothing need be alien to it, for there is nothing that
its masterful alchemy cannot transform. To speak of the imagination as a separate element of the mind — as the pure part,
for example, that must be isolated from the coarser elements,
lest it suffer contamination — is to fall into a paralyzing error.
Mrs. Colum's theory of the two consciences leads her almost
into absurdity when she writes:

> He [the artist] has to make his work as sincere and as fine as he
> can, without allowing other provinces of human achievement to
> shove their laws or rules onto him. Pure literature, therefore, can
> never be propaganda, for propaganda is the turning aside of liter-
> ature from the expression of life, which is its field, to the praise or
> advertisement of some policy, some endeavor, some side line of
> life, which may represent a public good.

What "pure" literature is I do not know, nor why a side line
is any less a part of life than a line. Whenever people begin to
talk about propaganda — and nearly everyone is ready to
begin at the drop of a hat — I am reminded of those demor-
alizing advertisements that warn us that we ourselves can't
tell when we're "offensive." Propaganda is what somebody
else is guilty of when he advocates something that you don't
believe in.

Mrs. Colum exhibits the nature of this fallacy when she
refers, in another context, to the Declaration of Independence
as a work of American literature. It is; but it is also, like Milton's *Areopagitica* and the Communist Manifesto, a provocative document — a piece of propaganda, if you will — and you
could not read it aloud in Jersey City today without being
clapped into jail. When the word "literature" is employed as
though it were a badge of honor to be pinned on the breast of a
Nobel Prize winner but not on any lesser mortal's common,
run-of-the-mill breast, the critic is enabled to exclude pe-

remptorily from his sacred garden any writer whose manners or opinions annoy him. Actually, the difference between the works of Jonathan Swift and those, say, of Brann the Iconoclast is one of quality and not of kind. Any valid critical method must be able to note and define such qualitative differences without establishing a Lipari for political offenders.

The artist need not apologize for being tormented and driven by humanitarian motives. Every true disciple of the creative intelligence is, to borrow Zola's epitaph, a moment in the conscience of man. In a time of the breaking of nations and classes the artist suffers the violence of the race, its corruption, and its deep, searing agony of hope. Like the victim-hero of Kafka, he stands in the prisoner's dock and is accused. Of what precisely he is accused he does not know, nor does it matter, since the namelessness of his crime does not minimize his guilt. The rules of the court are preposterously unintelligible, but that does not matter either, for by being what he is, imperfect, traduced, and human; by standing on trial, in his skin and with all his heritage; by receiving into himself the wounds of his brotherhood, he seizes on his destiny and adds it to the historic sum.

The past is forever dying; it needs continually to be revived, lest it suffer dissolution and sift into oblivion. Malraux has expressed the view that the supremely ethical function of a work of art is not only to create itself but to re-create the long tradition that has made it possible. As the human embryo recapitulates the evolutionary development of the primate body, so the poem repeats for us man's spiritual ascent, reaching back to those obscure thousands under the hill of time who once climbed up the forbidding slope. Without that triumphant leap of sympathy back to the Cro-Magnon cave artists, the singers of the Psalms, the clay-befriending worker at the potter's wheel, — without that healing and redeeming bond, time itself would crumble and expose the worm. There is only one artist, the true, recurrent undying wanderer, the eternally guilty, invincibly friendly man.

A purged and etiolated art, one separated from the desire for a good life, is vain and unfructifying. The artist — and this is why the dictators fear him — will speak, because he must, for those souls and values that have been dispossessed; ironically, tragically cry out with the guilty heart of those who have dispossessed them or permitted the usurpation. Even in the abstract, without overt accusation, a good poem rejects all bad poetry and all loose thinking. The aim of the authoritarian state is to fasten on the population a common, changeless, and submissive mask. The artists are squashed or expelled, because, being independent makers of masks whose virtue is to permit man to see himself perfect and ennobled, they compete with the national monopoly in false-faces. Against the superimposition on civilization of the State-manufactured *persona*, the artist, with those who stand beside him, forms the last line of resistance, tougher than armies, for armies find it easier to win a war than a victory. The general and the Führer, though they may fight against each other, are both of them, in the end, face-grinders. You will find in the soldier's kit a bundle of undifferentiated masks.

What hope we have lies in the single, integrating, humanitarian conscience of the men of culture, nourished by participation in the tremendous striving of the masses for a life less mean, less blighted, less ignoble, more light and free. We need to turn from the men of will and order, those with the fanatic righteous eye and the unmarried ethical principle, who have no dedication but to the rules and regulations for the efficient conduct of life in an organized society. "O ye Religious," cried outraged Blake, "discountenance every one among you who shall pretend to despise Art and Science!" The New Moralists of our age, with their death-dealing hatreds and abominations, have taught us to understand the sterilizing passion of the desert saints and the hitherto almost inconceivable brutality of the holy massacres, inquisitions, and wars. Moralism divides — church from church, nation from nation, race from race, and man from man.

If Morality was Christianity, Socrates was the Saviour.
Art degraded, Imagination denied, War governed the Nations.

To those who complain of the futility of creative effort in a time so shaken, I would say that no time has been in greater need of a compelling and representative art. The only measure of a man's usefulness is the extent to which he exercises his talent, according to the laws of his own growth, for the common good. The artist is wasted driving nails. Let the painter go back to his easel and the writer to his desk. Whatever has long endured in the veneration of mankind — even the Eternal Being — has been the product of the poetic genius. It would be arrogant for us to presume that the most benevolent of deities would be willing forever to save a civilization that does not carry in its heart those two companion humilities named by Keats: the principle of beauty and the memory of great men.

Land of Dust and Flame

On the jacket of this omnibus volume of Louise Bogan's work, containing in all some ninety poems, Allen Tate is quoted in praise of Miss Bogan as "the most accomplished woman poet of our time." The praise, to my mind, is justified; but I suspect that to be perennially classified and reviewed as a "woman poet" must prove discomfiting, at the least, to a poet of Miss Bogan's superlative gifts and power. It is true that she is a woman and a poet and that her motivations and themes, like those of her sister poets, relate essentially to her special experiences in a man-world — and why not? — but the virtue of her work is not a quality of gender. Stephen Spender recently made the somewhat rash generalization that when men write poetry they have their eyes fixed on several things at once — the form of the poem, the effect of the poem on the reader, their own personalities — whereas women lose themselves in the subject-matter, the experience behind the po-

A review of *Poems and New Poems*, by Louise Bogan, originally published, under the title "Pentagons and Pomegranates," in *Poetry*, April 1942.

etry, and are careless of words themselves and the rhythmic pattern. This indictment cannot even be applied to Miss Bogan's earliest poems, of which the following, with its conspicuously familiar theme, is an example:

> *Men loved wholly beyond wisdom*
> *Have the staff without the banner.*
> *Like a fire in a dry thicket*
> *Rising within women's eyes*
> *Is the love men must return.*
> *Heart, so subtle now, and trembling,*
> *What a marvel to be wise,*
> *To love never in this manner!*
> *To be quiet in the fern*
> *Like a thing gone dead and still,*
> *Listening to the prisoned cricket*
> *Shake its terrible, dissembling*
> *Music in the granite hill.*

Miss Bogan's work is occasionally pretty, with a deliberately wrought elegance of lyric style; it is never, or almost never, girlishly arch or matronly sticky. She is exempted from sentimentality by her respect for her art; by her discipline in self-seeing; by that nervous capacity for self-disdain without which the romantic poet, in an age of non-romantic values, no longer can endure.

Miss Bogan understands form: she writes a poem from beginning to end disdaining the use of filler. Her ear is good: she is sensitive to verbal quantity and quality. When she succeeds — and she succeeds remarkably often — the surface of her poem is only the other side of its substance, without holes to fall through. In the poem already quoted I doubt that there is a word that could be changed without impairing the whole structure. The distillation of her talent is in a deceptively simple quatrain, so just in style, so mature and witty in sensibility, that a long life can safely be predicted for it:*

---

* It is gratifying to see a prophecy confirmed. The posthumous publication of the first draft of this quatrain in *What the Woman Lived: Selected Letters of Louise Bogan, 1920–1970*, p. 82, provides a valuable insight into the poet's working habits, as well as a lesson in the art of revision. Her extemporaneous

> *Slipping in blood, by his own hand, through pride,*
> *Hamlet, Othello, Coriolanus fall.*
> *Upon his bed, however, Shakespeare died,*
> *Having endured them all.*

Aside from this quatrain and two other pieces, "The Dream" and "The Daemon," her new poems seem to me less consummately organized than before. (I am not discussing the silly section of *New Yorker*ish verses, which might well have been omitted.) In the new poems there are indications that Miss Bogan is experimenting in an effort to release her poetic energies more fully and to extend her range. Her long-held ideal of geometric perfection, her creative illusion of "cool nights, when laurel builds up, without haste,/ its precise flower, like a pentagon," has undoubtedly, in some respects, fettered her talent, so that one feels at times that she has re-worked her materials to excess, at the expense of associative spontaneity. I should like to see further manifestations of the mood of savage irony that produced "Hypocrite Swift"; and I find in "Kept," with its cold abnegating pity — "the playthings of the young/ get broken in the play,/ get broken, as they should" — a kind of writing that no one else can do half as well.

---

lines, as they appeared in a letter to Edmund Wilson, dated October 16, 1934, read:

For every great soul who died in his house and his wisdom
Several did otherwise.
God, keep me from the fat heart that looks vaingloriously toward peace and
  maturity;
Protect me not from lies.
In Thy infinite certitude, tenderness and mercy
Allow me to be sick and well,
So that I may never tread with swollen foot the calm and obscene intentions
That pave hell.
Shakespeare, Milton, Matthew Arnold died in their beds,
Dante above the stranger's stair.
They were not absolved from either the courage or the cowardice
With which they bore what they had to bear.
Swift died blind, deaf and mad;
Socrates died in his cell;
Baudelaire died in his drool;
Proving no rule.

But I am persuaded that the true world of Miss Bogan's imagination, of which she has up to now given us only fragmentary impressions, is "the sunk land of dust and flame," where an unknown terror is king, presiding over the fable of a life, in the deep night swarming with images of reproach and desire. Out of that underworld she has emerged with her three greatest poems, spaced years between, of which the latest is "The Dream":

O God, in the dream the terrible horse began
To paw at the air, and make for me with his blows.
Fear kept for thirty-five years poured through his mane,
And retribution equally old, or nearly, breathed through his
*   nose.*

Coward complete, I lay and wept on the ground
When some strong creature appeared, and leapt for the rein.
Another woman, as I lay half in a swound,
Leapt in the air, and clutched at the leather and chain.

Give him, she said, something of yours as a charm.
Throw him, she said, some poor thing you alone claim.
No, no, I cried, he hates me; he's out for harm,
And whether I yield or not, it is all the same.

But, like a lion in a legend, when I flung the glove
Pulled from my sweating, my cold right hand,
The terrible beast, that no one may understand,
Came to my side, and put down his head in love.

In the body of Miss Bogan's work "The Dream" stands with "Medusa" and "The Sleeping Fury" in violence of statement, in depth of evocation. They give off the taste of pomegranates: Persephone might have written them.

Barbaric Omens

Looking back in his flight, Robinson Jeffers sees the world turning to salt, as he had prophesied in his long crying of violence and doom. Mixed with his horror is a pardonable trace of pride, such as might become a vehement old warlock who, after interminable conjurings, suddenly produces a fell spirit from his kettle of bones and excrement.

Well: the day is a poem: but too much
Like one of Jeffers's, crusted with blood and barbaric omens,
Painful to excess, inhuman as a hawk's cry.

With this stricken world, dyed in the "noble, rich glowing color of blood," Jeffers can be friend: it is the familiar world of his imagination. Now that he begins to retrace his footsteps, it may be pertinent to inquire why he left us in the first place and to what fellowship he may return.

A review of *Be Angry at the Sun*, by Robinson Jeffers, originally published in *Poetry*, December 1941, under the title "The Day Is a Poem."

The picture of Jeffers as avatar, stone-breasted and prehistorical, living in ma tic isolation with a gang of clacking Furies for company, has been one of the formidable illusions of twentieth-century poetry. To have created that illusion is in itself a triumph. Actually, like the early nineteenth-century Romantic poets, he has been wielding his bright sword against the Industrial Revolution and the rise of scientific materialism. Since the time was late and the fight seemed lost, he could only renounce the civilization that had suffered itself to be tainted. All this disaffection, carried to the extreme of nihilism, stems from an overpowering disgust with "the immense vulgarities of misapplied science and decaying Christianity." What Taine said of Byron may be said, with equal appropriateness, of Jeffers:

> Inevitably imprisoned within himself, he could see nothing but himself; if he must come to other existences, it is that they may reply to him; and through this pretended epic he persisted in his eternal monologue.

Continuing his "pretended epic," Jeffers opens this volume with a long narrative poem entitled "Mara," which does no more than restate, with a new cast of incestuous phantoms, the allegory he has been writing for some twenty years. With practised hand he flicks his long whip-like lines; the rhythms are beautifully controlled; the story leaps from one explosion of emotion to another. If at times the language turns tasteless and gauche, particularly in expressions of sentiment, at other times it redeems itself effortlessly, as when "the artery sprayed like a fire-hose," or "the slow flies vultured the table." But nowhere does it match his best writing, when the language turns all to light, as in saying of a man's dying, "It is only someone dropping a mask./ A little personality lost, and the wild/ Beauty of the world resumed." That is from another and better poem in this book.

"Mara" itself is only a mask, and when it is dropped, a monumental ennui stares out at us. Here are "a cancerous old man, a jealous wife . . . , and a little young hot adulteress between her two men," one of whom is her husband, the other his brother. It is old stuff to Jeffers; he is bored writing it, and, what is worse, we are permitted to sense his boredom, his feeling that he has spun too many myths out of himself, that they have turned on him and are devouring him. He wants a living symbol who can project his sense of tragic destiny; who can enact on the world's stage the grandiose drama of Romantic irony and Romantic despair; into whom he can pour the disastrous vials of his spirit. Into the midst of "Mara," as though he had been waiting restlessly in the wings all the time, bursts, if only for a moment to take his bow, the Person for whom Jeffers has been waiting, the genius of his dire prophecies. We do not actually see him; our only contact with him is through his voice, his passionate high bark heard on the radio, bringing "scorn and dog wrath" from the pits of Europe, as the war starts and an old man wearily handles his pain.

Bruce Ferguson, the protagonist of "Mara," who hangs himself "by a horse-hair hackamore under a beam in the barn," may be the last of an ill-starred dynasty beginning with Tamar Cauldwell from Lobos. For better or worse, Jeffers has found his flesh-and-blood Manfred. In "The Bowl of Blood," a 27-page masque following "Mara," he introduces, for the first time in English poetry, Hitler as hero.

The scene of "The Bowl of Blood" — a magnificent accomplishment, by all odds the most important poem in the book — is a desolate cabin on the Schleswig shore of the North Sea. Attended by three maskers, a fishwife with a gift for prophecy leans over a basin of blood. Hitler has come to her for consultation. Out of her trance appear first the visions of Frederick the Great and Napoleon, enacted by the maskers. Reminding the Leader of how they failed, these apparitions serve only to agitate him:

This is my Gethsemane night, Christ's agony in the garden:
*   only to great artists*
Come these dark hours.

At last appears the spirit of his friend Ernst Friedenau, a young German soldier of 1917. The seance takes a turn for the better. The British, it is predicted, will be "howked out" of Norway. Holland and Flanders will submit. France will fall within sixty days. But Friedenau gives one emphatic warning: "Strike not England too soon . . . Strike in September; or if later, better."

This is false advice. Why is it given?

> Because a prompt invasion would catch England in anguish and end the war this year; which is not intended. The war must grind on, and grind small. It must not end when France falls, nor when England is beaten. It must not end when the ends of the earth are drawn in. God is less humane than Hitler, and has larger views.

The tragedy must be played out, "down into dreary revolution and despair, exhaustion and shabby horrors and squalid slavery," down to the death of "the boys without blemish," down to the finish of Europe.

At the close of the masque the medium, struggling to regain consciousness, upsets the basin of blood at Hitler's feet. He cries out in horror, pays her "the usual small fee," and leaves the cabin.

> *Watch this man, half conscious of the future,*
> *Pass to his tragic destiny.*

Jeffers's work has always had the force and the torment of great art. This poem contains, in addition, virtues for which he had not consistently prepared us: beauty of form; imagination of a high order; a style economical, just, bone-clean. Of the quality of the writing I need say only that it is maintained not far below the level of this passage:

> *Listen: power is a great hollow spirit*
> *That needs a center.*
> *It chooses one man almost at random*
> *And clouds him and clots around him and it possesses him.*
> *Listen: the man does not have power,*
> *Power has the man.*

Yes, the masque is undoubtedly a success — I am even tempted to call it the greatest masque since *Comus* — but when Jeffers takes, as it were, the somnambulant Leader's arm and conducts him sympathetically from the scene, I cannot help experiencing a curious shiver of apprehension, not so much for what he has here done with Hitler as for what Hitler may do to him. What is the nature of the impulse that led Jeffers to treat Hitler as a tragic figure, instead of as the ubiquitous Beast of Berchtesgaden? Rationalizing, one may say that Hitler is to Jeffers what Lucifer was to Milton, and one would rest content with that analogy if only it were possible to regard politics as a fiction. To my mind, Hitler is Jeffers's hero not because Jeffers condones the fascist program but because Hitler is the instrument of that destruction of civilization, that obliteration of humankind, which Jeffers has long invoked as both necessary and good. Violence is all. It is the recurrent theme of the lyrics that close this book:

> *It is not bad. Let them play*
> *Let the guns bark and the bombing-plane*
> *Speak his prodigious blasphemies.*
> *It is not bad, it is high time,*
> *Stark violence is still the sire of all the world's values.*

Jeffers's myth of himself is that he stands beyond moral judgment, so far removed from the hot human struggle that he is like Fawn Ferguson bathing in the mountain stream and watching, without a tremor, as a cream-colored car far down the mountain crashes through the bridge-rails and goes pitching down the canyon. "There was nothing to do about it at this distance."

Jeffers stood "at this distance" when he wrote "The Bowl of Blood." His dilemma is that as he approaches the contemporary scene in other poems, written on a lower level of the imagination, his symbols of violence and his death-wish for our civilization assume inevitably a political coloring. The nature of that coloring may be deduced from his observations on our world at war.

Roosevelt and Hitler are one to him, "the two hands of the destroyer." Germany and England are one to him. What does it matter?

If England goes down and Germany up
The stronger dog will still be on top.
All in the turning of time.

"Beware of taking sides," he warns.

In order to elucidate Jeffers's world-views I have had to oversimplify his position. Actually, in this book he is not a consistent thinker: frequently he does not think at all; what I wish to stress is that in becoming a topical poet he has forfeited the detachment on which he prides himself. He *does* take sides, sometimes contradictory sides. England he praises — "bleeding, at bay, magnificent, at last a lion" — when he is not dispassionately watching her go under; Russia he sneers at; Finland he eulogizes — "the best nation in Europe." To "the dupes that talk democracy" he is unkind, for he is one who, like the old boar of the mountains, believes in tusks. He projects a vision of "armed, imperial America," powerful, guilty, doomed, and this albeit with qualms he celebrates in the manner of Henry Luce proclaiming the American Century. Doctor of doom, with the works of Spengler in his bag, he prescribes, for the mass he despises, mass-suicide.

Perhaps a certain confusion has developed in Jeffers's mind between the non-human and the in-human. His pursuit of the one endowed him with a ferocity and grandeur of spirit that made him a legend in his time, as if he summed up, in a gesture of unappeasable nihilism, man's distaste for his own corruptibility. Now that he returns to the historical scene, it must be as one of us in a world of moral obligations and human values. For him to abnegate these responsibilities would be to range himself on the side of the destroyers. It is a critical moment in his career.

H. D.'s War Trilogy

The publication of *The Flowering of the Rod* brings to a close H. D.'s war trilogy, which has received less attention than it merits. "War trilogy" (the publisher's phrase) requires some qualification. It is true that the poem, which will be considered here *in toto*, begins amid the ruins of London, in the flaming terror of the Blitz, but it is equally true that it ends in an ox-stall in Bethlehem. The war was the occasion, it is not the subject-matter of the poem. Neither is "trilogy" wholly satisfactory, since it implies more of temporal continuity and progressive narrative line than the three parts possess. The relation between the parts seems to me more that of a triptych than of a trilogy, each book being a compositional unit, though conceptually and emotionally enriched by association with its companion units; each composition, furthermore, embodying a dream or vision. This formal arrangement is particularly

Originally published in *Poetry*, April 1947, under the title "Tale of a Jar." H. D.'s *Trilogy* has recently been reissued in a single volume (New Directions, 1973).

suited to H. D., whose art has unmistakable affinities with the pictorial.

Pursuing the triptych analogy, we find the second book, *Tribute to the Angels* (1945), falling naturally into place as the central composition; in the background "a half-burnt-out apple-tree blossoming," in the foreground the luminous figure of the Lady, who carries, under her drift of veils, a book.

> *her book is our book; written*
> *or unwritten, its pages will reveal*
>
> *a tale of a Fisherman,*
> *a tale of a jar or jars.*

The left side-panel, titled *The Walls Do Not Fall* (1944), shows the ruins of bombed-out London. They have an Egyptian desolation, like the ruins of the Temple of Luxor. The ascendant Dream-figure is Amen, not as the local deity of Thebes, ram-headed god of life and reproduction, nor even in his greater manifestation as Amen-Ra, when he joined with the sun-god to become a supreme divinity incorporating the other gods into his members, but the Amen of Revelation (III.14) with the face and bearing of the Christos.

> *Ra, Osiris, Amen appeared*
> *in a spacious, bare meeting-house;*
>
> *he is the world-father,*
> *father of past aeons,*
>
> *present and future equally.*

The background figure recording the scene is Thoth (to the Greeks, Hermes Trismegistus), scribe of the gods, in whose ibis-head magic and art married and flourished.

The interior of an Arab merchant's booth is represented in the foreground of the right side-panel *The Flowering of the Rod*. Half-turned towards the door stands a woman, frail and slender, wearing no bracelet or other ornament, with her scarf slipping from her head, revealing the light on her hair. ("I am Mary of Magdala,/ I am Mary, a great tower;/ through my will and my power,/ Mary shall be myrrh.") The noble merchant with the alabaster jar is Kaspar, youngest and wisest of the Three Wise Men, transfixed in the moment of recognition, of prophetic vision, before he will present her with the jar containing "the myrrh or the spikenard, very costly." In the background he is seen again, making his earlier gift, also a jar, to the other Mary of the manger.

Much has been omitted in this simplified presentation, but enough has been given at least to suggest the materials of the poem and its psychological extensions out of the modern world into pre-history, religion, legend, and myth. "This search for historical parallels,/ research into psychic affinities,/ has been done to death before,/ will be done again," writes H. D. in a self-critical passage. No hint of staleness or weariness, however, blemishes the page. On the contrary, the poem radiates a kind of spiritual enthusiasm. (The composition-period for two of the books is given: a fortnight apiece.) What H. D. is seeking for, what she has obviously found, is a faith: faith that "there was One/ in the beginning, Creator,/ Fosterer, Begetter, the Same-forever/ in the papyrus-swamp,/ in the Judaean meadow"; faith that even to the bitter, flawed Mary is given the gift of grace, the Genius of the jar; faith in the survival of values, however the world shakes; faith in the blossoming, the resurrection, of the half-dead tree.

> *When in the company of the gods,*
> *I loved and was loved,*
>
> *never was my mind stirred*
> *to such rapture,*
>
> *my heart moved*
> *to such pleasure,*
>
> *as now, to discover*
> *over Love, a new Master:*

> *His the track in the sand*
> *from a plum-tree in flower . . .*
>
> *His, the Genius in the jar*
> *which the Fisherman finds,*
>
> *He is Mage,*
> *bringing myrrh.*

Each of the three parts comprises a sequence of forty-three poems, and all the hundred and twenty-nine poems, except for the very first, are written in (basically) unrhymed couplets. The modulations and variety of effects that H. D. achieves within this limited pattern are a tribute to her technical resourcefulness and to her almost infallible ear. Her primary reliance, orally, is on the breath-unit; aurally, on assonance, with an occasional admixture, as in the following passage, of slant or imperfect rhyme:

> *I escaped, I explored*
> *rose-thorn forest,*
>
> *was rain-swept*
> *down the valley of a leaf;*
>
> *was deposited on grass,*
> *where mast by jewelled mast*
>
> *bore separate ravellings*
> *of encrusted gem-stuff*
>
> *of the mist*
> *from each banner-staff.*

Like Yeats, though with a different set of disciplines, founded on her Imagist beginnings, H. D. has learned how to contain the short line, to keep it from spilling over into the margins. For straight narrative or exposition she usually employs a longer, more casual line that approaches prose without becoming, in context, fuzzy or spineless:

It was easy to see that he was not an ordinary merchant;
she saw that certainly — he was an ambassador;

there was hardly anyone you could trust
with this precious merchandise.

The lyric passages have, at once, purity and tension, delicacy and strength, seeming to rejoice in the uncorrupted innocence of the worshiping eye:

> *And the snow fell on Hermon,*
> *the place of the Transfiguration,*
>
> *and the snow fell on Hebron*
> *where, last spring, the anemones grew,*
>
> *whose scarlet and rose and red and blue,*
> *He compared to a King's robes,*
>
> *but* even Solomon, *he said,*
> was not arrayed like one of these;
>
> *and the snow fell on the almond-trees*
> *and the mulberries were domed over*
>
> *like a forester's hut or a shepherd's hut*
> *on the slopes of Lebanon,*
>
> *and the snow fell*
> *silently . . . silently . . .*

One of H. D.'s innovations is a form of word-play that might be called associational semantics. "I know, I feel," she writes, "the meanings that words hide." She sees them as "anagrams, cryptograms,/ little boxes, conditioned/ to hatch butterflies." To a large extent her poem develops spontaneously out of her quest for the ultimate distillations of meaning sealed in the jars of language. ("Though the jars were sealed,/ the fragrance got out somehow.") She takes, for example, the

Hebrew word "marah," meaning "bitter," fuses it with "a word bitterer still, *mar*," and emerges triumphantly with "mer, mere, mère, mater, Maia, Mary,/ Star of the Sea, Mother." Mary of Magdala, bitter Mary, becomes Mary-myrrh, akin "to the Mother of Mutilations,/ to Attis-Adonis-Tammuz and his mother who was myrrh." Osiris is equated with the star Sirius and, on a punning level, with "O-sir-is or O-sire-is." Devil is written "dev-ill" in order to wrench a meaning out of the second syllable. The poet even complains that the name of Venus has been desecrated by the word "venery" . . . "Venus whose name is kin/ to venerate,/ venerator." Most of these passages impress me as being too self-conscious, too "literary," in the bad sense, though I recognize their catalytic function.

Although the significant fusion, the mutation into a new kind of experience, a new large meaning, does not take place in the body of the poem, it would be wrong to say that this ingenious, admirably sustained, and moving work fails because it does not achieve monumentality. H. D.'s is not a monumental art. Her poem remains as precise as it is ambitious. It is like the vision seen by the Mage on the occasion of his meeting with Mary of Magdala:

> *and though it was all on a very grand scale*
> *yet it was small and intimate.*

or like Mary herself, of whom it is written:

> *she was impersonal, not a servant*

> *sent on an errand, but, as it were,*
> *a confidential friend, sent by some great lady.*

Private Eye

The voice of Kenneth Fearing is an unmistakable one. No contemporary poet has more effectively dedicated his career to the representation of what T. S. Eliot, in his essay on Baudelaire, described as "the sordid life of a great metropolis." It cannot be said flatly that Fearing either loves or hates New York, but he is not seduced by it, he does not habitually celebrate it, and he never forgets, in the role of the quizzical pedestrian, those bleak images of the city's meanness and indifference and violence that crowded his eyes in the Depression years when his art matured.

In *New and Selected Poems*, his seventh book of verse, which affords a welcome opportunity to review the work of some thirty years, we cannot fail to note the constancy of his vision. The same cards, however reshuffled, keep turning up;

Originally published in the *Saturday Review*, June 29, 1957. *New and Selected Poems* was Kenneth Fearing's last collection — he died in 1961. For another examination of the role of the poet as detective, see my comments on Hugh Seidman's *Collecting Evidence*, p. 265.

we are in a world threatened by newspaper headlines and sudden death; a world of cops and gangsters, the hunters and the hunted; of stuffed shirts and frightened little men; of cigar stores and drugstores and seedy barrooms and pinball arcades; of doubts and guilts and inquisitions. Such material would seem to posit a poet of rage and revolution, but Fearing does not characteristically climb to that level of intensity. His tone, for the most part, remains ironic. If he is a revolutionary poet, out of the proletarian tradition of the thirties, and the best survivor of that tradition, he is one without a revolution to propose. One of his favorite disguises is that of the investigator, the private eye, whose professional pride constrains him, almost against his will, to crack the case.

Fearing's poems are always asking questions: "What will you do when the phone rings and they say to you: What will you do?" . . . "But what if the police find out? What if the wires are down? What if credit is refused? What if the banks fail?" . . . "What is one more night in a lifetime of nights?" The structures are incremental, largely based on repetitions, with little impulse towards the grandeur of resolution.

Question mark, question mark, question mark, question mark,
And you, fantasy Frank, and dreamworld Dora and hallucination Harold, and delusion Dick, and nightmare Ned,
What is it, how do you say it, what does it mean, what's the word. . . .

Though a handful of Fearing's poems evince a degree of optimism about man's destiny, he is usually too aware of the malady of our time to deceive himself with easy formulas for salvation. At times indeed he seems to settle a bit too comfortably, with a shrug of his shoulders, into the resignation of spiritual fatigue. "I am tired of following invisible lives down intangible avenues to fathomless ends."

Somewhat paradoxically, this realist speaks to us of the unreality of modern existence. His poems are populated by cliff-dwellers who own neither gods nor heroes, and who have lost finally their faith in themselves. It is by no means an accident that Fearing so frequently introduces sorcerers, wizards, astrologers, and other apostles of the degraded miracle into the world of his invention.

Fearing's ear for speech rhythms is remarkably keen, and he handles the vernacular without any trace of self-consciousness. His long cadenced line derives from Whitman, but he has made it very much his own, tinctured with an acidulous wit and sensitive to varying pressures. He aims at a poetry that is at once exciting and understandable: "Everything in this volume has been written with the intention that its meaning should disclose itself at ordinary reading tempo." I am not inclined to quarrel with the virtues of excitement and readability, but I wonder, as I look back at Fearing's career, with a good deal of admiration for his gifts and accomplishment, whether his development has not been restricted by the stubborn limitations of his esthetics. His art of brilliant surfaces and quick contemporaneity seemed more daring once, as a poetic configuration, than it does today, though the best poems keep their early lustre.

No Middle Flight

Hover, utter, still
A sourcing   whom my lost candle like the firefly loves.

The ambitiousness of John Berryman's poem resides not so much in its length — it runs to only 458 lines — as in its material and style. This is no middle flight. Despite the discrepancy in scale, the manifest intention of the poet inevitably recalls that of Hart Crane in *The Bridge:* to relate himself to the American past through the discovery of a viable myth, and to create for his vehicle a grand and exalted language, a language of transfiguration. If Berryman has been less fortunate than his predecessor in his search for a theme and a language, his failure nevertheless, like Crane's, is worth more than most successes.

The historical justification for Berryman's return to Anne

A review of *Homage to Mistress Bradstreet*, by John Berryman, originally published in *Poetry,* July 1957.

Bradstreet as "a sourcing" seems clear enough. As the first woman to write verse in English in America — *The Tenth Muse, Lately Sprung up in America* appeared originally in England in 1650 — she survives in the annals of our literature, companioned always by her florid title. To imagine her as the symbolic mother-muse of American poetry is, however, to stretch the point, as Berryman himself is well aware, for the mediocrity of her performance is too blatant.

> *. . . all this bald*
> *abstract didactic rime I read appalled*
> *harassed for your fame*
> *mistress neither of fiery nor velvet verse. . . .*

It is the life, the spirit, rather than the work, to which Berryman pays his homage. In a sense Anne Bradstreet prefigures "the alienated poet" with whose image we are all too familiar in our own time. The rugged environment of Massachusetts Bay, first glimpsed at eighteen, was scarcely of the kind to appeal to this fastidious, well-bred young English lady, despite her devotion to her so-much-older husband Simon, eventually governor of the colony, to whom she bore in due course eight children. "Pioneering is not feeling well." Modeling her style on DuBartas and Quarles, she sought refuge in her versifying (some 7,000 lines in all) and meanwhile labored to recreate in her immediate circle some of the lost amenities of the polite tradition. Her many descendants include Oliver Wendell Holmes, Richard Henry Dana, and Wendell Phillips. Obviously, in a consideration of the American heritage, Anne Bradstreet is not to be dismissed lightly; but just as obviously she cannot easily be cast in an heroic mold. Part of the imaginative sweat of Berryman's poem is produced by his wrestle with his subject.

Berryman opens with an invocation to Anne Bradstreet which gradually flows into her own speech: her crossing on the *Arbella*, nostalgia for England, remorse that at fourteen she found her heart "carnal and sitting loose from God," her punishment by the pox, Simon's reciprocated love for her despite her "sorry face," and now belatedly the bearing of her first child. In the mid-section the contemporary poet, or his creative spirit, engages in what can only be called a love-dialogue, a passionate confessional on both sides, with the ghost of Anne. In the third part, devoted largely to a recital of domestic woes, steeped in the odor of the body's decay, Anne resumes her narrative. While the children grow, "the proportioned, spiritless poems accumulate"; father throws "a saffron scum"; "baby John breaks out"; illness and death are ubiquitous attendants ("this our land has ghosted with our dead"); her married daughter Dorothy, mother of nine, declines and is "inearthed"; Anne herself is beset by rheumatic fever and dropsy; in her mortal delirium she leaps to God. The poem closes with a three-stanza coda in which the poet bids farewell to Anne. "I must pretend to leave you. Only you draw off/ a benevolent phantom."

Berryman's poem seethes with an almost terrifying activity, as must be evident even in the fragmentary phrases I have already quoted, where the peculiar energy of the language compels attention. Time and time again the medium comes powerfully alive, packed with original metaphor and galvanic with nouns and verbs that seem interchangeably charged with inventive excitement. At his best, in his moments of superlative force and concentration, Berryman writes with dramatic brilliance: "I am a closet of secrets dying," or again, ". . . they starch their minds./ Folkmoots, & blether, blether. John Cotton rakes/ to the synod of Cambridge." *Homage to Mistress Bradstreet*, I began by saying, is a failure, for reasons I must proceed to demonstrate, but it succeeds in convincing me that Berryman is now entitled to rank among our most gifted poets.

After at least half-a-dozen readings, in which many of the difficulties of the text and the form have been resolved, I still retain my first impression that the scaffolding of the poem is too frail to bear the weight imposed upon it. To put it in other terms, the substance of the poem as a whole lacks inherent imaginative grandeur: whatever effect of magnitude it achieves has been beaten into it. The display of so much exacerbated sensibility, psychic torment, religious ecstasy seems to be intermittently in excess of what the secular occasion requires; the feelings persist in belonging to the poet instead of becoming the property of the poem.

> *I am a man of griefs & fits*
> *trying to be my friend. And the brown smock splits,*
> *down the pale flesh a gash*
> *broadens and Time holds up your heart against my eyes.*

In particular, the love-duet in the central section tends to collapse into a bathos somewhat reminiscent of Crashaw's extravagant compounding of religion and sex. Anne speaks:

> *—Hard and divided heaven! creases me. Shame*
> *is failing. My breath is scented, and I throw*
> *hostile glances towards God.*
> *Crumpling plunge of a pestle, bray:*
> *sin cross & opposite, wherein I survive*
> *nightmares of Eden. Reaches foul & live*
> *he for me, this soul*
> *to crunch, a minute tangle of eternal flame. . . .*

> *a male great pestle smashes*
> *small women swarming towards the mortar's rim in vain.*

Intent on "leaguering her image," the poet interrupts Mistress Bradstreet's flights with protestations of devotion that strike me as being curiously incongruous: "I miss you, Anne." . . . "I have earned the right to be alone with you," etc., to which she at length replies, "I know./ I want to take you for my lover." It is presumptuous to be arbitrary about matters of taste and tone, but I cannot gainsay that I find such lapses damaging. The explanation for them is not that the poet suffers from emotional compulsions — these are the very fountainhead of art — but that he has been unable to canalize them totally into the creative process, with the result that they appear as extraneous to his fiction instead of subsuming it.

From the beginning of his career Berryman has been concerned with the problems of his craft. In the prefatory note to twenty of his poems first collected in *Five Young American Poets* (1940) he wrote: "One of the reasons for writing verse is a delight in craftsmanship — rarely for its own sake, mainly as it seizes and makes visible its subject. Versification, rime, stanzaform, trope are the tools. They provide the means by which the writer can shape from an experience in itself usually vague, a mere feeling or phrase, something that is coherent, directed, intelligible." In his new work, as I have already indicated, Berryman has evolved, for his language of rapture and of the "delirium of the grand depths," a dense and involuted style which in its very compression and distortion is best adapted for the production of extraordinary, not ordinary, effects. There is much that is extraordinary in his poem, often as a consequence of the magnificent conversion of the ordinary, but it is in the nature of the long poem that it must sweep into its embrace certain phenomena whose virtue is to be what they are, to resist transubstantiation — and here Berryman is tempted to inflate what he cannot subjugate. "Without the commonplace," remarked Hölderlin, "nobility cannot be represented, and so I shall always say to myself, when I come up against something common in the world: You need this as urgently as a potter needs clay, and for that reason always take it in, and do not reject it, and do not take fright at it."

A portion of Berryman's vocabulary and most of the idiosyncrasies of his technique can be traced back to Hopkins, witness such lines as these, spoken by Anne in the crisis of childbirth:

Monster you are killing me Be sure
I'll have you later Women do endure
I can can no longer
and it passes the wretched trap whelming and I am me

drencht & powerful, I did it with my body!

But Hopkins, to be sure, would have known better than to let the last phrase get by. (Hysteria is not an intensity of tone, but a laxness, a giving in. By the time Anne has pressed out her child — we are spared few of the physiological details — we must be prepared to accede to the premise that never has there been such an excruciating, such a miraculous birth, and we boggle at the superfluity of the assault on our disbelief.)

In his uncompromising election of a language of artifice

Berryman, like Hopkins, does not hesitate, for the sake of the emphasis and tension he aims at, to wrench his syntax, invert his word-order. The rewards of his daring are not to be minimized. The opening stanza, for example, seems to me to move with beautiful ease and dignity; the tone, the pressures, delicately controlled; the details small and particular, but the air charged with momentousness:

> *The Governor your husband lived so long*
> *moved you not, restless, waiting for him? Still,*
> *you were a patient woman. —*
> *I seem to see you pause here still:*
> *Sylvester, Quarles, in moments odd you pored*
> *before a fire at, bright eyes on the Lord,*
> *all the children still.*
> *'Simon . . .' Simon will listen while you read a Song.*

But when the dislocations have nothing to recommend them beyond their mechanical violence, the ear recoils:

> *Out of maize & air*
> *your body's made, and moves. I summon, see*
> *from the centuries it.*

> *They say thro' the fading winter Dorothy fails,*
> *my second, who than I bore one more, nine.*

.xamine a pair of lines from Hopkins,

> *When will you ever, Peace, wild wooddove, shy wings shut,*
> *Your round me roaming end, and under be my boughs?*

we can see that the older poet, however radical his deflections from the linguistic norm, keeps mindful of the natural flow and rhythms of speech, which serves him as his contrapuntal ground.

Throughout his poem Berryman handles his varied eight-line stanza, derived perhaps from *The Wreck of the Deutschland* and composed in a system of functional stressing adapted from Hopkins's sprung rhythm, with admirable assurance. Few modern poets, I think, can even approximate his command of the stanzaic structure. The alterations of pace through his juxtaposition of short and long lines are beautifully controlled; and the narrative-lyrical functions are kept in fluid relation, with the action riding through the stanza, which nevertheless preserves intact the music suspended within it.

Homage to Mistress Bradstreet can bear the kind of scrutiny that an important poem exacts. The flaws are real for me, but the work remains impressive in its ambition and virtuosity. Other poets and critics, it should be noted, have been far less qualified in their praise than I. Both Conrad Aiken and Robert Fitzgerald have not hesitated to apply the epithet "classic" to it. Robert Lowell has called it "a very big achievement." And Edmund Wilson has acclaimed it as "the most distinguished long poem by an American since *The Waste Land*."

The book is handsomely designed and printed, with drawings by Ben Shahn.

Pangolin of Poets

Miss Moore is unique, and she never argues. Like peace she is indivisible, and of her verse it can be said that nothing resembles it so much as her prose. Not the least of her accomplishments is that her readers, unprovoked to question her definition of poetry, accept its premises implicitly, without supererogatory judgment or comparisons, because it is their pleasure to do so. These fifteen poems, of which five were published in London in 1936 as *The Pangolin and Other Poems*, will add to that pleasure.

One would like to be able, if only as a reciprocal gesture, to describe Miss Moore's peculiar faculties with the same exactness of detail, founded on the microscopic patience of the eye, with which she delineates the antic physiology of a reindeer, an ostrich, a butterfly, a paper nautilus, or the elaborate pangolin, of which she is constrained to remark, "To explain grace requires a curious hand."

A review of *What Are Years*, by Marianne Moore, originally published in *Poetry*, November 1941.

The dictionary informs us that the pangolin is "a manoid edentate mammal of Asia and Africa, having large horny imbricated scales covering most of the body except the under surface and the inside of the limbs." That is good, but Miss Moore, in a poem that is a triumphant demonstration of her style, is infinitely better. We see "scale lapping scale with spruce-cone regularity" . . . "the flattened sword-edged leafpoints on the tail and artichoke-set leg and body plates" . . . "the giant-pangolin-tail, graceful tool, as prop or hand or broom or axe, tipped like the elephant's trunk with special skin"; we confront, clear-eyed, one of the monsters of creation, "strongly intailed, neat head for core, on neck not breaking off, with curled-in feet," and because we are given understanding, because it is our prerogative both to wonder and to smile, the idea of the pangolin loses its formidable eccentricity: we take him in, we domesticate him, we make him a usable concept.

> *. . . Among animals, one has a*
> *sense of humor. Humor saves a*
> *few steps, it saves years. Unig-*
> *norant, modest and*
> *unemotional, and all emo-*
> *tion, he has everlasting vig-*
> *or, power to grow*
> *though there are*
> *few creatures who can make one*
> *breathe faster, and make one erecter.*

Miss Moore's metrics must be classified *sui generis*. Few of her poems — the stately title-piece of the present volume is an exception — move on the flood of an internal rhythm. Since her rhythms, by design, are generally extensions of prose rhythms, with frequent word-breaks as run-overs to contradict the line-divisions, Miss Moore's intricate rhyme-schemes and stanzaic structures are actually extra-prosodic and contribute little or nothing to the ear. (The eye, of course, is thankful for white spaces.) Miss Moore even goes to the painful extreme of syllable-counting. But if these are devices to tempt and test her creative spirit, it would be ungrateful for us to cavil. "In writing," she has said, "it is my one principle that nothing is too much trouble." And elsewhere, in one of those quotations that stud the "hybrid composition" of her poems: "Difficulty is ordained to check poltroons."

For obvious reasons, modern poetry is largely a cry of confusion and anguish. The face of Miss Moore's poetry is serene. Shall we look into her mind for signs of travail? The mind of Miss Moore is astonishingly clean. Cluttered, to be sure, like your grandmother's attic; but with everything dusted and in place, labeled, catalogued, usable. The tensions are in the things themselves. The poetry is not in the self-pity:

> . . . *He*
> *"gives his opinion and then rests on it";*
> *he renders service when there is*
> *no reward, and is too reclusive for*
> *   some things to seem to touch*
> *him, not because he*
> *   has no feeling but because he has so much.*

Responses, Glosses,
Refractions

I.

It could not be dangerous to be living
*   in a town like this, of simple people,*
who have a steeple-jack placing danger-signs by the church
while he is gilding the solid-
*   pointed star, which on a steeple*
stands for hope.

*   —From "The Steeple-Jack"*

Poets in our time are supposed, for good reason, to be "alienated," and nearly all of them are. Our only domesticated poet,
at least the only one whom we can take seriously, is Marianne
Moore. Her vital optimism and good will have a Christian
source and an American flavor. She is at home in the community of her imagination, just as "the hero, the student, the
steeple-jack, each in his way, is at home." However much we

Originally published in *Festschrift for Marianne Moore's Seventy-Seventh
Birthday*, edited by Tambimuttu; Tambimuttu & Mass, New York, 1964.

may be tempted to impute an ironic meaning — conditioned as we are by modern verse — to the job of the steeple-jack and to his danger-sign, we must not suppose that Miss Moore is, even obliquely, mocking the "simple people" of this town or being acerbic about their faith. It is prudent and right for a man to protect his neighbors against injury. And the church, though it appeals to the townsfolk as a provident and practical institution, is also the house of mystery and transcendence — hence fittingly labeled "dangerous." This fishing town, with its stranded whales and proliferating seaside vegetation, has its elements of fantasy, but we realize in the clear light that, after all, "the climate is not right for the banyan, frangipani, or jack-fruit trees; or an exotic serpent life . . . They've cats, not cobras, to keep down the rats." Neither is it a town meant for an exotic spirituality, a fanatic religious life. Maybe hope is as much transcendence as it can bear. The last lines of the poem, with their forthright explication of the symbolism of "the solid-pointed star," are appropriately matter-of-fact. Miss Moore, indeed, almost never seeks the smash ending. Her poems are not orchestrated for brasses and kettledrums. Suspended at the close, by-passing the full stop, they seem to drift back into life.

II.
Silence

My father used to say,
"Superior people never make long visits,"
have to be shown Longfellow's grave
or the glass flowers at Harvard.
Self-reliant like the cat —
that takes its prey to privacy,
the mouse's limp tail hanging like a shoelace from its mouth —
they sometimes enjoy solitude,
and can be robbed of speech
by speech which has delighted them.
The deepest feeling always shows itself in silence;
not in silence, but restraint.
Nor was he insincere in saying, "Make my house your inn,"
Inns are not residences.

Miss Moore's inductive method of composition is not conducive to economy. Generally she needs to accumulate a palpable mass of data before she is willing to let go of her poem. If she seems to be in no hurry to reach her destination, it may be that she has no destination in view. Her mind is like Stendhal's mirror dawdling along a road, enchanted by the succession of unpredictable reflections, which we in turn are permitted to enjoy. She will know, when she gets there, where to stop. If she did not have a conviction about the unity of experience, she would get nowhere.

"Silence" is among the very best of her short poems: every word of it is fine. The moment of intense particularity in the image of "the mouse's limp tail" is the point of perception on which the whole poem is deftly balanced by a sure hand. Remove that image and the entire structure collapses into a heap of more or less interesting observations.

With its air of artless intimacy, the poem reads like a family anecdote. It is something of a shock to discover, from Miss Moore's appended notes, that the opening quotation derives from a Miss A. M. Homans, who wrote (or said): "My father used to say, 'Superior people never make long visits. When I am visiting, I like to go about by myself. I never had to be shown Longfellow's grave or the glass flowers at Harvard.'" The other remark attributed, in the poem, to Miss Moore's father is equally foreign in its source, going back to Prior's *Life* of Edmund Burke: " 'Throw yourself into a coach,' said he [Burke]. 'Come down and make my house your inn.' "

We need constantly to remind ourselves that Miss Moore's poems are works of the imagination, despite their lack of afflatus. Their quality depends on her gift for picking and choosing. Miss Moore, who does not pretend to be a bard, has a scrupulous sense of limits. On this rock she has built her house. The workmanship is more than honest: it is passionately fastidious. I suspect it will stand.

III.

*There is a great amount of poetry in unconscious
    fastidiousness. Certain Ming
        products, imperial floor-coverings of coach-*

*wheel yellow, are well enough in their way but I have seen
      something*
  that I like better — a
    *mere childish attempt to make an imperfectly ballasted
        animal stand up,*
    similar determination to make a pup
      eat his meat from the plate.
                          —from "Critics and Connoisseurs"

Literature is a phase of life. If
  one is afraid of it, the situation is irremediable; if
one approaches it familiarly
  what one says of it is worthless. Words are constructive
when they are true; the opaque allusion — the simulated flight

upward — accomplishes nothing. Why cloud the fact
  *that Shaw is self-conscious in the field of sentiment but is
      otherwise re-*
warding; that James is all that has been
  said of him if feeling is profound? It is not Hardy
the distinguished novelist and Hardy the poet, but one man

'interpreting life through the medium of the
  emotions.' . . .
                          —from "Picking and Choosing"

The enemy of the poem is poetry. A precious art, rooted in a convention of formal perfection, can be exquisite, but it would be better if it were true, which means true to life, touched with the human, founded in the reality of the encounter between self and others, between self and universe. The world of intellect is not to be separated from the world of feeling.

Miss Moore has a strange affinity for the writers she mentions. The authors she reads consolidate into a single presiding spirit. Like GBS she is "self-conscious in the field of sentiment but is otherwise rewarding"; T. S. Eliot could have applied to her what he said of James . . . "he had a mind so fine that no idea could violate it"; like Hardy she is two writers in one, in her case poet and critic. In a later stanza of "Picking and Choosing" she writes of "Burke" (whom I take to be Kenneth, not Edmund) that he "is a psychologist — of acute, raccoon-like curiosity" — and what might be said of her that would be more apt?

Fastidiousness is the other face of truth. The poet does not abdicate human responsibility when he turns to language. On the contrary, every time he decides between a right and a wrong word he is compelled to make a moral choice. Language stands in the service of honor: words are deeds. In effect, the probity of a man of understanding is tested by the precision of his speech: "Inns are not residences."

Miss Moore has made a great triumph by building an art out of a lifetime of trust in small, real virtues. She is our Moral Eye, saved from platitude by accuracy, by honesty, by coolness, and by joy. One of her convictions is that "poetry watches life with affection." She is fond of quoting from Confucius, who taught her, "If there be a knife of resentment in the heart, the mind will not attain precision."

Sea Son of the Wave

When Dylan Thomas was not yet nineteen, he wrote a series of articles on the poets of his birthplace, Swansea, for the *South Wales Daily Post*. His essay on Llewellyn Prichard, an all-but-forgotten writer of the early nineteenth century, begins: "No one can deny that the most attractive figures in literature are always those around whom a world of lies and legend has been woven, those half mythical artists whose real characters become cloaked forever under a veil of the bizarre."

The essay continues with a garishly lighted résumé of Prichard's "strange and disordered" life "as poet, artist and strolling player, trembling on the verge of disease, one foot in the grave and the other in the workhouse." And it ends: "Prichard, coming home late one night to the cottage in Thomas Street, attempted to write in his room. But he soon fell asleep. The candle fell onto the papers surrounding him. He was too drunk to know what to do, and died as strangely and tragically

A review of *The Life of Dylan Thomas*, by Constantine FitzGibbon, originally published in the *New York Times*, October 31, 1965.

SEA SON OF THE WAVE 229

as he had lived, 'caught in a chaos of unrestrained words and passions, caught by the fire and the flames.' . . . He failed to be great, but he failed with genius."

The article is headed, "A Figure Lost in Lies and Legends," and though its author had not yet published a serious poem, it indicates that he was neither unprepared nor reluctant to lose himself in a role to which nature and circumstances and his own sense of romantic destiny assigned him. Though he is no longer the fashionable bard of the moment and though his influence on young writers has steadily declined since his death in 1953, Dylan Thomas remains one of the famous poets of the century, perhaps the best-loved since Rupert Brooke (whom he admired as a schoolboy). The proliferation of words in print about him suggests that his life, like that of Keats, belongs as much to legend as to literary history.

Not that he was unaware of the parallel. At sixteen, when he terminated his formal education on leaving Swansea Grammar School — the record shows him at the bottom of the class in every subject except English, where he was at the top — he confided to his mother that all he wanted to be was a poet, "as good as Keats, if not better." At the close of his life he told a friend, "I can't go on. I've already had twice as much of it as Keats had."

Like Keats, too, he had a lovely gift for friendship, though it was a gift he abused, along with all his others. One of his many friends in wartime London was Constantine FitzGibbon, then an intelligence officer, at whose wedding Dylan served as best man and in whose guest room Dylan practiced his sullen craft. Despite these bonds, FitzGibbon disclaims any degree of intimacy with the chameleon poet: "I realize now that my knowledge of him was as superficial as was most other people's."

Unlike previous memorialists of Thomas who had egos and consciences to appease, FitzGibbon deliberately effaces himself from the *Life*, which is easily the best all-around biographical study of its subject to date. The story is told with the unobtrusive skill that we might expect from the novelist who wrote *When the Kissing Had to Stop* and the essayist responsible for *Random Thoughts of a Fascist Hyena*. In a rare excursion into personal anecdote, he recalls with equanimity that his guest once tried to walk off with an electric sewing machine, and again with a small rug tucked under his arm. "Dylan," he comments, "quite simply did not believe in property, just as some men do not believe in God."

Even when one detects the cutting edge in a remark, one is disinclined to attribute it to malice or self-interest, for the work, wherever it can be tested, proves diligently just. The style reflects the mind of the writer in its coolness and efficiency; and the tone of professional authority, as befits a proper biography, is set in the very first paragraph:

"Dylan Marlais Thomas was born on the 27th of October, 1914, in his parents' house, No. 5 Cwmdonkin Drive, which lies in that part of Swansea called the Uplands. He was the only son and younger child of D. J. Thomas and of his wife Florence Hannah, née Williams; their daughter Nancy being some eight and a half years older than the new baby."

FitzGibbon is particularly thorough in his treatment of Thomas's family background and early years, and most enlightening in his portrait of the father, an awesome, embittered provincial schoolmaster, "the human beer-barrel," the failed poet, who called his son Dylan — Sea Son of the Wave — after the golden-haired boy in the "Mabinogion"; and who then added, for good measure, the bardic name of the most renowned of the Thomases, the infant's preacher-poet great-uncle, known as Gwylym Marles or Marlais. Dylan was marked for poetry from the start. D. J., who applied the brand, predicted that his son would die young.

Dylan enjoyed an early flourishing. By the time of his first visit to London in 1934, at the age of 20, he had already experienced the three most important years of his creative life: "three-quarters of his work as a poet date in style, in concept and often in composition from this Swansea period." Already the pattern was set: he was a heavy smoker and drinker; his health was bad, but not so bad as he made it out to be; he was preoccupied with death; he was half in love with a young London writer, Pamela Hansford Johnson, whom he had never met, but with whom he conducted an ardent correspondence; and he was head-over-heels in love with words, with "the color of saying."

He became famous in 1936, with the publication of his second collection, "Twenty-five Poems." The following year he married a madcap Irish girl, Caitlin MacNamara, whose flaming temper and fierce devotion were to become part of his legend. FitzGibbon writes with tact and understanding of their stormy relationship, but he makes clear that "the alcoholic cherub" from Swansea was ill-suited to the financial and moral responsibility of marriage, let alone parenthood. Undoubtedly the squalor, disorder and hysteria of a feckless household contributed to Dylan's rapid disintegration.

To put it bluntly, Dylan lacked the strength of character to support his genius. Having lost his Eden and his innocence, he learned all too quickly, in Traherne's immortal phrase, "the dirty devices of this world." If we accept the record at face-value, he was a sponger, a liar, a thief, a drunkard and an adulterer. But his outrageous behavior was not mean or perverse: it was simply infantile. He could be generous to excess — with his praise, his affection, his charm, his company, and even his money when he had a windfall to squander. As his friend Richard Hughes commented: "He may have sponged on us economically but spiritually it was more the other way about."

He was badly educated and intellectually lazy, but he cared passionately about poems and tried to make his own come right and true.

The man whom Caitlin learned to despise was the sot and entertainer, basking in the flattery of his toadies . . . "instant Dylan," the life-and-soul of whose desperation stemmed from the fear that he had exhausted, if not betrayed, his lyric gift; who had the honesty to rate himself "top of the second eleven"; who put so much faith in the Word that he would write and rewrite a line fifty or a hundred times; who took so much pride in his craft that he could affirm in reply to a student's naïve questionnaire: "Yes. I am a painstaking, conscientious, involved and devious craftsman in words. . . . I use everything and anything to make my poems work and move in the directions I want them to: old tricks, new tricks, puns, portmanteau-words, paradox, allusion, paronomasia, paragram, catachresis, slang, assonantal rhymes, vowel rhymes, sprung rhythm."

Despite the many lies that Dylan Thomas spoke and lived, he remained in possession of a great truth that John Donne's *Devotions* first announced to him: the fact of our human "earthness," that man is "earth of the earth, his body earth, his hair a wild shrub growing out of the land." The best words that he wrote had their roots in what he described as "my small, bonebound island."

FitzGibbon's account of Thomas's adventures in America, 1950 to 1953, his four triumphant and disastrous journeys in quest of American dollars and of "naked women in wet mackintoshes," is a rather flat and truncated version of John Malcolm Brinnin's more vivid memoir. In the proportions of the narrative it gives the effect of an epilogue. Thomas was already celebrated, corrupted, and sick; he was more than ripe for the *coup de grâce*.

On October 24 and 25, 1953, though he was near collapse, he managed, with the aid of an injection of ACTH (a cortisone-type drug), to participate in the memorable performances of "Under Milk Wood" at The Poetry Center–Y.M.H.A. in New York. On November 5, after more alcohol, more ACTH (with which alcohol is contra-indicated), and an injection of morphine to relieve delirium tremens, he was taken to St. Vincent's Hospital in a coma, from which he never recovered. Negligence and confusion attended him to the last. When Caitlin, who had been hastily summoned from England, arrived, she asked, "Is the bloody man dead yet?" She was too bitter to mourn for "instant Dylan"; but the death of the poet shattered her.

According to the autopsy, the cause of Dylan Thomas's death on November 9 was: "Insult to the brain." The phrase appears to have no meaning in medicine, but it bears a load of tragic irony.

The Vice-President of Insurance

Wallace Stevens was so fine and rare a poet, such a dazzling virtuoso on the keyboard of language, that he became one with his instrument: the man disappeared. Or so it seemed in his lifetime. He did not move in literary circles or condescend, with two or three exceptions at the last, to read his poems in public. To be sure, we knew, or thought we knew, a few hard facts about him: birthday 1879, Pennsylvania Dutch background, Harvard education, Hartford insurance connection. But these scarcely defined a character, and when he died in 1955, having just rounded off his 75 years with the publication of his *Collected Poems*, the event seemed neither final nor shattering: he had simply eluded us once more. Stevens was not a magisterial force like Eliot and Pound, who put western civilization under their jurisdiction, or an American culture hero like Frost and Williams. He was a voice, different from

A review of *The Letters of Wallace Stevens*, edited by Holly Stevens, originally published in *The New Republic*, November 12, 1966.

others, that "sang beyond the genius of the sea." The disembodied voice was what we heard.

Holly Stevens must have been aware of the risk she took in letting us see her father plain. Inevitably the man, as he appears in his voluminous correspondence, is more flawed than his art; but this is only to confirm Yeats's warning that "the intellect of man is forced to choose perfection of the life or of the work." Only an artist could have sustained, over a span of sixty years, so much epistolary verve, even when he was dictating as he usually did, to a stenographer. Out of almost thirty-three hundred letters that were available for inclusion, Miss Stevens has made a bountiful selection, excising the dead-wood at her discretion. Her biographical interpolations and occasional notes are models of editorial taste and intelligence.

Even as a high school boy in Reading, Stevens was mad about language. On a visit to his grandmother, in his sixteenth summer, he wrote home euphorically, anticipating the sweep and crackle of his mature style:

> The piping of flamboyant flutes, the wriggling of shrieking fifes with rasping dagger-voices, the sighing of bass-viols, drums that beat and rattle, the crescendo of cracked trombones — harmonized, that is Innes band. Red geraniums, sweet-lyssoms, low, heavy quince trees, the mayor's lamps, Garrett playing on the organ, water-lilies and poultry — that is Ivyland. A shade tree, meagre grass, a peaky, waxen house, a zither, several books of poetry, a pleasant room — mine — that is our house.

I cannot help wondering whether his schoolteacher mother smiled at the affectation of his signing-off: "Forever with supernal affection, thy rose-lipped arch-angelic jeune Wallace Stevens."

After closing out the century at Harvard, where he made the grade as president of the *Advocate* and of the Signet Club, Stevens hopefully moved to New York to try his wings as a writer. He was a generation too early to become a citizen of Bohemia. From the dispirited records of this period, I surmise that the years of struggle to earn a living and to find his place in the sun hardened his temper and put a permanent stamp on his character. He failed as a reporter on the *Tribune,* took up the study of law, and failed again as a practicing attorney. The occasional verse that he produced fell unpromisingly flat. "Living a strange, insane kind of life," he noted in his Journal in 1904. "Working savagely; but have been so desperately poor at times as not to be able to buy sufficient food — and sometimes not any." Apparently he was too proud to ask for help from his father, a successful lawyer and businessman, who had four other children to think about and who was the sort of man, in any case, to keep a close watch on his accounts — a trait that his son inherited. In 1908 he began his lifetime association, in a legal capacity, with the insurance business; in 1909 he married; in 1915, in reply to Harriet Monroe, who was planning to publish his phenomenal "Sunday Morning" in *Poetry* (albeit in a mutilated version), he wrote laconically: "I was born in Reading, Pennsylvania, am thirty-five years old, a lawyer, reside in New York and have published no books."

Although he intermittently complained that business occupied too much of his mind and day, he appears to have enjoyed his work at the office and to have taken pride in it. "Yes, I am still here," he wrote to a former business associate during World War II, "doing exactly the same thing day after day. This is very largely my own fault, because I think I am happier so. The Company has made prodigious strides all during the war, and done a tremendous amount of business; we are now by far the largest company of the kind in the country." By that time he was vice-president of the Hartford Accident & Indemnity Co., immured in "a solemn affair of granite, with a portico resting on five of the grimmest possible columns." The clink of money made a satisfying background music.

One of the hidden blessings of his routine existence was that it compelled him to invent a kind of walking poetry, verse that reflects the energy of a man in stride.

I have to jot things down as I go along since, otherwise, by the time I got to the end of the poem I should have forgotten the beginning. Often, when I reach the office, I hand my notes to my stenographer who does a better job of deciphering them than I should be able to do myself. Then I pull and tug at the typed script until I have the thing the way I want it, and then I put it away for a week or two until I have forgotten about it and can take it up as if it was something entirely fresh. If it satisfies me at that time, that is the end of it.

Some of the dash and spontaneity of Stevens's verse may be attributed to his method of composition, determined though it was by circumstance. Except for the hiatus after the indifferent reception of *Harmonium* in 1923, the year of the furor about Eliot's *The Waste Land*, he scarcely ever stopped producing verse. He was lucky enough to find, as every poet dreams of finding, a way to be inexhaustibly fecund. The gross events of the life were not his meat; he did not cannibalize himself in his poems. As long as his mind kept turning, there was no way in which he could use up the materials of his art. Words beget words . . . "poetry is the subject of the poem." In the natural universe he found his lights and colors, things in themselves, an infinite store of metaphors. He did not get much sustenance from the drama of human relationships, nor was he stirred by a confessional impulse.

One can only guess how inordinately difficult it was for him to get down to a first-name basis with others. In his correspondence, even with those who might be considered his intimates, the formal mode of address tends to persist for years, or for a lifetime. Perhaps his formality, his air of imperturbable urbanity, his coolness, his assiduous cultivation of the role of burgher and connoisseur, of "spiritual epicure," as he styled himself, masked a fundamental insecurity, a crack in his psyche that could be traced back to the time of his early struggle for survival in New York, when he stared in depression out of his downtown "window in the slums." A pattern that repeats itself is his fantasy that in company he has blurted out something unmentionably offensive that will be held against him. In the follow-up it turns out that his fantasy was real.

What shall we say of his politics other than that they were deplorable? He complained consistently about taxes, the New Deal, the welfare state, foreign aid. How grateful we should be that his theory of poetics prevented him from writing as an opinionated man! A poetry of Republican irony would not have amused us long: "This year [1950] there is so much more to be thankful for: The Eskimos have corrugated roofs on their houses at your expense and mine; Tito is passing around sandwiches and lemonade on the USA; and we are giving a million Chinese a little outdoor exercise which is probably good for them." Without blinking an eye he could say, "I am pro-Mussolini. . . . The Italians have as much right to take Ethiopia from the coons as the coons had to take it from the boa constrictors." The subsequent correction, under pressure, to the effect that "my sympathies are the other way: with the coons and the boa constrictors" does not help matters much. Communism fascinated him as much as it repelled him, for after all it, too, like fascism, presented itself as a principle of order. His "rage for order" subsumed what was best and worst in him. "I do very much have a dislike of disorder," he admitted. "One of the first things I do when I get home at night is to make people take things off the radiator tops." In the pursuit of domestic order Stevens took on several tasks to help his wife, washing the dishes and, among other chores, scrubbing the kitchen floor — surely the most ingratiating picture that we get of him after his arch-angelic adolescence.

Though he stands today as one of the unchallenged masters of modern poetry, he deprecated the quality of modern life and the symptomatic modernism of the arts. "What has this last year [1948] meant to me as a reasonably intelligent and reasonably imaginative person? What music have I heard that has not been the music of an orchestra of parrots and what books have I read that were not written for money and how many men of ardent spirit and star-scimitar mind have I met? Not a goddam one. And I think it is because the world in general is not really moving forward. There is no music because the only music tolerated is modern music. There is no painting because the only painting permitted is painting derived from Picasso or Matisse. And of course there are very few living individuals because we are all compelled to live in clusters: unions, classes, the West, etc." He made a point of refraining from reading his fellow-poets. An avowed Francophile, he had an agent in Paris who regularly shipped him French books of verse and philosophy and who picked up for his modest art collection a number of second-rate still-life and

landscape paintings at bargain prices. Paris was the un-
disputed capital of civilization for him: he never took time out
to visit it.

He was not generous in his appraisal of his peers, excepting
Marianne Moore, for whom he held a long and affectionate
regard as "a moral force 'in light blue' at a time when moral
forces of any kind are few and far between." On inspection,
his celebrated friendship with William Carlos Williams
emerges as a rather tenuous affair. He never really warmed up
to the poems, for to him they represented "an exhausted phase
of the romantic." After Williams and Cummings, with their
"mobile-like arrangement of lines" and their "verbal con-
glomerates," what could we expect in the next generation but
the bare page, "for that alone would be new"?

When Williams, in his sick old age, "the least subversive
man in the world," was denied the opportunity to serve as
poetry consultant to the Library of Congress, as a consequence
of the McCarthy hysteria, Stevens could only come to the lame
conclusion:

> I don't see how the government could be expected to counte-
> nance any man who is committed to throw bricks at it. Of all
> people, Williams would be the least justified in throwing bricks
> at it anyhow because his case is typical of the philosophy with
> which America treats those who came to it from elsewhere. It is
> true that he was born in this country but neither one of his par-
> ents were [sic], unless I am mistaken.

In this connection it is relevant to note that Stevens hired
professional genealogists to establish the purity of his ancestry. He had his heart set on admission to the Holland Society,
which requires, for eligibility, an ancestor in a male line who
lived in New York before 1675. To his disappointment, Stevens was able to go back before this date only through female
lines.

Prior to the Williams contretemps he had refused to participate in a symposium on Ezra Pound, when the poet was being
brought here to stand trial for treason: "While he may have
many excuses, I must say that I don't consider the fact that he
is a man of genius as an excuse. Surely, such men are subject
to the common disciplines."

On Eliot (1950): "After all, Eliot and I are dead opposites and I have been doing everything that he would not be likely to do." On Frost (1954): "Frost is greatly admired by many people. I do not know his work well enough to be either impressed or unimpressed." On Dylan Thomas (1953): "Someone telephoned me yesterday to ask that I come down and speak at a memorial meeting for Dylan Thomas to which I said no. . . . He was an utterly improvident person. He spent what little money he made without regard to his responsibilities."

Wallace Stevens, let it be said, was not great-hearted; but he emerges from this book, with its relentless documentation of his passage, as a superior presence. The choice of an occupation that he made early in his career more or less determined the limitations of his sympathies and the backwardness of his politics; but the style of life that he perfected and the virtues that he cultivated were resolutely his own. His word of praise for others was "rectitude," and in its weight and measure the word seems right for him. I can admire his capacity to say No without equivocation, even when he did so for the wrong reasons. It may be that the most tangible thing about him was the solidity of his honor. "I don't profess to be erudite," he wrote. "My whole point is that, if I refer to a book as if I have read it, I have in fact read it." He brought his "tireless conscience" to bear on the smallest matters.

Students of Stevens will rejoice at the number of letters in which he patiently elucidates the most difficult of his poems, line by line and image by image — the most extensive commentary that any major poet has ever provided on his own work. Nobody will be able to write again on Stevens's poetics; on his philosophic assumptions about imagination and reality; or on his *idée fixe*, the Supreme Fiction, without reference to the recurrent exposition of these themes in his correspondence. Even more to the point, perhaps nobody will have to write about them, since Stevens has already supplied whatever gloss is needed.

It used to be said pejoratively of Stevens that he was a decorative poet, a charge that he resented. "I know exactly why I write poetry," he once commented, "and it is not for an audience. I write it because for me it is one of the sanctions of life." He quoted with approval "a precious sentence in Henry James":

> To live *in* the world of creation — to get into it and stay in it — to frequent it and haunt it — to *think* intensely and fruitfully — to woo combinations and inspirations into being by a depth and continuity of attention and meditation — this is the only thing.

The vice-president of insurance was privileged to quote that sentence from the Notebooks because he shared the Master's passion for "the only thing." He was a flawed and consecrated man who had been visited by the necessary angel . . . the angel of *reality*, he kept insisting. For years he had been trying to get it down on paper. "The object is of course to purge oneself of anything false." Crispin, Peter Quince, Connoisseur of Chaos, The Man with the Blue Guitar, Ariel . . . it was Ariel at last who said it best for him, when he was almost ready to die. He called it "The Planet on the Table":

> *Ariel was glad he had written his poems.*
> *They were of a remembered time*
> *Or of something seen that he liked.*
>
> *Other makings of the sun*
> *Were waste and welter*
> *And the ripe shrub writhed.*
>
> *His self and the sun were one*
> *And his poems, although makings of his self,*
> *Were no less makings of the sun.*
>
> *It was not important that they survive.*
> *What mattered was that they should bear*
> *Some lineament or character,*
>
> *Some affluence, if only half-perceived,*
> *In the poverty of their words,*
> *Of the planet of which they were a part.*

Out of the Cage

I wish I had known Randall Jarrell earlier. We met in the
mid-fifties, when he called to discuss an abortive publishing
project. There were others in my Village apartment, but his
was the presence that filled and disturbed the room. He was
bearded, formidable, bristling, with a high-pitched nervous
voice and the wariness of a porcupine. That was my dominant
image of him for a decade, until the turn of '65, when he came
north for a visit from Greensboro, with his beard deleted, and
I saw at dinner for the first and last time the naked vulnerability of his countenance. A few months later he was dead.

One of the most revealing poems that he ever wrote, and
one of his best, was "The Woman at the Washington Zoo."
The speaker is, of course, the woman of the title — one of
the many female voices to whom he gave, in his poetry, a
language:

Originally published in *Randall Jarrell 1914–1965*, edited by Robert Lowell, Peter Taylor, and Robert Penn Warren; Farrar, Straus & Giroux, New
York, 1967.

The saris go by me from the embassies.

Cloth from the moon. Cloth from another planet.
They look back at the leopard like the leopard.

And I. . . .
            this print of mine, that has kept its color
Alive through so many cleanings; this dull null
Navy I wear to work, and wear from work, and so
To my bed, so to my grave, with no
Complaints, no comment: neither from my chief,
The Deputy Chief Assistant, nor his chief —
Only I complain. . . . this serviceable
Body that no sunlight dyes, no hand suffuses
But, dome-shadowed, withering among columns,
Wavy beneath fountains — small, far-off, shining
In the eyes of animals, these beings trapped
As I am trapped but not, themselves, the trap,
Aging, but without knowledge of their age,
Kept safe here, knowing not of death, for death —
Oh, bars of my own body, open, open!

With a dramatic single stroke in the opening line — "The saris go by me from the embassies" — a colorful and cosmopolitan world is evoked. The next movement is toward the dark, for the speaker who stands before the cages, this government clerk in her "dull null navy," knows that the colors and the possibility of colors have been washed out of her life. She senses her kinship with and yet her difference from the animals.

The world goes by my cage and never sees me.
And there come not to me, as come to these,
The wild beasts, sparrows pecking the llamas' grain,
Pigeons settling on the bears' bread, buzzards
Tearing the meat the flies have clouded. . . .

Trapped in her lonely and defeated flesh, she is worse off than the captive beasts, for "the world goes by my cage and never sees me." Nor is she visited, as are the beasts, by those who feed on their leavings: sparrows, pigeons, buzzards. Her life is too starved for leavings. What a gray world! What a bleakness! And just when we are ready to turn away, Jarrell does something magical and triumphant with his woman at the zoo. He has her cry out, addressing the predatory bird who is the figure of lover-death, such words of shameless agony that the despair is transmuted into a fierce exaltation, as the true colors of the world, terrible though they may be, pour back into the poem:

> *Vulture,*
> *When you come for the white rat that the foxes left,*
> *Take off the red helmet of your head, the black*
> *Wings that have shadowed me, and step to me as man:*
> *The wild brother at whose feet the white wolves fawn,*
> *To whose hand of power the great lioness*
> *Stalks, purring. . . .*
> *You know what I was,*
> *You see what I am: change me, change me!*

All the voices in all of Jarrell's poems are crying, "Change me!" The young yearn to be old in order to escape from their nocturnal fears; the old long for the time of their youth, no matter how poor and miserable it was, for "in those days everything was better"; life is moving toward the death; the dead are moving back into life, and wherever they come, they come in disguises. It is a world of shifts and changes, as in a fairy tale, and the only reason you suspect it is more is that Cinderella and the Dwarfs and the Frog Prince have had a curse put on them: they have real memories and real fears. Karl Shapiro once acutely observed that Jarrell's "almost obsessive return to the great childhood myths is sometimes as painful as psychoanalysis," and that the subtitle of his work might well be "Hansel and Gretel in America." What Hansel and Gretel tell us is that the woods are dark and that the creatures who inhabit them change their skins. In the mythic imagination metamorphosis is the great theme underlying all others. To the individual psyche it is the way out of the cage. "Self-transformation," said Rilke, whom Jarrell revered and translated, "is precisely what life is."

E. E. Cummings:
A Personal Note

It scarcely seems possible that Cummings died as long ago as 1962 — but of course he has never left us. The critics these days have other fish to fry, but that may be all to the good. He led them a merry chase all his lifetime, and perhaps they have a right to feel tired. One thing I know, from beating around college campuses — his reputation rests in firm young hands.

Our house — in Greenwich Village, just around the corner from Patchin Place, indelibly associated with his name — keeps reminding us of his impudent, elusive spirit, since it is furnished with the carved, green-plush Victorian chairs that he and Marion treasured. The proof of their comfort is that we have to fight each day with our fat cat Celia for possession of the seats . . . a losing battle. How he would have enjoyed that comedy!

I am also the caretaker of the Cummings houseplants, and can report that they are greener, more flourishing than ever, as

Based on my introduction to the first showing of Harold Mantell's film on Cummings, at the Museum of Modern Art, New York, November 9, 1971.

is only appropriate. In fact, I have made a small industry out of distributing cuttings of those plants to his true admirers.

He was a marvelous mimic and could bring to vivid life, out of memory, any scene or person. There was the story, as he told it, of the first time he made a recording of his poems — it may have been for the Harvard Vocarium. Machinery always frightened him, for he was intrinsically a shy man, one of the shyest. There he stood in the recording room, quaking, leaning on a grand piano for support, swallowing hard. The signal was given to him to start. He couldn't open his mouth. He wanted to fall through the floor. Suddenly a tinny voice erupted from the bowels of the piano: "JUST-BE-PER-FECTLY-NATURAL!" That broke him up!

When Marianne Moore was editor of *The Dial* she politely but sternly requested him to change an inelegant word in one of his poems. The word was *spittoon*. She preferred *cuspidor*. Cummings's account of that dialogue was a classic of a sort. But she was always Miss Moore to him — a mark of respect.

Gallantry was second nature to him. There was a young woman — a friend of his and Marion's — whose heart had just been broken, for the usual domestic reasons. Cummings came to comfort her. She wept. A few minutes after he left, she heard her doorbell ring. When she opened the door, she discovered him standing there with an offering in his extended hand. "You need a yellow rose," he said and gave her one, then turned away without an extra syllable. I know the story about that young woman is true, because eventually I married her.

Cummings respected the privacy of others and stanchly defended his own. On one occasion, when somebody tried to bluster his way into his summer retreat in New Hampshire, Cummings picked up an old .38 that just happened to be handy and let go with it. On another occasion, when Ed Murrow and his "Person to Person" TV crew appeared at Patchin Place to film an interview, Cummings suddenly exploded at the commotion, the snaking wires, the battery of lights, the aggression on his territory, and ordered them to leave.

"I will not," he announced, "be photographed in my underwear."

Perhaps more than any other poet of his generation Cummings cherished and nurtured the image of himself as poet, rejecting the many flattering temptations that the world offers to attractive people, if only they will be less like themselves and more like others, if only they will permit themselves to be slightly corrupted. In a society of gladhanders and backslappers and self-advertisers he insisted not so much on his uniqueness as on his right to be unique, to sequester himself from mediocrity, to spit on progress when he felt like it, to remain unconcessive in his fierce enterprise.

Other poets in their maturity — the ones who manage to live that long — seek wisdom. On the contrary, the light, the joy that breaks from Cummings's work is the product of his lifelong pursuit of folly, the folly of selfhood in a society of automatons, the folly of art in a time of the degradation of values.

In the diligence of this pursuit he kept alive for all of us the very idea itself of Poet, the romantic idea — which is still the only one that all poets secretly entertain.

Poet of Terribilità

Robert Lowell is the American poet of his generation who has most conspicuously made his mark. T. S. Eliot must have had this thought in mind when at his valedictory reading at the Poetry Center in New York some dozen years ago he requested that Mr. Lowell, who was introducing him, should remain seated on stage during the entire program. The request, coming from Mr. Eliot, had the authority of a dynastic gesture. What one noticed, in the younger man's act of compliance, was his characteristic mixture of awkwardness and graciousness, a quality present in the poems as well as in the person.

America is a bad nurse of poets: it either withers them with neglect or — exceptionally — kills them with success. Robert Lowell is one of less than a handful, after the senatorial gener-

From my introductory remarks to a reading by Robert Lowell at The Pierpont Morgan Library, New York, November 8, 1973; subsequently published as a pamphlet (1974) by the library. An earlier version of my comments appeared in *Salmagundi*, Vol. 1, No. 4. Lowell's quoted remarks are from my conversation with him, pp. 153 f.

ation, who have had the opportunity of being done in by admirers and imitators. The fact that he is still an unpredictable — some would say an uneven — poet suggests that in his mid-fifties he is neither self-satisfied nor becalmed. This past spring he called attention to his survival with a bravura gesture, publishing three books of his poems on the same day. I cannot think of anyone else who would have the poems — or, for that matter, the publisher — to rival that performance.

In the twentieth century we prefer to think of our poets as rebels and innovators, and it is not difficult to fit Lowell into these categories. At the same time he remains very much a traditionalist, nourished by his New England roots, steeped in the classics, preoccupied with technique, shored up by Christian and post-Christian values.

"In life," he has said, "we speak with many false voices; occasionally, if we are lucky, we find a true one in our poems. A poem needs to include a man's contradictions. One side of me, for example, is a conventional liberal, concerned with causes, agitated about peace and justice and equality, as so many people are. My other side is deeply conservative, wanting to get at the roots of things, wanting to slow down the whole modern process of mechanization and dehumanization, knowing that liberalism can be a form of death too. In the writing of a poem all our compulsions and biases should get in, so that finally we don't know what we mean."

If he were less of a traditionalist, his sporadic radical decisions and statements, including his stand as a conscientious objector in World War II, his celebrated rebuff to President Johnson on the occasion of the disastrous White House Festival of the Arts, his march on the Pentagon, would be less meaningful. Though he is not a man of action, he has a great intuitive gift for symbolic gesture. And though he is more deeply committed to the past than most contemporaries, the vibrant touch of his poetry is on the nerve of the modern.

At one time Lowell was regarded as a New England poet, but despite his family connections he is no Yankee versifier and is not to be classified among the regionalists. Among his mentors were Allen Tate and John Crowe Ransom, with whom he studied, majoring in classics, at Kenyon College. Several of his formative years were spent in the South, and for many years a trace of Southern accent lingered in his speech. His abortive conversion to Catholicism, the influence of which dominated his early work, must be considered among his radical dissents. He remains an essentially Protestant spirit.

Lowell is fascinated by "the prose grip on things." In *Life Studies*, which looms as one of the watersheds of modern literature, he attempted to recapture a portion of the territory that poetry has for so long yielded to the novel. In *Notebook*, now retitled *History* in its expanded form, he has aimed at closing the gap between public and private events. One of his signal intuitions is the connection between terror as a fact of our political life and as a principle of the imagination, what Burckhardt in his study of the Renaissance called "terribilità," a term equally applicable to the sculpture of Michelangelo and the politics of Cesare Borgia. The two dominant figures in his landscape are Milton's Lucifer and Captain Ahab, "these two sublime ambitions," as he defines them, "that are doomed and ready, for their idealism, to face any amount of violence." In his poetry Lowell investigates states of crisis as permanent aspects of being. His work is invested with the quality of a mind that suffers history. Evil, guilt, and power are his insistent themes. Sometimes he magnifies the trivial to satisfy his taste for enormity.

To comment in this abrupt and detached manner on a poet is to make him sound like a machine for producing verse. One of the disarming features of Lowell's work is that it does not pretend to aspire to the condition of an absolute art. He tells us the time in the right kind of voice for the day. He does not try to overpower us with a show of strength; instead, with his nervous vivacity, he hurries to build a chain of fortifications out of sand, or even dust. A revisionist by nature, he is forever tinkering with his old lines, rewriting his old poems, revamping his syntax, and periodically reordering his existence.

"It may be," he has remarked, "that some people have turned to my poems because of the very things that are wrong with me, I mean the difficulty I have with ordinary living, the impracticability, the myopia." Nobody else sounds quite like that. He makes us excruciatingly aware of the thrashing of the self behind the lines; of the intense fragility of the psyche trying to get a foothold in an "air of lost connections," struggling to stay human and alive. He is a poet who will even take the risk of sounding flat or dawdling in the hope that it might be true. What we get from these poems is the sense of a life . . . a life that has been turned into a style.

Quick Studies

John Crowe Ransom

In one of his essays John Crowe Ransom remarked, with his characteristic dry inflection: "Every poet finds his place in the company of poets, and there is no necessity for killing one poet to make room for another." It would seem, from their behavior, that not all poets are persuaded there is that much space on Parnassus, but who among them would have been silly enough to believe in the advantage of liquidating Mr. Ransom? Almost from the beginning he seemed unique and irreplaceable.

A minister's son, born in Pulaski, Tennessee, he never deviated, till his death at eighty-six, from his love for the graces of a civilization and from his faith in the rituals and sanctions of a tradition. This is not to say that he was a conventional writer or thinker — his sensibility was much too keen, his mind much too fine, for sterile conformism.

His spare output of poems, exquisitely tuned, oblique, ardent but understated, leavened by irony, is the gift of his that we treasure most, because it delights us and because it encourages us to believe in the possibility of perfection.

Golden Codgers: Frost and Williams

In 1962, which must surely be considered *annus mirabilis* for the remnant tribe of octogenarians, Robert Frost, aged eighty-eight, and William Carlos Williams, a mere child just short of eighty, published their valedictory collections. A year later both of them were dead. They were unlike each other in their person and in their art, and the difference in the reception of their books is equally instructive.

Frost's *In the Clearing* was celebrated as a great public event, with an appropriate burst of sentimental and patriotic flourishes. His late elevation to the post of fireside bard to the American people and laureate of the Kennedy administration, officiating at the vaunted marriage of Poetry and Power, had certain comic overtones, for he was anything but "progressive" (in the liberal Democratic tradition), his characteristic vision could scarcely be described as optimistic, and in the main body of his work, forgetting the embarrassing doggerel towards the end, he was to be seen as hermetic, idiosyncratic, and egocentric — qualities that he shared with many other famous poets.

Even in his decline one gets occasional flashes of the intrinsic Frost, as when he notes, of butterflies, in "Pod of the Milkweed": "They knock the dyestuff off each other's wings," after which he appends his undeceived reflection, "But waste was of the essence of the scheme." In the title-poem ("A Cabin in the Clearing") the speakers are Mist and Smoke, and the subject of their dialogue is the uncertainty of the human condition. The final lines, though too stiffly articulated, carry a recognizable beat and moral: "Than smoke and mist who better would appraise/ The kindred spirit of an inner haze."

One of the most profound of his aphorisms stresses the necessity coupled with the difficulty of making choices: "Nature within her inmost self divides/ To trouble men with having to take sides." The theme is a recurrent one. Years before he had written in lines that every schoolboy thinks he understands: "Two roads diverged in a wood, and I — / I took the one less traveled by,/ And that has made all the difference." What, in passing, could be more artful than that suspended first person singular? This traveler's pride in his ability to confront his fate and to make up his mind, despite the persistence of the "inner haze," induces him to call one of his last lyrics, "Escapist — Never." The title has a ring of defiance, perhaps a hollow ring. As the poem reaches its climax we are given a momentary glimpse of a redemptive pathos: "His life is a pursuit of a pursuit forever./ It is the future that creates his present./ All is an interminable chain of longing."

No fireworks or testimonial dinners greeted the publication of William Carlos Williams's *Pictures from Breughel*. Not a single review is listed for it in the *Book Review Digest* for 1962 — or, for that matter, in the following year, when the Pulitzer Prize, an honor he had never been deemed worthy of before, was awarded to him posthumously. Frost had been given the prize four times during his lifetime. Dr. Williams's volume presented the work of his last decade, containing more than fifty poems not previously available in book form, as well as the complete texts of *The Desert Music* (1954) and *Journey to Love* (1955), the latter including "Asphodel, That Greeny Flower," a modern love poem that stands comparison with the best in the language.

An extraordinary aspect of Dr. Williams's book is that the reader is not tempted to make apologies for the poems of his seventh decade: they dance as smartly as anything he ever wrote. His responsiveness to experience is a kind of beauty in itself; he remains awake at the controls of his technique — what a joy it is to watch him tinkering with his "variable foot"!; in truth he never stopped tuning his ear to catch the true idiom of the living tongue. The final image that he presents to us is not that of the wise ancient or of the poet-as-hero: the man who walks through his poems is the man of our time, fallible, vulnerable, full of marvels.

In "The Stone Crock," to cite an example, the style is characteristically open, almost casual, on the verge of flatness, yet at the same time exquisitely taut, partly as the result of the felt discipline of the mind in its motion, and partly because the sensitive manipulation of the short fourth line of each stanza — a departure from his habitual tercets — culminates in the isolated power of the very last word of the poem after we have been led to expect it to be thrown away:

> *In my hand I hold*
> *a postcard*
> *addressed to me*
> >*by a lady*
>
> *Stoneware crock*
> *salt-glazed*
> *a dandelion embossed*
> >*dark blue*
>
> *She selected it*
> *for me to*
> *admire casually*
> >*in passing*
>
> *she was a Jewess*
> *intimate of*
> *a man I*
> >*admired*
>
> *We often met in*
> *her studio*
> *and talked*
> >*of him*
>
> *he loved the early*
> *art of this*
> *country*
> >*blue stoneware*
>
> *stamped on the*
> *bulge of it*
> *Albany reminding me*
> >*of him*

> *Now he is dead how*
> *gentle he*
> *was and*
> > *persistent*

James Wright

James Wright's is an art of nostalgia and memory and of something more, an almost hypnotic concentration on the object till it yields up its secret to him. He sees the earth folded in mystery, of which not the least element is the phenomenon of life itself, that lonely disturbance. He cracks the kernel of the particular in order to release a visionary energy. Standing in the streets of Minneapolis, the poet inquires, "Where is the sea, that once solved the whole loneliness/ Of the Midwest? Where is Minneapolis? I can see nothing/ But the great terrible oak tree darkening with winter."

"Dark" is indubitably his favorite adjective. In the violent Gothic landscape of his poems, where murderers and animals run for cover, the protagonist runs with them, seeking the mother-comfort of the dark. It is a landscape of caves, mines, slag heaps, stagnant waters, ruins, curiously suggestive of an America in the depression period, though Wright was only a child in the thirties. The depression now is the same and not the same: it is of the spirit.

In his earlier poems he was a humanist, asking, as he has put it, "moral questions," such as: "Exactly what *is* a good and humane action?" After *Saint Judas* (1959), he announced: "Whatever I do from now on will be entirely different. I don't know what it will be, but I am finished with what I was doing in that book." And it is true that his more recent work is different, more fluid and associative, riding with the image rather than pinned to a theme, but yet I still recognize the same person banging his fists on a wall. Though he now seeks what Wallace Stevens called "the morality of the right sensation," he is still capable of a big rage in a world ripe with abominations. He casts his lot with the hunted and persecuted and with all animals, especially those subject to predatory man.

In one of his epigraphs he quotes Unamuno: "We die of cold, and not of darkness." His poems include terrible revelations: I am sick . . . I am lost . . . I am dying . . . I have wasted my life . . . I am the dark Bone I was born to be. But these revelations are not introduced for theatrical effect, or to make you feel sorry for him. Having watched his career from the beginning, I am witness to a recurrent pattern. He is perpetually arriving at a crisis of style . . . of which the meaning is that he is perpetually discovering a crisis of conscience. At that level of experience things are capable of changing into their opposites, as suffering into joy, as despair into radiance. "The Branch Will Not Break" is the title of one of his books — and we believe him. Of course it won't.

Jean Garrigue

Jean Garrigue was a wildly gifted poet, the most baroque and extravagant of spirits, whose art took the road of excess that leads to the palace of wisdom. She was our one lyric poet who made ecstasy her home. Her world of angels, demons, ghosts, moon and roses, fabulous beasts and birds, fireworks and fountains would seem Gothic and artificial if a real anguish, countered by the most sumptuous of joys, did not hold its ingredients together. The flushed and impulsive quality of her poems and even their flaws reflect her lifelong pursuit of the romantic ideal. Of all the writers and artists I have known Jean Garrigue most vividly embodied, in her person, the ardor of the poetic imagination. Another generation may be better tuned to the freshness of her lines:

> This day is not like that day.
> That was a day majestic with clouds,
> Barrows of fruit, ices, and birds,
> And in the pink stalls the melon,
> While the mango, magniloquent stem,
> Steeped him in baskets, Othello's green,
> And there were strawberries, the plums and the figs.
> This day is not.

Robert Graves

Some people have the impression that Robert Graves is not a man but a syndicate. How else explain the prodigality and variety of his production? Even if we ignore his novels, stories, memoirs, essays, criticisms, polemics, translations, mythologies, exegeses, lectures, and miscellaneous what-nots, we are left with a formidable body of work in verse, all of it stamped with the characteristic quality of a style that Graves himself once described as "hand-made, individual craftsmanship."

He has such command of his medium and such persuasive confidence in his voice — call it ego, if you will — that even when he is reworking the most familiar of his themes, the romantic ordeal of thwarted passion, as he has done for years, he can manage to sound at once proud of his fate and spontaneous in his confession of injury. One of his gifts is to write with so little sense of strain as to make poetry seem immediately easy.

Graves does not always avoid stereotypes of language and of feeling, and, in truth, the White Goddess has gotten to be a bit of a bore who cries to be kicked out of his poems; but this is a writer who has the luck to be endearing even in his faults.

Although he made his mark as a poet of World War I, Graves has not yet retired to the company of the Ancients. One can still learn from him what Rilke learned from Goethe: "I need to realize that greatness is not superhuman exertion but naturalness."

Charles Olson & Co.

Undeniably the fifties was the most innovative decade in American poetry since the twenties. In *The New American Poetry 1945–1960* (Grove Press), edited by Donald M. Allen, the Beat poets comprise one section of the anthology; other sections are devoted to the Black Mountain group, the San Franciscans, and a New York contingent. The unifying characteristics that Mr. Allen finds among his "strong third gener-ation" of forty-four poets is "a total rejection of all those qual-ities typical of academic verse." Their preceptors, in evolving "new conceptions of the poem," have been Ezra Pound and William Carlos Williams. Many of them stand in close relation-ship to modern jazz, and others have been affected by abstract expressionist painting. Several of Mr. Allen's poets, who seem to have crept into the *avant-garde* on the shirttails of their friends, sound tired and conventional; some are crass or illiter-ate or both; a solid core of honest work nevertheless remains, particularly in the Black Mountain and New York sections, with Charles Olson looming large as the dominant figure of the entire anthology.

Olson aimed "to cut this new instant open." How? By de-claring war on iambics and rhyme ("the dross of verse"); by striving for an open organic form ("no line must sleep"), by producing a live look on the page, with benefit of typography; by insisting, sometimes in Latin, that the idiom must be colloquial; by professing inside information about history and women; by attacking fools and enemies and false ancestors; by sounding direct and walking crosswise; by paying homage to Confucius-Pound:

> *Words, form*
> *but the extension of*
> *content*
>
> *Style, est verbum*
>
> *The word*
> *is image, and the reverend reverse is*
> *Eliot*
>
> *Pound*
> *is verse*

As codified in Olson's helter-skelter essay on "projective verse," reprinted by Mr. Allen along with other manifestoes of the period, the three major premises of "the new poetry" are

(1) open composition, or composition by field, "as opposed to inherited line, stanza, over-all form"; (2) form conceived as never more than an extension of content; (3) process as the over-riding principle of energy in the poem — "one perception must immediately and directly lead to a further perception."

These doctrines are scarcely as revolutionary as the editor supposes, nor are they the exclusive property of the writers anthologized. Most of the poets of our time, including the despised "academics," would assent to them, as did Hopkins and Coleridge previously, and even Milton in part. In practice, the concept of process is the central one, the verse conceived as projecting the very action of the mind, the poem conceived as a way of breathing in words. The difficulty is not only to convey the sense of the process, the feeling of the mind-flow, but in the course of the action, and as a result of it, to make a *thing*, a whole, an entity. The poets of this anthology are inclined to give all to process; the *thing* tends to escape them. Which brings to mind Robert Lowell's comment about "the raw, huge blood-dripping gobbets of unseasoned experience . . . dished up for midnight listeners." and W. H. Auden's animadversion on "a mechanized generation to whom/ Haphazard oracular grunts are profound wisdom."

Robert Creeley

No one has more successfully practiced the hard, dry, anti-poetic style that represents a significant strain in modern writing than Robert Creeley. It is the kind of verse that illiterates claim not to be literature, since it lacks the sentimental effusiveness that is popularly associated with poetry. What is one to make of a poet who is prepared to expose his most trivial domestic complaints?

> *Let me say (in anger) that since*
> *the day we married*
> *we have never had a towel*
> *where anyone could find it,*
> *the fact.*

I recognize, though my own system of documentation is different from his, that "the fact" is terribly important to Creeley, as it is to me, and that he is relentless in his determination to record it as strictly, as sparely as he can. He is chary even of metaphor, as though it were a form of decoration. This purism breeds a cold and narrow strength. His aesthetic is related to that of several painters of his generation — Jasper Johns is the most familiar name — who insisted on presenting, in explicit detail, the American flag as American flag (a composition of stripes and stars) or a slice of blueberry pie as a slice of blueberry pie, stripped of all background, connotation, or symbolic aura, as if to say, "Here is the thing-in-itself: take it for what it is, and take it now." One could argue that the reality of "the fact," given the findings of modern physics, is a supreme fiction, but this objection has not inhibited a strong tendency in the modern arts that can be called actualism. Creeley, it seems to me, is the most persuasive of the actualist poets, all of whom derive in varying degrees from W. C. Williams. In the best of his collections, *For Love*, Creeley is emotionally freer than he has been before, without rejecting his minimalist technique:

> *Love, if you love me,*
> *lie next to me.*
> *Be for me, like rain,*
> *the getting out*
>
> *of the tiredness, the fatuousness,*
> *   the semi-*
> *lust of intentional indifference.*
> *Be wet*
> *with a decent happiness.*

More recently Creeley's work, which has always shown a predilection for word-play, has moved in the direction of conceptual art. The increasing dryness, impersonality, and abstraction of his new poems would seem to betoken a temporary exhaustion or numbness of feeling rather than the hardening of an aesthetic credo.

Ruth Pitter

In some ways Ruth Pitter seems to have been the loneliest poet of her generation, though marked by a self-reliant joy. From the first she was precocious and irreconcilable. One of her perilous triumphs was to have written as well as she did without permitting herself, until middle life, to concede the existence of the twentieth century. Conventional poesy and piety were pitfalls she did not always escape, out of her dogged loyalty to traditional measures and archaic diction, to Elizabethan song and Jacobean air.

She became a modern poet without forfeiting her right to deal with sacred experience. The natural world remained miraculous to her. Her later poems are harder fought, less touched with innocence, but the best of them, however knowingly desolate, are still fortified by her sense of musical delight, her idiosyncratic purity of heart and eye. "But for lust we could be friends. . . ."

Her poems are so sensitively tuned that they are liable, with a breath, to fail, but even when they do they are never failures of spirit. I like to pick my way among her pieces, in that small Eden, half peaceable kingdom, half battleground, which is yet spacious enough for passion and betrayal, faith and its absence, cottage and cave, angels and military harpists, creatures of earth and air (including the only real swan in poetry) and their "mind-infected" predators, the eloquent coffin-worm and the rose.

7

On the Threshold:
Five Young Poets

> The future of poetry is immense,
> because in poetry, where it is worthy of
> its high destinies, our race, as time goes
> on, will find an ever surer and surer
> stay. There is not a creed which is not
> shaken, not an accredited dogma which
> is not shown to be questionable, not a
> received tradition which does not
> threaten to dissolve. Our religion has
> materialized itself in the fact, in the
> supposed fact, and now the fact is failing
> it.
>
> — Matthew Arnold

> I am the truth, since I am part of what
> is real, but neither more nor less than
> those around me. And I am imagination,
> in a leaden time and in a world that does
> not move for the weight of its own
> heaviness.
>
> — Wallace Stevens

Hugh Seidman

In his extraordinary study of Baudelaire, Walter Benjamin projects the image of the poet as detective, who — like the paid ferrets and informers so much a part of the scene in the Paris of his time — tirelessly explores the streets of the metropolis, scanning the behavior of the crowd for signs of its secret guilts and derelictions. Peering into the faces of the sick, the harried, the lost, Baudelaire found the clues he needed to confirm his own elusive identity. Hugh Seidman is a twentieth-century urban investigator with related characteristics. He borrows the title of his book from a passage in his sequence, "The Modes of Vallejo Street," and the phrase itself goes back to Resnais's film *Muriel*, in which boy tells girl friend why he is so busy taking pictures of Boulogne. It should be no surprise that a poet born in 1940 counts a film-maker among his literary ancestors.

Seidman became a poet after advanced study as a mathema-

Originally published as the Foreword to *Collecting Evidence*, by Hugh Seidman, 1970, Vol. 65 of the Yale Series of Younger Poets.

tician and physicist and after employment as a computer programmer. The "scientist of poetry" whom he addresses in one of his poems might be Einstein or Oppenheimer, but it might also be himself. When he refers to the unified field, or to "the sine curves of emotion," or to "the subtle magnet bending the signals out of shape," he does so almost casually and with an authority that we at once recognize.

> A woman consults me concerning
> her misfortune in FORTRAN.
> Her long glazed fingernail
> is polished pink & glides over
> the 132 character per line
> printer output. We examine
> her logic & sources of error.
> A scale factor is incorrect.
> Her face registers the desire
> I have awakened in her.
> The jargon of acronyms & chance
> encounters. Later we make it.
>   from "The Days: Cycle"

The impressive feature of this passage is not so much the precision of the allusion to the computer language FORTRAN as it is the ability of the poet to incorporate what he knows into a structure of feeling. "Later we make it" is the transcendent pay-off for the IBM discipline, albeit with ironic overtones. I like, too, the shock of that effortless leap from technical vocabulary to blunt vernacular.

The city that Seidman walks through is a city in ruins, like San Francisco after the earthquake or Hiroshima. Existence is marginal, as in the forms of algae, lichen, mushrooms, or as in the fibrillations of the rejected heart. His two obsessive themes are the end of love and the death of society. In "Washington's Square" he addresses the General in a voice that surely is touched with glee: "It's coming to an end George." One notes the terminal implications of his images of dread: "The teeth marks on the end/ of the rope that binds./ The wall at the edge/ of the field before fall." He can say, "This is a poem of absolute resignation." And again, "the loss of love does not cease in this world." When he produces a case-history of loss, as in "The Modes of Vallejo Street," his clinical analysis of the details of a hopeless passion proceeds irresistibly to an epiphany of desperate exaltation. He discovers the sources of his strength, the reality of his manhood, in the blaze of desire. Incidentally, is there a better account in modern literature of a lovers' quarrel than in the ninth poem of "The Modes"?

It is characteristic of Seidman that he should open his "Diary of the Revolution" — presumably based on the disturbances at Columbia University in the spring of 1968 — with the observation, "He felt himself despicable. On the grass with her —." Eventually he sums up the character of his protagonist, who could occupy the post of central intelligence in almost any of his poems:

> *watcher of events and men*
> *expresser of disparity*
> *man of the inward force*
> *for whom everything is closed*
> *soldier of anger*
> *who is shut in solitude.*

Similarly, the public event that dominates "The Last American Dream" is the burning of Newark one riotous summer; but the poet's attention is focused on a situation of personal crisis:

> *and when she went away*
> *I turned in my sleep*
> *and the deepest synapse in my brain*
> *sparked and broke.*

The poet who refuses to see himself as a hero on the stage of history, who insists, rather, on writing of defeats, incapacities, humiliations, is not perforce expressing his contempt for humanity. The self, he may be saying, is of course only a wound, a peculiarly nasty kind of psychic efflorescence, but it is at the center of a universe, and at least it is a great wound:

> *Creature of the genital despair.*
> *Thalassal regressor.*
> *Stander upon the world.*
> *Conjoiner of the great circles.*

Some of the poems have deceptive surfaces. One of my favorites, "Tale of Genji," begins with a ravishingly elegiac tone: "In Murasaki's time/ they wept at the sunsets." The life of the court and the calligraphic art of that epoch were fine, ritualized, delicate. Perspective and chiaroscuro came later, signifying a different kind of life and vision, a fracturing of the plane:

> *The cold light defining shadow*
> *Poetry leading nowhere*
>
> *Occurrence made meaningless*
> *The injustice of history*

What are we supposed to do? Weep for a golden age nearly a thousand years gone? The poet will not buy that easy sentiment. The past must not be falsified. With a stroke he shatters the glass:

> *Not that it mattered*
> > *Or the light*
> > *they wept at*

"O rose, thou art sick!" wrote Blake at the dawn of the Industrial Revolution, and poets ever since have been studying the pathology of our society, In "Atavist" Seidman lists "the civilized diseases: gonorrhea, falling hair, bad skin, neurasthenia." Others have made similar diagnoses. But he goes a step beyond to ask a troubling question: "Is it moral to get better?" And the poem closes with an image of St. Francis kissing the leper who disdained him — that pariah who betokens all the outcasts of a system — "cursed and dragged off,/ jangling his bell on the landscape."

Like so many of the poets of his generation, as well as some of his elders, Seidman feels compelled to assume a renegade role. The air is freer and purer outside the system. Yet he seems already aware that art, as Goethe said, exists in limitations and that the creative imagination, though it adores freedom, remains irrevocably bound to a private identity, to human necessities, and to the rigors of a craft. Vessel of a rage, he seeks to master "the technique of rage." At one point he repeats the phrase "in consummate craft and artistry," as though it were a litany. If a poem occasionally appears tighter and denser than it needs to be, we are all the more mindful that a deep violence is being contained and that the poet has been as open as he has learned to dare.

Hugh Seidman's work is alive with energizing contradictions. It combines dryness with vehemence, order with obsessiveness, knowledge with terror. This is a poet who has listened, for survival's sake, to the language of psychoanalysts, physicists, revolutionaries, statisticians, and saints; and who has made a hard vocabulary out of the mixture. The moral pressure that his imagination exerts originates in aesthetic scruples and choices and is so evenly distributed through the syntax, the nerves and sinews, of the poem that its existence is scarcely perceptible.

One of his differences from others is in the measure and quality of his discipline, which does not find its expression in conventional modes, since it is a discipline of risks, like adventuring in space. Perhaps his education as a scientist has prepared him for dealing with the absurd. His yearning for form, his need to organize and illuminate experience, is matched by his gravitation toward chaos.

Wallace Stevens once remarked that the mind is "a violence from within that protects us from a violence without." In Seidman's version ("The Pillar") it is "the core against disturbance that was itself disturbance/ in its fixity and need to be."

In this disturbed and disturbing first book he makes me think of someone battering his way out of the cellar of a computer factory to prowl the streets, raging for a new life, but still tormented by desire, pursued by the old furies. Or perhaps he comes out of a gothic laboratory, where smoke-smudged al-

chemists, who are a breed of poet, forever seek the philosopher's stone in the glow of their alembics. If the analogy
seems remote, I advise you to read the concluding poem in
this collection. "The Making of Color," where color mounts
on color, pigment on pigment, each in the semblance of its
base ingredients, until we arrive at the extreme temperature of
transubstantiation, as if the matter of the life were being con-
verted into pure gold, pure fire, pure spiritual energy:

> *The pages are stained with purple*
> *The letters are written in gold*
> *The covers are encrusted with gems*
> *St. Jerome remonstrates*
> *The curling writhes*
> *Molten gold on carbon*
> *Ink burnt ash grey*
> *Emerald into vapor*
> *The book, the codex, the manuscript*
> *The canvas, the panel, the wall*
> *Conflagrant world against world.*

Peter Klappert

Peter Klappert is such a recklessly clever poet that one's first inclination is to mistrust his seriousness. His wit, his sophistication, his delight in word-play are constituent elements of his craft. Among some five hundred manuscripts submitted to the 1970 Yale competition, *Lugging Vegetables to Nantucket* is the only one, to the best of my recollection, that made me laugh, and perhaps in a sorry world that is as good a reason as any for being partial to it. Who else could have rewarded me with the little joke of the lady anthropologist, otherwise known as the dean of menopause: "But I have lost touch with the Touchwas"? I do not mean to suggest that this is a light-hearted poet. If one fails to catch the joke, one might as well shudder.

The gift for nonsense is one of the signs of the poetic character. Some of Peter Klappert's simplest inventions have the auditory smack of a child's counting-rhyme:

Originally published as the Foreword to *Lugging Vegetables to Nantucket*, by Peter Klappert, 1971, Vol. 66 of the Yale Series of Younger Poets.

> *Up in my attic I've got a bazooka*
> *That used to belong to Joe Palooka.*

When Klappert takes aim at the human comedy, his "bazooka" transforms itself into a more complicated instrument of social satire, as in "The Babysitters," the central poem of his first collection:

> *When I wriggled my big toe in under*
> *Her dichotomous athletic ass, she took off*
> *Ostrogoth's shoe and stroked his sole.*
> *When I ran my right hand under her jersey*
> *And tweaked her left breast, she ran her left hand*
> *Up his leg as far as the crotch. Loyal*
> *Faithfully watched.*

In its offhand polymorphous way the passage exemplifies Klappert's impertinent assurance as a writer — some might call it his "nerve"— and his cool, almost allegorical, vivacity. An examination of "The Babysitters" may help to reveal the disciplines he works with and certain of his characteristic poetic strategies.

The poem's title alludes to the poet's friends, "who have seen me through these troublous times, who have indulged my weaknesses and returned kindness where I have been bitter, who have been my babysitter." The action occurs in the mind of the protagonist at a literary party, where the main preoccupation of the guests is with one-upmanship and sexual conquest. (The analogy, in a larger context, would be a concern for power and self-interest rather than for truth or beauty.) The different "voices" of the poem represent aspects of the speaker's personality. Sometimes he asserts his presence as a detached observer, sometimes as a resentful participant, sometimes as a self-pitying introspective sensitive plant; sometimes he lapses into free-association, and sometimes, as in his letters to Elsie, he attempts (generally without success) to be honest. The poem opens formally, with everything, it would seem, under reasonable control. As the situation gets out of hand, we experience a gradual process of disintegration, with both language and sentiment running down.

The seven sections of the poem, I am advised by the author,

take their titles from "the Lasswell Formula," by which any communication is divided into seven elements: (1) who, (2) says what, (3) to whom, (4) under what circumstances, (5) by what means, (6) with what purpose, and (7) with what effect. The poem ends with the knowledge of the loss of Elsie and with an effort to live with the knowledge. Having failed to establish communication with others, the protagonist faces the necessity of reconciling himself to himself, of finding his place in the scheme of things.

Here as elsewhere one of the implications of Klappert's work, never directly stated, is that he must mediate between his sense of a poetic vocation and his other role as bemused guest at the festival of life, the higher nonsense of a dissolving universe. He must pass beyond the flippancy that permits him, or one of his voices, to say, "We are all caught up in a masquerade,/ It's in moments like these that poets get made"; and he must search within himself for the grain of authentic feeling: "Elsie, I am so angry, and so lonely, and sorry about everything."

Another key work in the collection is the opening poem, "Pieces of the One and a Half Legged Man," a nightmarish vision, as powerful as it is outrageous, of the mutilated self, "Jesus Christ Remnant," sitting in the center of the world's zoo, suffering obscene indignities at the hands of others, vainly appealing for succor to the malign authority of The Court of Divine Justice, before which he must plead "filthy or not filthy."

> *"What were you looking for when*
> *the leg came off?"*   *"Looking*
> *for God, looking for the great totem."*
> *"How many totems have you found lately?"*

Even here a savage humor comes into play, as the merciless interrogation continues:

> *"Have you ever loved?" (I*
> *kissed her) "and what*
> *was it like?"*
> *(I kissed her).*

> *She*
> *arched her heart*
> *up from the mattress*
> *and took the room*
> *into her eyes:*
> *"It was like*
> *driving the car."*

"Pieces of the One and a Half Legged Man" is more than simply ironic or satiric. It is one of the cruelest poems I know, a cleverly brutal phantasmagoria, swarming with images of the grotesque and ugly, and creating out of them a kind of triumph, a bravura spectacle of human entrapment. If there is an easy way out, the speaker's naked voice at the last does not pretend to have found it:

> *I can betray you*
> *with no resolution; this is the metropolis*
> *and you are in danger here, but where will you go?*

Peter Klappert's speech is natural and colloquial, though steeped in his literary information and sometimes deliberately salted with echoes, as in the Eliotish rhythms of the first movement of "The Babysitters." The search for a form is part of his poetic process, and when it suits his purpose he lets the process show or simulates its effect — for instance, in the canceled portions of his letters to Elsie. On the other hand, his poems are full of prosodic secrets. "Rowayton at 4 P.M." is based on the principle of alternating nine- and seven-syllable lines. "A Man I Knew" is essentially syllabic, but it conceals an internal, irregularly spaced Petrarchan rhyme scheme (strong, guest, request, belong, wrong, invest, rest, long, fence, table, block, sense, fable, locks). He is so confident of his ear and of his technical virtuosity that he does not hesitate to ring repeated changes on a rhyme or to build a towering pyramid of redundancies. In the breakdown phase of "The Babysitters" he alternates between semidoggerel and gross invective, of which he proves himself a master. When the burden of his voice is elegiac, he is capable of a broad, deep-

channeled music that reaches back in time to·a great tradition.
I quote from his moving lines "In Memory of H. F.":

> *Summer upon summer the Sound*
> *fell upon the mouthing river,*
> *striped bass and bluefish wandered*
> *among the rocks, weed creatures scavenged*
> *in the breakwater wash. Broad summers*
> *we have known the land would shift;*
> *we could not catch the momentary trembles*
> *but saw, on morning walks, sand fill*
> *our footprints, and found new boulders*
> *in the sea below the bluff. We know*
> *of sea, that it breaks the whole world down,*
> *or builds it, in some other sea.*

Peter Klappert has made an elegant and bold beginning.
Few poets of his age — or you may multiply his age — can
equal him in his command of craft. He has a wicked eye, a
nimble mind, audacity, and zest. Nothing fools him long, even
his own postures. As he has written, "*Camera* is a childhood
game, almost as much fun as *Doctor*."

Despite his taste for extravagances, he has too much existential awareness and too highly developed a critical faculty ever
to settle for an ornamental art. "Melville," he observes, "knew
the cost/ of falling off the portico/ into a design of hanging
vines."

For a young man he has already disburdened himself of
much of the gear and baggage of his adolescence, those guilts
and hangups that make so many poets hobble for a lifetime.
He is strong enough to contemplate the ultimate absurdity of
being alive, and free enough to keep on searching for
ancestors and meanings. At twenty-nine Klappert has already
made a brilliant voyage and caught a vision of those hills on the
islands where "men are raising broccoli, grapes, bayberries,
beach plums, and lighting their lamps with whale oil." I wish
for him that he will continue lugging vegetables to Nantucket.

Michael Casey

Michael Casey's *Obscenities* is, to my knowledge, the first significant book of poems written by an American to spring from the war in Vietnam, though for more than seven years, since the passage of the Gulf of Tonkin resolution, the American experience — and, in particular, the experience of American youth — has been radically transformed by that ill-starred adventure. Other comparable poems out of Indochina have foundered in declamatory indignation or bored us with their redundance. We can no longer respond to rhetorical flourishes and sentiments borrowed from the poets who fought — and too often died — in the earlier wars of the century. Casey begins as a poet with an act of rejection. He has had the original insight and the controls to produce a kind of anti-poetry that befits a kind of war empty of any kind of glory.

"This book is not about heroes. English Poetry is not yet fit to speak of them," wrote Wilfred Owen in the stillborn Preface

Originally published as the Foreword to *Obscenities*, by Michael Casey, 1972, Vol. 67 of the Yale Series of Younger Poets.

found among his papers. He wanted above all to depict the senseless horrors and inhumanity of war — "All a poet can do today is warn" — but the scale of his compassion and the elevation of his style inevitably exalted his agonists-in-khaki. Despite his disclaimer, the imagination at work in his poems can only be described as heroic, subsuming his subject matter:

> *Nevertheless, except you share*
> *With them in hell the sorrowful dark of hell,*
> *Whose world is but the trembling of a flare,*
> *And heaven but as the highway for a shell,*
>
> *You shall not hear their mirth:*
> *You shall not come to think them well content*
> *By any jest of mine. These men are worth*
> *Your tears. You are not worth their merriment.*

The outstanding poets of World War I — Owen, Sassoon, Isaac Rosenberg — all fought in the front lines and wrote directly of what they knew of hell, under "the monstrous anger of the guns." Their verse is as much a by-product of trench warfare as trench foot or shell shock. In World War II the action climbed out of the muck into the wild blue sky or rolled across open plains and deserts in armored tanks. Mobility, automation, depersonalization marked the new order of hell, a stupefying extension of modern city life, not calculated to shock the imagination into other states of awareness. Performed at a distance, even killing lost its moral and aesthetic force. "How easy it is to make a ghost," wrote Keith Douglas. Except for the Air Force, few soldiers preserved the legend of belonging to a doomed elite. Death distributed his favors with an equal hand, converting civilians as indifferently as it did combatants into "men of dust." Often the civilian ordeal was the more harrowing. "In the fourth year of this war," observed Douglas in a posthumously published essay, "we have not a single poet who seems likely to be an impressive commentator on it." In fact, no poet — American or British — was to achieve superlative distinction or special identity from a distillation of his World War II experiences. Douglas's own ad-

mired poem on the desert war, written in Egypt shortly before
Montgomery's attack, appears rather stilted and formalistic
now:

> To-night's a moonlit cup
> and holds the liquid time
> that will run out in flame
> in poison we shall sup.
>
> The moon's at home in a passion
> of foreboding. Her lord,
> the martial sun, abroad
> this month will see time fashion
>
> the action we begin
> and Time will cage again
> the devils we let run
> whether we lose or win.

Randall Jarrell's war poems of the period were more vital and
clever — he had the curious gift of making the whole grim
business sound like a sinister fairy tale — but the irony, I fear,
begins to wear a bit thin in places:

> And the world ends here, in the sand of a grave,
> All my wars over? . . . It was easy as that!
> Has my wife a pension of so many mice?
> Did the medals go home to my cat?

Unlike his predecessors, Michael Casey did not see action
as either infantryman or airman. His appropriately inglorious
assignment in Vietnam, given the nature of the war, was to
serve in the Military Police as a highway patrolman over a
thirty-mile stretch of Vietnamese National Highway One, a
two-lane macadam road, and as a gate guard at LZ Bayonet,
across the highway from the big Chu Lai air base. These loca-
tions provide the setting for most of the poems in this book.
Specifically, LZ Bayonet was the headquarters of the 198th
Infantry Brigade (commanded by a celebrated colonel, who
wore the Congressional Medal of Honor and who was nick-

named The Reaper by his men) and the 6th ARVN Infantry Regiment. Some readers may want to fill in the landscape with a picture of the steep hills, pockmarked with defense bunkers, that surrounded the base and protected it from rockets. "Last year [1970] on my birthday," notes Casey in an account of his military service, "was the only time the base was mortared while I was there. Sappers hit us too then. My squad under the Sgt. Booboo of the book was sent to the headquarters building to guard it. From there I could see two of the perimeter bunkers that had been blown up by satchel charges. That day was the most war I got to see. I was lucky. Two of my friends died near my hooch then. One was a Vietnamese interpreter who was mistaken for a sapper by an MP and shot five times in the stomach. Another friend saw this, backed into a nail on a bunker wall, and died of a heart attack."

Casey's assignment brought him into close contact with Vietnamese nationals. He made friends among them and studied their language. For this, he recalls, "I was considered a dink lover." He has strong feelings about the war, but he did not write his poems in order to exploit them as propaganda. His poems express no opinions, and the closest he comes to a generalization — one of the few times his voice is even slightly raised — is in the lines:

> *If you have a farm in Vietnam*
> *And a house in hell*
> *Sell the farm*
> *And go home*

Obscenities is conceived as a book, not as a random collection of poems. The anecdotal mode of narration that Casey has adopted is a risky one, since it calls for great energies and skill to prevent it from going slack and nerveless. In this case it works, perhaps partly because of the inherent excitement of his material, but mostly because he is a natural and frugal storyteller, not given to self-indulgence; and because he does not have to strain for credibility — his honesty shines through; and because he listens. How beautifully he listens, and with what a fine ear for speech patterns!

> *Gentlemen*
> *One year over there*
> *An you'll age ten*
> *Am I exaggeratin, Sergeant Rock?*
> *You ask Sergeant Rock*
> *If I'm exaggeratin*
> *Sergeant Rock was in the army*
> *Since the day he was born*
> *He was in the war of the babies*

I recommend reading this book straight through, from first to last, as though it were a novel or a play, in order to follow the implicit development of the action, a progress of awareness, and to make the acquaintance of a sterling cast of recurring characters, including bluff, profane Bagley; Boston Booboo, the ineffable sergeant; his Canadian counterpart, Sergeant JohnJohn, who played a dirty trick on his music-loving captain (see "Sentiment"); bereaved and spunky Stanley, one of a pair of Vietnamese girls employed as police matrons, whom the men, for apparently obvious reasons, called Stanley and Ollie, after Laurel and Hardy; and the GI named Casey, "Sort of big/ Sort of doofus looking," who threads his way from episode to episode, not always announcing his presence, not always self-respectful.

Obscenities is full of what the title suggests. War has its scatology, even its hilarity at times. This young poet enjoys his joke as much as any man. But the manifestation of the ultimate obscenity, as revealed to "The LZ Gator Body Collector," is beyond either tears or laughter:

> *See*
> *Her back is arched*
> *Like something's under it*
> *That's why I thought*
> *It was booby trapped*
> *But it's not*
> *It just must have been*
> *Over this rock here*
> *And somebody moved it*

After corpus morta stiffened it
I didn't know it was
A woman at first
I couldn't tell
But then I grabbed
Down there
It's a woman or was
It's all right
I didn't mind
I had gloves on then

Here as elsewhere the language is so simple and open, so plausible, that one scarcely notices the artfulness of the compression, the understatement, the nice distortion of "rigor mortis," the rightness of the unpunctuated linear structure based (but not slavishly) on the short span of the breath units.

One of the last poems in this sequence is entitled "Learning," The speaker is unnamed, but we can guess his identity.

I like learning useless things
Like Latin
I really enjoyed Latin
Caesar and the Gallic Wars
Enjoyed his fighting
The Helvetians and Germans
And Gauls
I enjoyed Vietnamese too
The language
Its five intonations
Its no conjugations
A good language to learn
Vietnam is divided in
Three parts too
It makes me wonder
Who will write their book

I submit that Michael Casey, with his first volume of poems, has already written at least one chapter of that book.

Robert Hass

Some poems present themselves as cliffs that need to be climbed. Others are so defensive that when you approach their enclosure you half expect to be met by a snarling dog at the gate. Still others want to smother you with their sticky charms. Reading a poem by Robert Hass is like stepping into the ocean when the temperature of the water is not much different from that of the air. You scarcely know, until you feel the undertow tug at you, that you have entered into another element. Suddenly the deep is there, with its teeming life.

Consider the opening lines of "On the Coast near Sausalito":

> *I won't say much for the sea*
> *except that it was, almost,*
> *the color of sour milk.*
> *The sun in that clear*

Originally published as the Foreword to *Field Guide*, by Robert Hass, 1973, Vol. 68 of the Yale Series of Younger Poets.

unmenacing sky was low,
angled off the grey fissure of the cliffs,
hills dark green with manzanita.

It was as if the voice were the continuation of a long solil-
oquy that had only just now become audible, without straining to be heard, without breathing harder — a clear musical
voice that modulates itself as it flows and that enjoys caressing
the long vowel sounds.

Later in the poem we are introduced to "an ugly atavistic
fish," the cabezone, a variety of Pacific sculpin that with its
duck's-web fins and bloated head "resembles a prehistoric
toad." It belongs to the category of trash fish, but Italians prize
it for the savor of its bluish meat when fried in olive oil "with a
sprig of fresh rosemary." (Hass is characteristically explicit
with his culinary instructions.)

At the close of the poem the fisherman confronts his squirm-
ing catch, that "spiny monster" held in his hands:

his bulging purple eyes
were eyes and the sun was
almost tangent to the planet
on our uneasy coast.
Creature and creature,
we stared down centuries.

Hass's poetry is permeated with the awareness of his creature self, his affinity with the animal and vegetable kingdoms,
with the whole chain of being. The country from which he has
his passport is the natural universe, to which he pledges his
imagination. He is most at home writing of his native Pacific
coast, but he carries his passport with him wherever he goes.
Natural universe and moral universe coincide for him, cen-
tered in a nexus of personal affections, his stay against what he
describes as "the wilderness of history and political violence."
For one so caring, an occasional lapse into sentimentality
would be understandable, but a reliable sense of humor and a
certain aspect of down-to-earth plainness in his makeup

prevent him from going soft. He does not, for example, break into tears over the sufferings of his skillet-bound cabezone: it is enough that he has transformed its ugliness into beauty and dignified its fate in the act of confrontation. To a troubled friend in another poem he remarks, "This world did not invite us."

In his mid-twenties, for an anthology of young poets, Hass composed a brief statement of poetics that remains revealing:

"I like poems for the peace involved in reading and writing them. I began writing seriously when I found that I could write about myself and the world I knew, San Francisco and the country around it, in a fairly simple and direct way. For a long time I felt a compulsion to direct myself to large issues; this was mainly due to the cant I acquired around universities about alienation. About the time that the Vietnam War broke out, it became clear to me that alienation was a state approaching to sanity, a way of being human in a monstrously inhuman world, and that feeling human was a useful form of political subversion.*

The shapes of evil in his poems are identifiable as spoilers and predators; inheritors of "the old fury of land grants, maps, and deeds of trust"; robber barons east and west; warmongers and bigots. In "Palo Alto: The Marshes" Kit Carson is glimpsed anticipating the rape of California with the torch he puts to an Indian village, a vision mounted on the apparition of "ten wagonloads of fresh-caught salmon" and dissolving to the harsh reality of a tanker lugging "bomb-shaped napalm tins toward port at Redwood City," site of the chemical factory whose business is with death by fire. "Palo Alto: The Marshes" is a brilliant and profound poem of American history. Its ending, with its crystalline detail and authority of tone — remarkable in a poet so young — typifies Hass's style at its best:

> *The otters are gone from the bay*
> *and I have seen five horses*
> *easy in the grassy marsh*
> *beside three snowy egrets.*

* Paul Carroll, ed., *The Young American Poets* (Chicago: Follett, 1968).

Bird cries and the unembittered sun,
wings and the white bodies of the birds,
it is morning. Citizens are rising
to murder in their moral dreams.

At first glance Hass appears to be an expansive poet in the open tradition of Walt Whitman and William Carlos Williams; but gradually we perceive his attachment to more private imaginations, including those of Wallace Stevens and Theodore Roethke. Some of the energy of his writing can be attributed to the contradictions of this ancestral line. An added element is the influence on his work of Chinese and Japanese poetry, evident in the scrupulous purity of his observation — as in the ending of "Song," one of the most buoyant and delightful of his lyrics:

On the oak table
filets of sole
stewing in the juice of tangerines,
slices of green pepper
on a bone-white dish.

Hass's debt to the Orient is acknowledged in the sequence entitled "After the Gentle Poet Kobayashi Issa," based on the standard haiku translations by R. H. Blyth. A comparison of texts may serve to indicate the extent of Hass's stylistic accomplishment. Blyth's version of the eighth haiku reads:

Spiders in the corners,
Don't worry!
I'm not going to sweep them.

Hass's transpositions and modifications are subtle:

Don't worry, spiders,
I keep house
casually.

The exquisite differences are what make poetry.

Eastern influence is only one of the factors contributing to the particularity of Hass's style. The underlying assumptions are inherently philosophical. Was it Sartre who said, "Evil is making abstract that which is concrete"?

Haiku and other poems of literary reference are gathered in the middle of *Field Guide* under the heading "A Pencil." Included in this group is a series of "pornographer poems," as if to underscore the bond between sexuality and art. Presumably the section heading has Freudian connotations, though its origin is innocent enough. Faulkner, it seems, was once asked by an interviewer what it took to be a writer. "A pencil," he replied. It will be recalled that Renoir, in his arthritic age, when he could scarcely lift his hand, employed a blunter term to designate his painting tool. My favorite in this section is "The Nineteenth Century as a Song," a witty tour de force — but it is only slightly pornographic.

Two of Hass's most ambitious poems, "In Weather" and "Lament for the Poles of Buffalo," considered in conjunction, display the versatility of his gifts. The former is that rare contemporary phenomenon, a testimony to the persistence of married love through a long winter and the metamorphoses of the heart. Hass already knows what it took Pound a lifetime to learn: "If love be not in the house there is nothing" (Canto 116). "In Weather" is intimate, reflective, tortuous, sensuous, a compulsive journey through the labyrinth of landscape into the mystery of affections:

> o spider cunt, o raw devourer.
> I wondered what to make
> of myself. There had been a thaw.
> I looked for green shoots
> in the garden, wild flowers in the woods.
> I found none.
> . . . .
> I could not sleep.
> I imagined the panic
> of the meadow mouse,
> the star-nosed mole.
> Slowly at first, I

made a solemn face
and tried the almost human wail
of owls, ecstatic
in the winter trees, twoo, twoo.
I drew long breaths.
My wife stirred in our bed.
Joy seized me.

In contrast, "Lament for the Poles of Buffalo" is a public poem with a documentary base, dense with allusions to the local history of upper New York State, agitated and propelled by the thrust of current affairs. It is the most topical of Hass's poems, and the one best served by a commentary. A note on its background will illuminate many of its details.

In 1970, at the time of the Cambodian escalation, Hass was faculty adviser — an entirely titular position — to SDS (Students for a Democratic Society) at the State University of New York at Buffalo. In this capacity he was subpoenaed by the grand jury convened to investigate antiwar activity on the campus. At one level this is a poem of civic conscience, an outcry of sorrow and dismay, complicated by the irony of the poet's investiture as a leader of mad bombers and subversives. At another, more meditative level it is a probing for the meaning of roots in a deracinated community, by a man who is himself cut off, at least temporarily, from his Pacific source as well as from the mainstream of the national will.

"I had been teaching in the night school," he recalls, in a letter that is as informative as it is casual. His students were "Polish working class people who lived on streets named after poets and revolutionaries they had never heard of, ashamed of their nationality, some of the younger ones speaking very affectedly because they were trying to get rid of the whine in their vowels. There are not even Polish restaurants in the city, not one Polish bookstore. After San Francisco it was puzzling to me at first. I started teaching Polish books and they didn't like the idea at all. By the end we were trying out the Lithuanian salads in *Pan Tadeusz*. I was getting mason jars of their grandmothers' sauerkraut and in one case directions to a stretch of woods that held a treasure of birch mushrooms. . . ."

Robert Hass is a poet who sits easy in his skin. One is not accustomed to encounter, in the work of a contemporary, this much élan, this much celebration of "the quick pulse of blood." Almost every page demonstrates, with singular clarity, the satisfactions of an art committed to making "felt connections" between words and body, between body and world. These poems are as much an expression of an organic principle as the activities of which they are an extension — walking, eating, sleeping, love-making — and they are equally pleasurable, equally real.

> *It is an ancient*
> *imagination and it begets,*
> *this order with the random symmetries*
> *of mallow poppies in the field,*
> *the dying and green leafing of the grass,*
> *meadows crackling in the midday heat,*
> *alive with seed. It translates easily.*

Michael Ryan

Michael Ryan is a poet of secrets and dislocations. The air of his poems is charged and ominous. Even the love poems admit feelings of doubt and dread. Their order embraces a violent reality. He has a mind that rejoices in the play of concepts, in the embodiment of "thought as experience." The imagination that presides over his work is elusive, complex, and singularly restless.

At the traumatic center of a young man's world is the death of the father. In poem after poem Ryan returns to this theme, no matter from what starting point, partly because it is what his memory most fears, partly because it is that event by which he is renewed. In "The Beginning of Sympathy" he writes:

> *I've never left my father.*
> *He's getting colder,*
> *his voice thin as an angel's,*

Originally published as the Foreword to *Threats Instead of Trees*, by Michael Ryan, 1974, Vol. 69 of the Yale Series of Younger Poets.

> *although his tongue is stuck in death.*
> *Don't waste the dead, he says sympathetically,*
> *Come sit in my mouth.*

Another poem, "Transformations," opens with the line, "In this house, death is a closet," and concludes: "I feel silent & changed, like a house/ when the father dies." Elsewhere he sees "dead fathers circling the universe."

This death, he realizes, is not only for others: it is for himself. He is locked in the house of the dead with no key to salvation except his sex, his cunning, and his art. Metaphors of enclosure appear on almost every page: closets, rooms, caves, shells, the tube of the body. Another syndrome projects images of suffocation and drowning. In one climactic moment ("What Keeps You Thinking") the self burrows through the self: "A deep winding hole./ As you squeeze through yourself all night/ you feel the pressure letting go."

Ryan's commitment is to seek exact verbal equivalents for ambiguous inner states. In reading certain of his lines one can almost detect the *frisson* of the poet when he hits it right:

> *Even thought was clear, like watching a lover*
> *explore the bottom of a deep lake.*

> *I'm honestly grateful there's breath*
> *to make noise with, and many words*
> *have meaning. I feel lucky*
> *when hello doesn't hurt.*
> *On a bus, I could love anyone.*

> *I say she does belong. I say sometimes*
> *I'm not alone, even if love imposes*
> *its limits like a gangleader and this razor*
> *of a brain makes me the enforcer.*

> *You think constantly*
> *of silk, how it must feel good*
> *as the skin melts, lying there,*
> *eyes rolled inward, looking at yourself.*

Imagining pain, you wear out your body
slowly, like a favored article.

Still, those wings inside you.
At the hot stove all day you feel yourself
rising, the kids wrapping themselves
around your legs oh it's sexual
this nourishing food for the family
your father stumbling through the door
calling to you Honey I'm home.

The poems have their separate identities, but at the same time they exist in an elaborate system of cross-references. This room of any poem is like that room, "a closet of secrets"; at every window the moist animals of the night are nuzzling; the same blind swimmer propels himself underwater from page to page; nobody can stop the dead father from walking. Few young poets have constructed so self-contained a world.

The sound of the verse is mostly desperate, but it is not a leaden or a sodden desperation. A subtle and mercurial *persona* inhabits this poetry of interiors, subject to periodic crises of the spirit, responsive to every metabolic change of weather. In the passage that gives the book its title Ryan writes:

We're learning how to walk unlit streets,
to see threats instead of trees,
the right answer to a teenager
opening his knife. The answer is yes.
Always we couldn't do otherwise.
                    —("Prothalamion")

The landscape here is characteristically emblematic; but the danger is real. What matters is survival.

Most contemporary poets are attached to particulars; their act of the imagination depends on a concatenation of perceptions; they draw their sustenance from the visible universe. Ryan, on the contrary, is enamored of ideas, as well as of more conventional objects of desire, and rejoices in the capacity of the intellect to reason, to make fine discriminations, to move towards some tentative order, to categorize, to achieve the hard-edged beauty of abstraction. He is a poet who can speak of "kissing a concept," who is tempted by "the violence of strict edges," who acknowledges that "the other desire" (after sex) is "to sharpen the brain/ to a fine edge." In "A Post-humous Poetics," which reviews, not without a touch of self-mockery, the history of his aesthetics, he speaks of abstractions "insisting on their fine edges,/ asking to be used to open cans," and appropriately concludes with an example: "our first kiss, perfect as gravity."

Ryan does not usually conceive his poems in dramatic terms. When he does, as in "Lincoln Inward" and "The Janitor's Coffin," the protagonists emerge as aspects of the poet's own identity. The rhetorician who wonders how he sounds exposes his vulnerability: "I begin to listen to myself/ freeing the slaves: don't come back, I say,/ don't come back." The janitor who, like Pluto, is lord of the dead and the lower world, carries shapes of words in his nocturnal rounds that connect like a ring of keys. Essentially the structure of the poems is dialectical, as of a man conducting a running argument, or at least an urgent dialogue, with himself. Ryan's deceptively colloquial inflections oppose an abstract vocabulary, without excluding it, and resist, without negating, the formal pattern. In his usual strategy he tries to set the measure and tone of a poem, its integrity, with the very first line, to be tested against the flow and momentum of the syntax. He is adept at preserving the tension of the line and at controlling the tone.

In "Negatives," his most ambitious poem, he explores the meaning of a relationship with a woman in a sequence of thirty octaves that suggests a sonnet cycle. What he discovers in the process of composition, as he lets his poem think about itself, is the degree of denial in him. Hence the title, with its implicit allusion to undeveloped images in photography. Throughout "Negatives" the focus is on the loved one, but another presence insists on getting into the picture:

> Let me say a word for orgasm
> which isn't death, but don't we speak
> as relief from the loneliness of sex,

me feeling like a crowd as I push
toward a way out of my body,
you saying my name as if my name
could let you in. I'm the stranger
who rubs against you & grins.

. . . . . .

Let me put this straight:
if I taste my death in the back
of my mouth, don't expect a kiss.
It comes out in every word,
crawling through breath like a whip.
I believe it more than my life,
because more desperate, this friend,
my big woman, the only fact.

Threats Instead of Trees is an obsessive book, producing in at least one reader intermittent sensations of vertigo and claustrophobia, but it is redeemed from narrowness and made strangely exhilarating by the mobility of Ryan's mind. "As soon as the mind is involved," Valéry once observed, "everything is involved." He understood, as his own work demonstrated, the aesthetic possibilities of monomania: "I can see for my part that the selfsame subject, and even the selfsame words, could be taken up again and again, indefinitely, and could occupy the whole of a lifetime."

Not only does Michael Ryan let his poems think about themselves; he gives them rope enough, without letting go, to think about the mind that is making them and its load of memories. He may be on the way to fulfilling a prophetic sentence from one of Wallace Stevens's letters: "The pleasures of poetry are not yet the pleasures of thought; perhaps that is the work poetry must do in the future."

8

Recapitulations

To live is to fight with trolls in the caverns of both heart and mind; to write is to sit in judgment on oneself.
— Henrik Ibsen

We work in the dark — we do what we can — we give what we have. Our doubt is our passion and our passion is our task. The rest is the madness of art.
— Henry James

Seedcorn and Windfall

> The moon has set, and the Pleiades; it is the middle
> of the night and time passes, time passes, and I lie
> alone.
>
> — Sappho

"Do you think I have talent?" "Yes." "So you really think
I'll be a poet!" "It doesn't follow as the night the day. Talent is
cheap, you know. One of the attractive features of mediocrity
is that you can count on it — mediocrity infallibly begets the
mediocre. But you can never be sure what the gifted will do.
So many of them go straight to hell. Talent without character is
the worst kind of curse."

The Industrial Revolution succeeded in changing the landscape (mostly by fouling it) overnight; but a hundred and
fifty years, more or less, had to pass before it could produce a
race of unqualifiedly urban poets. As a people we are still
suspicious of our city-bred poets, whom we profess not to

Based on notebooks, articles, and transcripts of interviews. Published
sources include *Harper's*, for which I wrote an annual survey of poetry,
1959–1962; *Yale Literary Magazine*, May 1968; *New York Quarterly*, Fall
1970; *Quadrille* (Bennington College), Winter 1972; *Salmagundi*, Spring–
Summer 1973; *Contemporary Literature*, Winter 1974; *Iowa Review*, Spring
1974.

understand. Though Frost was not born in the New England countryside, he had the luck or the genius to become identified with it. His most successful work of the imagination was the legend he created about himself. We tend to picture him at some rural crossroads as proprietor of the general store, dispensing his honest wares with a benevolent seasoning of colloquial salt.

The American genius has historically had two natures and two poles — the one idealistic, metaphysical, living in abstraction and pure reason; the other shrewd, practical, individualistic, even self-centered. Emerson and Franklin respectively embody these contradictions. Now Frost, who wins your confidence by insisting that he talks nothing but common sense, is the heir of Franklin, from whom he borrows Poor Richard's voice; but remember that Franklin himself was thoroughly a man of the world. Frost's mind is tough and undeceived. Its rather special brand of urbanity is what his art conceals.

Paul Elmer More said of Emerson that he was "a kind of lay preacher to the world," and so was T. S. Eliot, the last of the literary Brahmins, with the same type of coldly nervous, eclectic, intellectual force as his predecessor, and with the same gift for composing memorable quotations. For a long time, for more than three decades, in fact, you could scarcely pick up a poem by a young writer without overhearing somewhere in the background, however faintly echoed, the breathless, reiterative, suspended rhythm of Eliot.

Wallace Stevens said of William Carlos Williams that he "spent his life in rejecting the accepted sense of things." It was a backhanded compliment, smacking a little of censoriousness. Williams was another kind of person, expansive, compassionate, emancipated. In his American lineage he goes back directly to Walt Whitman, but his even deeper kinship is with the village atheist and Huck Finn and — earlier still — with Natty Bumppo, the stanchly resourceful hero of Cooper's tales of the frontier.

Noise isn't virtue. It isn't even reputation. How can one talk seriously about a "school" of poets? Poets don't run in packs. And confessions aren't to be confused with public rants and exhibitions. If we are going to bait academic poets — one of the most wholesome of literary sports — we might as well keep in mind that the Beat poets constituted the most clearly defined and most widely publicized "academy" in the American world of poetry during my lifetime. Allen Ginsberg's *Howl* was an event of a kind, a rhetorical blockbuster, a stupefying increment of rage and prophecy, but the subsequent squeals and bleats of his disciples became something of a nuisance, as well as a bore.

Self-indulgence, automatism, is an escape from the risk of art. The poem does not lie easy in the mind for the picking. It must be fought for intimately through long days and nights. The actual process of composition is a solitary journey to the other side of fatigue and consciousness. There would be no poems if poets did not have boldness, compulsions, cunning, science, and luck.

Anthologies are like women that can't be lived with or without. Too often they seem to be compiled by cautious moles with an ear to the ground, not the right position for doing one's required homework. Moreover, they tend to perpetuate the kind of poem that is made up of the fashionable floating materials of a period. Some of our most distinguished poets have remained relatively obscure for years, even for decades, either through anthological caprice or simply because their work did not seem to lend itself to captivity in the standard zoos of the period.

Poets don't live: they get by.

The mind of the scientist, exploring space and matter, is closely related to the mind of the poet, whose task is to explore inner space and the reality of things. Like the scientist the poet is enchanted with an expanding universe of knowledge; but he keeps insisting that the new data must be incorporated into a moral universe, the universe that poetry originally created as myth and for which he must perpetually seek new metaphors. "After such knowledge, what forgiveness?" asked Eliot. Ideally the mind of the poet is pulled two ways at once: on the one hand, to the purity of the precision of mathematics; on the other, to the purity of the violence of love.

Question: How do publishers feel about accepting a book of verse by a new poet. Answer: Frankly, they feel sick at the thought. Some of the most successful trade publishers have not even considered it scandalous to admit they are dis-inclined to read *any* manuscripts of verse submitted to them. When will the publishing fraternity realize that poetry is the source, the seminal impulse, of all literature, the circumfluent air that gives all the arts of an epoch their weather? I have no patience with the Midas-fingered who complain that poetry resists being turned into gold. It is better than gold.

The first poems come to you out of nowhere. You are more of a conduit than a vessel. Later, those early efforts seem com-pletely extraordinary, because you realize how immature you were emotionally. A feeling for language is a kind of prehen-sile thing. You don't know why you're writing poems, any more than a cat knows why it claws at the bark of a tree.

Language comes to you with certain preordained con-ditions — it has, for example, syntax; it has vocabulary; it has symbolic meaning. Nobody owns it. When you touch lan-guage, you touch the evolution of consciousness and the his-tory of the tribe. You reach for a tool, a common tool, and you find to your surprise that it has a cuneiform inscription on the handle.

Periodicity is the great secret of the natural world. The day itself is periodic, from morning through noon to night; so, too, are the stars in their passage, the tides, the seasons, the beat of the heart, women in their courses. This awareness of periodic-ity is what gives us the sense of a universal pulse. And any art that does not convey that sense is a lesser art. In poetry it leads us, as Coleridge saw, to an organic principle, the most profound of all intuitions about the nature of the imagination. For a poet, even breathing comes under the heading of prosody.

My early writing was dense and involuted — so, I guess, was I. Now what I am seeking is a transparency of language and vision. Maybe age itself compels me to embrace the great simplicities, as I struggle to free myself from the knots and complications, the hangups, of my youth. In my sixties I am astonished by the depth of my affection for this life. It's equally true that I am no more reconciled than I ever was to the world's wrongs and the injustice of time.

A poet needs to keep his wilderness alive inside him. To remain a poet after forty requires an awareness of your darkest Africa, that part of your self that will never be tamed.

There's hope for you as long as you keep on being terrified by history.

A poet's beginnings are largely a generational phenomenon, a combination of accidents and influences, on which he builds. Maybe at a certain point he would prefer a fresh start, but the difficulty is that he has already established the condition of his art. Poets are always wanting to change their lives and their styles. Of the two, it's easier to change the life. Perhaps the style will follow. If poets lived long enough, they would become their opposites. No single kind of poetry is sufficient for a millennium.

I had just been graduated from college when I sent my first batch of poems to *The Dial*. Within ten days I received a handwritten note from Marianne Moore, who was editor then. "I have read your poems," she wrote, "and I do admire them. We shall be delighted to publish them." I felt I had been blessed by the gods. There are no magazines now that are even faintly analogous to *The Dial*. I don't really care where I publish anymore. Several of the young poets I know have that same feeling of diffidence. They have nowhere to turn for a sense of sanction. A great loss.

The audience for poetry, though it is far from representative of the whole community, is more numerous and more knowing than it has ever been. You find it in scattered urban cells and colleges, a community of friends, waiting, listening. When I was in college, and for a decade or two thereafter, no contemporary poetry was taught in the universities. Poets were not asked to give readings, let alone to teach. The underlying assumption was that poetry, after Kipling and Amy Lowell, was not a respectable vocation.

This is the day of the cult of the amateur. Anybody has the right to call himself poet, and anybody does. Sometimes I am tempted to echo Yeats's peevish remark at a meeting of The Rhymers' Club: "There are too many of us."

The ordeal of the artist, of which we hear so much, is real enough, God knows, but so are his joys. The poets of my acquaintance are doing precisely what they want to do and what they believe they do best. Nobody had to twist their arms to wring verses out of them.

In hierarchical societies, genius tends to flow from the top — it percolates down to the lesser fry from the towering few who dominate the age. As society becomes more and more democratized, the genius of the race is dispersed among larger and larger numbers. A dilution occurs, so that perhaps now there are twenty poets who together are the equivalent of a Milton. There is, however, no Milton. Maybe we're inching back to some sort of chorus of poets, as in certain primitive societies, where everybody composes songs. No great poets, but still, now and then, great poems.

The poets of my generation were born in the shadow of our formidable predecessors: Eliot, Pound, Frost, Robinson, Stevens, William Carlos Williams (the one democratic spirit among them), etc. Living in the country, I had no literary friends, except for Roethke, who visited me occasionally and with whom I corresponded, exchanging manuscripts. It didn't occur to me that the senatorial generation might be interested in what I was doing, and I didn't expect them to be. Today young poets feel perfectly free to converse with their elders, and this is one of the healthiest aspects of the contemporary scene, this ongoing conversation. But for me such a colloquy was inconceivable. Nothing happened till I was almost fifty to abate my deep sense of isolation. The truth is that I've never gotten over feeling like a loner.

I see no reason why an oral tradition and a written tradition shouldn't co-exist — they've done so for centuries. Historically the former have influenced the latter, as when the ballads entered into the stream of English Romanticism. Right now the contrary is true. Bob Dylan, Leonard Cohen, Rod McKuen, for example, in a descending scale of interest, are by-products, vulgarizations, of the literary tradition. Compare them with the jazz musicians or the gospel singers, who were authentic expressions of the folk.

Circumstances made Akhmatova a political poet, but the politics is invariably filtered through her lyric voice. For example, "Requiem," one of the masterpieces of modern Russian literature, is more than a diatribe against the Stalinist terror which blighted her life and took her son from her. What it conveys is a sense of tragic landscape, the desolation of hearts in a heartless epoch. Akhmatova learned from Dante the necessity for human scale in depicting the crimes of history.

I came to teaching late and found it second nature, but I recognize the danger of settling for its comforts and satisfactions and try to keep myself mobile, non-tenured, reasonably disaffiliated. One has to defend one's own image as poet or be prepared to lose it. The poets I admire are those who have preserved that image in their mind and mirrored it in their art.

In the beginning Nature threatened Man. Now their roles are reversed. Is there anything on earth more to be feared than the hairless biped *homo sapiens*, the beast that knows so much and loves so little?

I keep trying to improve my controls over language, so that I won't have to tell lies. And I keep reading the masters, because they infect me with human possibility. The vainest ambition is to want an art separated from its heritage, as though the tradition were a cistern full of toads instead of a life-giving fountain. A poet without a sense of history is a deprived child.

One of the prevailing illusions is that youth itself is a kind of genius . . . instead of a biological condition.

To say that one is aware of the comedy of life is not to deprive it of its dignity. The comic vision requires a certain distancing from the object. It enables us not to fall into the grotesqueries of self-pity or to become sentimental about our losses. The fatal temptation for any poet is to become grandiose, to write only in inflated emotional states. Hölderlin said that the way to achieve nobility in art is through the commonplace. Not to over-reach, not to strain for high-flown epithets or resolutions, but simply to be as true as we can to the grain of the life.

Poetry is the enemy of the poem.

There is an aspect of one's existence that has nothing to do with personal identity, but that falls away from self, blends into the natural universe. To be human is not to be apart from or superior to the whole marvelous show of creation.

I suppose I am too much of a Western man to be greatly influenced by the poetry of the Orient. Nevertheless I admire its spareness, its power of understatement, its willingness to let the natural image and its juxtapositions speak for themselves rather than to force the issue. "Never try to explain," I comment in one of my poems, and that's good advice, if I may say so, for any poet.

If we did not wear masks, we should be frightened of mirrors.

Memory is each man's poet-in-residence. It's curious how certain images out of the life — not necessarily the most spectacular — keep flashing signals from the depths, as if to say, "Come down to me . . . and be reborn." The words that reveal they've made that descent, when the mind is shaken, come up wet and shimmering and alive. They've been down in that well, where they've met the child you were.

I went back to Worcester, where I was born, and looked for the old house at the city's edge and those Indian woods. It was a most depressing adventure. The place had turned into a technological nightmare . . . an express highway running through my childhood. On the site of my nettled field stood a housing development ugly enough for tears. That's one reason why I had to write "The Testing-Tree."

How can one separate awareness from suffering? To be aware of mortality itself, the running down of the universe, the horrors of poverty, the abomination of bigotry, the monstrousness of war . . . that alone is suffering enough to last a thousand lifetimes. People don't have to be taught to suffer — they have to be taught how to live. Then they can begin to discover what joy is.

The words of a poem are language surprised in the act of changing into meaning. The poem is always becoming meaning, but is not meaning itself. Language overwhelms the poet in a shapeless rush. It's a montage, an overlapping of imagery, feelings, thoughts, sounds, sensations, which have not yet submitted to regimentation. Part of the freshness of the poem comes from leaving some of the primordial dew on it, not polishing the language down to the point where it becomes something made, not something born.

So many poems have an airy, even a gaseous, aspect. A vague poetic impulse was all that brought them into existence.

A poem needs to be nailed to the foundations of the life itself. Concrete instances — what Blake called Minute Particulars — are the nails for the job.

A few summers ago, on Cape Cod, a whale foundered on the beach, a sixty-three-foot finback whale. When the tide went out, I approached him. He was lying there, in monstrous desolation, making the most terrifying noises — rumbling — groaning. I put my hands on his flanks and I could feel the life inside him. And while I was standing there, suddenly he opened his eye. It was a big, red, cold eye, and it was staring directly at me. A shudder of recognition passed between us. Then the eye closed forever. I've been thinking about whales ever since.

I am not sure who invented the game, Roethke or I, but its object was to test how much we really knew about the poetry of the past. We would try to stump each other by reading aloud the most obscure poem from another century that we could find. If the identity of the author escaped us, the alternative requirement was to guess the date. We became so adept at the game that we were scarcely ever more than ten years off. Indeed, style and prosody are such sensitive variables that every poet, without realizing it, stamps a date line on his work.

Each poet has his pastness, which is different from any other's. Originality for him consists in tracking down those key images which will unlock his deepest and most secret reality. It is not to be found in seeking originality, for that is what everybody else is doing — an unoriginal pursuit.

Beware of the critic who pretends to be objective. Scratch his skin and you find a slave of fashion. In the twenties and thirties one had to follow Eliot in order to win a reputation or an audience. In the late thirties, into the forties, one had to be Audenesque. Then Thomas was the rage. Later the Beats, the Black Mountaineers, the New York School, and the Confessors had their respective turns. And so it goes. The easiest poet to neglect is one who resists classification.

The cult of novelty leads to the glorification of inventors among the poets. They are not necessarily the strongest voices of an age, though they may well be the most exciting. Pound (who coined the epithet) affected the style of modern verse more than, let us say, Yeats, who was not an inventor, but I would be willing to say flatly that Yeats is the greater poet. In the long run he may prove to be more influential.

An old poet ought never to be caught with his technique showing.

The way backward and the way forward are the same. A rediscovery of the past often leads to radical innovation. We know, for example, that Picasso was inspired by African sculpture, that the art of the Renaissance is linked with the resurgence of classic myth. Poetic technique follows the same route. I can think of Hopkins, who went back to Old English for his sprung rhythm; of Pound, who tuned his ear on Provençal song; of Berryman, who adapted inversion and minstrel patter for his *Dream Songs*. These are all acts of renewal, not tired replays of the style of another period. Pound was, of course, right, in his criticism of *The Waste Land* manuscript, when he dissuaded Eliot from trying to compete with Pope in the matter of composing heroic couplets. As he indicated, Pope could do it better. In general, a poet has to rework — not imitate — the past, and the success of his reworking is dependent on the degree of his contemporary awareness. If he has an ear for the living speech — whose rhythmic pulse is ever so slightly modified from generation to generation — he has at least the foundation of a style, the one into which he was born.

The innocence that I cherish in the arts derives from a capacity for perpetual self-renewal, as opposed to a condition of emotional exhaustion or world-weariness. It's waking each day to the wonder of possibility; it's being like a child — which is not to say being childish. "There lives the dearest freshness deep down things" — Hopkins's line — that's an expression of it. With Blake, it's the very essence of his rebel spirit. How I love those bright-eyed ones who stay obstreperously alive till the day they die!

Certain critics have seen fit to discuss me as a late convert to the school of confessional poetry. I guess I resent that. I've always admired a fierce subjectivity; but compulsive exhibitionism — and there's plenty of that around — gobs of sticky hysteria and self-pity — are an embarrassment. Perhaps I sound more censorious than I intend. One of my premises is that you can say anything as long as it is true . . . but not everything that's true is worth saying. Another is that you need not be a victim of your shames . . . but neither should you boast about them.

Why am I so taken with Mandelstam's line "Only the flash of recognition brings delight"? To strike the note of tragic exaltation is to echo the wild laughter of Oedipus and Lear, or to experience anew the metaphysical shudder of Pascal invoking "the eternal silence of the infinite spaces." It is the supreme rapture of the night. Imagine wrestling with an angel, the darkest one of the tribe. You know you're doomed to lose. But that weight on your shoulder!

I have no religion — perhaps that is why I think so much about God.

The problem of the long poem, like that of the novel, is related to our loss of faith in the validity of the narrative continuum. Joyce invented a technique for coping with a new time sense, but that required a superhuman effort, which no longer seems consistent with an anti-heroic age. The collapse of Pound's *Cantos* remains a central symptomatic event. Technically he understood the problem, as his contribution to the making of *The Waste Land* proves, but his own project was too indeterminate, and he had overreached himself in the matter of scale. As a collection of musical fragments, *The Waste Land* seems curiously adapted, like the ruins of antiquity, for enduring the weathers of an age. I suppose the last major effort to build a solid monument was Hart

Crane's — and *The Bridge* has its magnificence, but it is the magnificence of failure. *Mistress Bradstreet* and *Howl* are passionate apostrophes, but their architecture is too frail for the weight of their rhetoric. Berryman's *Dream Songs* and Lowell's *Notebook* don't aspire to the unity of the long poem. Essentially they're poetic sequences, like the sonnet cycles of the Elizabethans. I am half-persuaded that the modern mind is too distracted for the span of attention demanded by the long poem, and that no single theme, given the disorder of our epoch, is capable of mobilizing that attention. But I am only half-persuaded.

During the heyday of the New Criticism, there were poets who trafficked in obfuscation, providing grist for the critics who trafficked in the explication of obfuscation. A beautiful symbiotic relationship! Poets today tend to be clearer — sometimes all too clear. A poem is charged with a secret life. Some of its information ought to circulate continuously within its perimeter as verbal energy. That, indeed, is the function of form: to contain the energy of a poem, to prevent it from leaking out.

In an after-dinner conversation with Mark Rothko one evening I referred to Picasso — not without admiration — as a kind of monster. And then, for good measure, I added Joyce's name. Mark was troubled by the epithet. I argued that in the modern arts the terms "genius" and "monster" may be interchangeable. His face darkened. "You don't mean me, do you?" he asked. A few months later he was dead, by his own hand. What is it in our culture that drives so many artists and writers to suicide — or, failing that, mutilates them spiritually? At the root of the problem is the cruel discrepancy between the values of art and the values of society, which tends to make strangers and adversaries out of those who are most gifted, ambitious, and vulnerable. Sometimes I suspect that every artist has a touch of paranoia. But the word "monster" implies a special kind of greatness — Picasso's, Rothko's, Sylvia Plath's, for example.

When I speak of "the guilty man," I don't mean someone who has sinned more than others. I mean the person who, simply by virtue of being mortal, is in a way condemned: he's mortal and he's fallible, and his life is inevitably a series of errors and consequences. Since he cannot really see the true path — it is not given to him to see it, except in moments of revelation — he is denied the rapture of innocence.

A man's preoccupations and themes aren't likely to change. What changes is the extent to which he can put the full diversity of his moods and interests and information into his poems. Formal verse is a highly selective medium. A high style wants to be fed exclusively on high sentiments. Given the kind of person I am, I came to see the need for a middle style — for a low style, even, though that may be outside my range.

The poet is not to be thought of as set apart from others. On the contrary, he is more like others than anybody else — that's his intrinsic nature. A poetry of self-indulgence and self-advertisement is simply squalid. At Bennington, I recall, Martha Graham used to say to her classes, "Self-consciousness is ugly." (She also used to say, "Movement begets movement.") God knows a poet needs ego, but it has to be consumed in the fire of the poetic action

Standards were easier to maintain in an aristocratic society. Emerson said somewhere that democracy descends to meet. All the modern arts are being threatened by the cult of the amateur. And being nourished, too. You have to know the difference between naïveté and simplicity, novelty and originality, rhetoric and passion. The most insidious enemy of the good is not so much the bad as it is the good-enough, including the inferior productions of first-rate reputations. Anyone can see that we have plenty of talent around — what civilization had more? The trouble is that our gifts are not being used well. On the face of it, our literature reflects a mediocre or silly age, sometimes an angry one. When are we going to wake up to the fact that it's tragic?

Occasionally I am astonished to find, through all the devious windings of a poem, that my destination is something I've written months or years before, embedded in a notebook or recorded on a crumpled scrap of paper, perhaps the back of an envelope. That is what the poem, in its blind intuitive way, has been seeking out. The mind's stuff is wonderfully patient.

The variable pulse of a poem shows that it is alive. Too regular a beat is soporific. I like to hear a poem arguing with itself. Even before it is ready to change into language, a poem may begin to assert its buried life in the mind with wordless surges of rhythm and counter-rhythm. Gradually the rhythms attach themselves to objects and feelings. At this relatively advanced stage the movement of a poem is from the known to the unknown, even to the unknowable. Once you have left familiar things behind, you swim through levels of darkness towards some kind of light, uncertain where you will surface.

I doubt that a poet should expect to be rewarded for his voluntary choice of a vocation. If he has any sense at all, he should realize that he's going to have a hard time surviving, particularly in a society whose main drives are exactly opposite to his. If he chooses, against the odds, to be a poet, he ought to be tough enough, cunning enough, to take advantage of the system in order to survive. And if he doesn't, it's sad, but the world is full of the most terrible kinds of sadness.

By its nature poetry is hostile to opinions, and the opinions of a poet on public affairs are, in any case, of no special interest. The poems that attract me most, out of those that occur in a political context, are the peripheral ones that are yet in essence the product of a mind engaged with history. "The Mound-Builders," I can recall, came out of the resumption of nuclear testing by President Kennedy in 1962, when I was traveling through the South, and looking at the archeological traces of a civilization that flourished in this country between 900 and 1100 A.D., the greatest civilization north of Mexico, of which nothing now remains except a few shards. There in Georgia the inscription reads, "Macon is the seventh layer of civilization on this spot"— Macon, one of the seats of racist injustice in this country. So all these elements entered into the making of the poem, including the fact that I was traveling, and reading my work, and talking to college students in the South. But most readers would say, not without justification, "It's a poem about the history of mound-builders."

I have always hated the business of ranking poets. What was it Blake said? — "I cannot think that Real Poets have any competition. None are greatest in the Kingdom of Heaven."

I perish into work. I have a sense of using the life, of exhausting it in the poetic action. The analogue is the dying image involved with sex. As far as the poet is concerned, life is always dying into art.

The supreme morality of art is to endure.

The only reason you write about yourself is that this is what you know best. What else has half as much reality for you? Even so, certain details of your life can be clouded by pain, or fear, or shame, or other complications, so that you are scarcely ever free from the temptation to tell lies. But the truth about yourself is no more important than the truth about anybody else. And if you knew anybody else as well as you know yourself, you would write about that other.

It's fairly clear to me, as I near the end of my seventh decade, that I'm moving toward a more expansive universe. I propose to take more risks than I ever did. Thank God I don't have to ask anyone else's permission to do what I want to do. If I give it my imprimatur, it's OK. That's the privilege and insolence of age.

Index

Index